MEDIA AND COMMUNICATION RESEARCH METHODS

Second Edition

MEDIA AND COMMUNICATION RESEARCH METHODS

An Introduction to Qualitative and Quantitative Approaches

Second Edition

Arthur Asa Berger

San Francisco State University

Los Angeles | London | New Delhi
Singapore | Washington DC

For information:

SAGE Publications, Inc.
2455 Teller Road
Thousand Oaks,
    California 91320
E-mail: order@sagepub.com

SAGE Publications India Pvt. Ltd.
B 1/I 1 Mohan Cooperative
    Industrial Area
Mathura Road, New Delhi 110 044
India

SAGE Publications Ltd.
1 Oliver's Yard
55 City Road
London EC1Y 1SP
United Kingdom

SAGE Publications
    Asia-Pacific Pte. Ltd.
33 Pekin Street #02-01
Far East Square
Singapore 048763

Printed in the United States of America

Library of Congress Cataloging-in-Publication Data

Berger, Arthur Asa, 1933-
Media and communication research methods : an introduction to qualitative and quantitative approaches / Arthur Asa Berger. — 2nd ed.
    p. cm.
Includes bibliographical references and index.
ISBN 978-1-4129-8777-6 (pbk.)

    1. Mass media—Research—Methodology. 2. Communication—Research—Methodology. I. Title.

P91.3.B385 2011
302.23072—dc22   2010026693

This book is printed on acid-free paper.

10   11   12   13   14   10 9   8   7   6   5   4   3   2   1

Executive Editor:	Diane McDaniel
Editorial Assistant:	Nathan Davidson
Production Editor:	Astrid Virding
Copy Editor:	Gillian Dickens
Permissions Editor:	Karen Ehrmann
Typesetter:	C&M Digitals (P) Ltd.
Proofreader:	Dennis W. Webb
Cover Designer:	Candice Harman
Marketing Manager:	Helen Salmon

Brief Contents

Detailed Contents

Preface to the Second Edition

The world has changed a great deal since the first edition of this book was published in 2000. The impact of the Internet has been enormous, and now newspapers and magazines are struggling to survive because people have become used to getting their news, for free, on the Internet. Google is now a verb, and it has become a multi-billion dollar corporation that dominates the Internet search engine field. Cell phones have become ubiquitous, and thanks to their ability to take photographs and videos, everyone with a cell phone that can take images is now a potential news photographer or news video maker. Cameras are now digital, and Kodak no longer manufacturers film for cameras. Adolescents spend enormous amounts of time texting (and sometimes sexting) one another. We have iPhones, iPods, iPads, and any number of incredible new devices and gizmos. As a result of these changes and others that have occurred, we live in a world considerably different from the way it was in 2000.

This new edition has much new material in it. I have enhanced my discussions of a number of topics involving aspects of cultural studies, I have added a section on keeping a journal, updated all statistics cited in the book, updated all references, and added new images to make the book more visually attractive. You will find new material such as the following:

Applications and Exercises for every chapter on methods

How to read analytically

Clotaire Rapaille on culture codes

Roland Barthes on *Mythologies* and semiotic-Marxist analysis

A paradigmatic analysis of Humpty Dumpty

A discussion of facial expressions as signifiers

John Berger on glamour and advertising

Mary Douglas and "Grid-Group" theory

Freud's structural hypothesis applied to various topics

New developments in psychoanalytic theory

Janice Radway's participant observation study of romance novel readers

The Values and Lifestyle typology and surveys

Writing research reports

More considerations about ethics and research

Keeping a journal to aid in research

I faced a problem with this new edition similar to the one that all researchers face: Where do you begin and when do you end your research? In principle, I could have doubled or tripled the size of the book if I added new material on every topic in the book. For this new edition, I've been selective and chosen those topics that I believe could most benefit from updating and enhancing. I hope that you, my readers, will find this book both interesting and useful and after reading it you will have a much more informed view of how to conduct research.

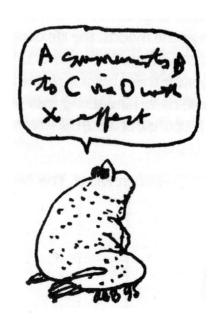

Acknowledgments

I would like to express my appreciation to my first editor, Margaret Seawell, for suggesting I write this book and to my editor, Todd Armstrong, for suggesting I write a new edition of this book and being extremely supportive and helpful. I enjoyed making the revision and offering new suggestions about how media and communication research might be undertaken. I am also grateful to Felianka Kaftandjieva, a Bulgarian scholar, who wrote the first part of the chapter on statistics and offered many useful suggestions on the chapter on surveys. Al Kielwasser was kind enough to send me his syllabus for the course he teaches on media research at San Francisco State University, which was very useful. I also want to thank my copy editor, Gillian Dickens, and the production editor, Astrid Virding, for their assistance.

I also gratefully acknowledge the contributions of the following reviewers:

John DiMarco (St. John's University)

Teri Gamble (College of New Rochelle)

Laurel Hellerstein (Endicott College)

Kevin M. Lerner (Marist College)

Rocci Luppicini (University of Ottawa)

Linda Holtzman (Webster University)

John H. Parmelee (University of North Florida)

Gregg A. Payne (Chapman University)

Karen Pitcher (Eckerd College)

Melinda B. Robins (Emerson College)

Katerina Tsetsura (University of Oklahoma)

This book is the second edition of one of eleven books that I've published with Sage Publications. I am happy to have had such a long and rewarding relationship with a publishing house of such distinction.

At this moment he wished to be a man without qualities. But this is probably not so different from what other people sometimes feel too. After all, by the time they have reached the middle of their life's journey few people remember how they have managed to arrive at themselves, at their amusements, their point of view, their wife, character, occupation and successes, but they cannot help feeling that not much is likely to change any more. It might even be asserted that they have been cheated, for one can nowhere discover any sufficient reason for everything's having come about as it has. It might just as well have turned out differently. The events of people's lives have, after all, only to the least degree originated in them, having generally depended on all sorts of circumstances such as the moods, the life or death of quite different people, and have, as it were, only at the given point of time come hurrying towards them—Something has had its way with them like a flypaper with a fly; it has caught them fast, here catching a little hair, there hampering their movements, and has gradually enveloped them, until they lie, buried under a thick coating that has only the remotest resemblance to their original shape.

—Robert Musil, *The Man Without Qualities* (1965)

Introduction

In this introduction, I describe myself as "The Man Without Quantities" or, in comic book lingo, Data-Free Man. In the past, I have sometimes described myself as The Secret Agent and at other times as Decoder Man. So you are getting, if you think about it, three "superheroes" for the price of one.

The Secret Agent.

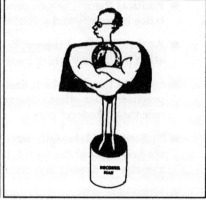

Decoder Man.

❖ ROUND UP THE USUAL SUSPECTS

There are, psychologists tell us, people who have multiple identities or multiple personalities. I have an analogous problem, although *problem* probably isn't the right word: I tend to see things not "from both sides now," as the song goes, but sometimes from 5 or 10 different "sides" or points of view or disciplinary perspectives. I suggest that doing this, using a multidisciplinary perspective, often offers us better ways of making sense of phenomena such as television commercials, common objects, fashions, popular culture, and humor than a single or unitary perspective does.

In a sense, when I find something I wish to analyze, I say to myself "round up the usual disciplines" and begin, often using a number of different perspectives, which I believe complement one another. These disciplines include the following:

- Semiotics, which deals with signs and how we find meaning in phenomena such as films, songs, fashions, and so on

- Aesthetic theory, which deals with how lighting, color, cutting, sound, music, camera shots, and related matters generate ideas, feelings, and emotions in audiences

- Psychoanalytic theory, which deals with unconscious elements in our thinking and behavior

- Sociological theory, which deals with institutions and groups and matters such as race, gender, religion, and class

- Political theory, which concerns itself with power, control, and resistance in groups and societies

- Anthropological theory, which focuses on culture and the enculturation process by which people are taught to fit into their cultures

- Literary theory, which investigates how literary works (of all kinds) generate their effects, the various artistic devices writers use, and the role that "readers" play

- Philosophical thought, which concerns itself with matters such as how we know about the world, the status of knowledge, ethical issues, and principles of reasoning and logic

- Historical perspectives, which study change over time—what happened, how it happened, and why it happened

- Comparative perspectives, which deal, when considering media, with how a given text (such as the TV show *Dallas*) or other phenomena are perceived and the role that the text plays in different societies and cultures

These methods are at the heart of a new subject or "metadiscipline" (some people say I never met a discipline I didn't like, but it's not true) called cultural studies, which, as I see things, developed out of an old one—popular culture. Cultural studies eliminates the boundaries between elite arts and popular arts, but what it represents, I would suggest, is really a formalization (and perhaps an elaboration) of what people who had been studying the mass media and popular culture were already doing. Or should have been doing. In the late 1960s, for example, I used to teach a course called "The Arts, Popular Culture and Society."

There are, I suggest, a number of focal points one might consider when doing cultural criticism. These are shown in Figure 0.1.

In this model, everything is connected to everything else, which is meant to suggest that each of the focal points may have an influence on each or all of the others. When we write about popular culture, mass communication, or media culture, we may focus on a text, such as a film or television program, but we also might want to concern ourselves with the creator(s) of the text, the audience of the text, and what impact the text might have on society and culture (the "effects" of the text). Communication researchers generally focus on one or more aspects of the communication process, such as sources, messages, channels/media, encoding and decoding, audiences/receivers, feedback, barriers and obstacles to communication, and communication contexts.

Figure 0.1   Focal Points Model

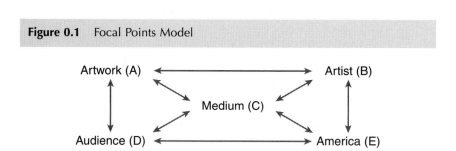

❖ HOW I BECAME A MAN WITHOUT QUANTITIES

Twenty some years ago, a colleague and I were having a chat. We were standing in one of the corridors of the expensive and very plush (although, in certain ways, remarkably dysfunctional) building that houses one of California's premier communication research schools. During the course of our conversation, my colleague, a noted quantitative researcher, said, "Arthur, did you ever think about the fact that you are data-free?"

"Data-free?" What could that mean?

I recognized, suddenly, in an epiphany, that I was a man without quantities. During the course of my academic career, I have argued that the dynamics of the McDonald's organization and their outlets were similar to the methods of evangelical religions; that television commercials showing "muscle" cars crashing through roadside signs and similar barriers represented, symbolically, the deflowering of virgins; and that our passion for using deodorants to remove body odor was tied, ultimately, to Puritanism, perfectionism, and a fear of death. I have also hypothesized, in an article in *Rolling Stone,* that traditional white or "American" bread reflected our lack of ideology in America, where political parties often compromise on important issues. (Nowadays, there is a revolution in American bread, and we're seeing hard-crusted breads in many American bakeries and stores, which reflects, I suggest, the fact that our politics is also getting more ideological.) I have also written about the importance of language in shaping people's consciousness. For example, words indicating masculine identity are part of so many words dealing with women, such as *women, she, her, female, menstruate,* and *menopause.* (The science that explains the power of language to shape consciousness is, of course, semantics.) All of these arguments I made without using statistics, or "data" in the sense that quantitative researchers use data. (Recall my "usual suspects.")

❖ DATA MAN VERSUS DATA-FREE MAN

Let us assume, using the perspective found in comic books, that we have two heroes, both of whom are researchers—Data Man and Data-Free Man. There are considerable differences in the way our two heroes see and make sense of the world, which I have sketched out in the chart of complementary opposites that follows.

Data Man	Data-Free Man
Information	Interpretation
The mean	The meaning
$N = \infty$	$N = 1$
Quantitative	Qualitative
Ingenuity in design	Ingenuity in analysis
Focus on audience	Focus on artwork (text)
Statistics	Concepts from various domains
Quantifiable subjects	Subjects useful for theorizing
Certainty but triviality	Uncertainty but significance
Getting data a problem	Getting ideas a problem
American pragmatic tradition	European philosophical tradition
Counts all grains of sand in the universe	Sees the universe in a grain of sand

This chart oversimplifies things, of course, but it does show how different the orientation of quantitative and qualitative scholars can be.

Quantitative researchers often use sophisticated statistical methods, but they sometimes (maybe often?) are forced to deal with relatively trivial matters—ones that lend themselves to quantification. Qualitative researchers, at the other extreme, often deal with important social, political, and economic matters and use concepts and theories from psychoanalytic thought, Marxist thought, semiotic thought, and the like—which may yield interesting ideas but are highly speculative and do not give certainty. This polarity is a gross simplification, but thinking about these two extremes can help us see the "middle ground" more clearly.

For Data Man, designing research so that one gets good data (and not the wrong data) is very difficult. For Data-Free Man, applying the right concepts correctly and "not going off the deep end" is the problem. The optimal situation is to figure out how to compare statistics and quantitative data with qualitative and theoretical material. The best scholars do this. They occupy some middle ground between the two extremes I've sketched out. But it isn't easy being both Data Man and Data-Free Man at the same time.

Consider the science of economics, probably the most scientific of the social sciences. Economists, using the same data—statistics from various governmental agencies, for example—often disagree about what they mean. So you can't escape from some kind of interpretation and "going beyond" one's data. (And that's assuming that the data are accurate and correct.)

❖ CONCLUSIONS OF A MAN WITHOUT QUANTITIES, WHO IS ALSO A PRACTICING THEORETICIAN

I am, as I have explained, a man without quantities, and since I am "data-free" and have no statistics to "massage," I cannot, so the logic of quantitative researchers suggests, do research. A number of years ago, when I told a colleague of mine that I had written *Media Research Techniques,* a book on research (one that, incidentally, has gone through a number of printings and is now in its second edition), he laughed and said, "What do you know about research, Arthur?"

Since I've published more than 100 articles and more than 60 books (this book is the second edition of my 35th book, it turns out), if I don't do research I must, at the very least, have a really fantastic imagination. Maybe being data-free is actually a kind of postmodernist stance? Maybe qualitative scholars should best be seen as fiction writers? Fiction writers use fiction to convey truths about people—and isn't truth what we're after? I may be data-free, a man without quantities, but I like to think that I, and other qualitative researchers, have qualities— imaginative, literary, artistic, ethical, and otherwise—and that these qualities count for something. But I am not as data-free as I pretend.

When I was a student at the University of Massachusetts many years ago, I had a philosophy teacher who explained the difference between science and philosophy as follows: "Science seeks to know more and more about less and less until it knows everything about nothing. Philosophy seeks to know less and less about more and more until it knows nothing about everything."

This book takes a middle course between these two extremes and aims to teach you something about research. If you think it teaches you everything about nothing or nothing about everything or, even worse, nothing about nothing, I will have failed. But if, by the end of the book, you think you have learned something about viewing the world in both qualitative and quantitative ways, then you will have succeeded in the course.

If you wish to get in touch with me, thanks to the magic of e-mail, you can do so easily now by e-mailing me at aberger@sfsu.edu, which is my e-mail address at San Francisco State University or arthurasa berger@gmail.com. I look forward to hearing from you.

❖ INTRODUCTION: APPLICATIONS AND EXERCISES

1. Find two articles on media and society—one for Data Man and one for Data-Free Man—and compare them. Which one do you find more compelling? Which is more interesting? Which has more important implications? Explain your answer.

2. The title of this introduction, "The Man Without Quantities," is based upon a famous novel by Musil, Robert. (1965). *The Man Without Qualities* (E. Wilkins & E. Kaiser, Trans.). New York: Capricorn Books (pp. 151–152). Let me add another paragraph that comes after the material I quoted earlier:

   And then they only dimly remember their youth when there was something like a force of resistance in them—this other force that tugs and whirrs and does not want to linger anywhere, releasing a storm of aimless attempts at flight. Youth's scorn and its revolt against the established order, youth's readiness for everything that is heroic, whether it is self-sacrifice or crime, its fiery seriousness and its unsteadiness—all this is nothing but its fluttering attempts to fly. Fundamentally it merely means that nothing of all that a young man undertakes appears to be the result of an unequivocal inner necessity, even if it expresses itself in such a manner as to suggest that everything he happens to dash at is exceedingly urgent and necessary.

   What response do you have to these passages? Do you think Musil is correct about people becoming stuck like flies on fly paper? Does he understand young people? Would you describe him as a pessimist or a realist? Explain your answers.

3. Examine the Focal Points Model. Which of the focal points interests you the most? Explain your answer.

Part I

Getting Started

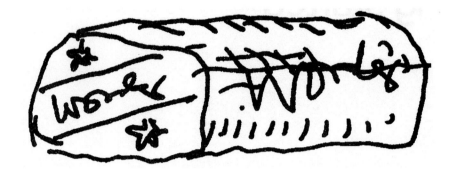

Our conceptions arise through comparison. "Were it always light we should not distinguish between light and dark, and accordingly could not have either the conception of, nor the word for light. . . ." "It is clear that everything on this planet is relative and has independent existence only in so far as it is distinguished in its relations to and from other things. . . ." "Since every conception is thus the twin of its opposite, how could it be thought of first, how could it be communicated to others who tried to think it, except by being measured against its opposite. . . ."

—Sigmund Freud, "The Antithetical Sense of Primal Words" (1910/1963a, p. 47) (a review of a pamphlet by Karl Abel, *Uber den Gegensinn der Urworte*, 1884)

1

What Is Research?

Thereisalook that comes over the faces of some of my students when they hear the word *research*. Their eyes glaze over, and their faces take on a pained expression as if they had a migraine or a bad stomachache. They see the required course on research as some kind of an ordeal they must survive before being allowed to take the courses they want and live a normal life.

❖ WE ALL DO RESEARCH, ALL THE TIME

Yet curiously, many students in my internship courses, when they describe what they do in their internships—that is, when they are out there in the "real world"—talk about looking for information and data, finding material on this or that subject, getting names and addresses— in other words, **research.** It turns out that research is one of the most valuable courses students take, as far as having practical uses are concerned, but there's something about the term *research* that generates lumps in throats and expressions of pain.

What is research? Literally it means "to search for, to find" and comes from the Latin *re* (again) and from *cercier* (to search). In French, the term *chercher* means "seek." In the most general sense, research means looking for information about something.

Like one of Molière's characters, Monsieur Jourdain, who didn't realize he was always speaking prose, most of us do what could be called "research" all the time—even though we may not think of what we are doing as research. For example, when people decide to buy a computer, they generally try to get some information about the brand and models of the computers they are thinking of buying. They may look in computer magazines, they may check in *Consumer Reports,* and they may ask their friends who have computers about the particular kind of computer they have. This is research.

Let me offer another example. In one of my classes, during a break, several of my students were discussing a professor. "What's he like?" asked one student. "Oh, he's easy," someone said. "He gives you a preliminary exam and then in the real exam, he always asks one of the questions in the preliminary exam. I'd take him." This was information of value to the student who was thinking of taking a course with that professor. This is research.

So we are always doing research, even though we don't think of what we are doing as such. We do this research because we have choices to make about matters such as what we want to buy, what we want to take at college (and whom we want to take the courses with), and where we want to live. Even when we have limited budgets, generally speaking, we still have choices to make.

A SHORT THEATRICAL PIECE ON RESEARCH

Grand Inquisitor:	*Who is John Q. Public?*
Arthur:	Nobody! It's just a name we use for the ordinary American.
Grand Inquisitor:	*Why is his middle initial Q?*
Arthur:	That's an interesting question. You can find out if you do a bit of research.
Grand Inquisitor:	*Is John Q. Public related to Joe Sixpack?*
Arthur:	Some people think they're both the same person. You can find out if you do some research.
Grand Inquisitor:	*Why do people do research?*

Arthur:	To find the answer to questions that interest them or problems they want to solve, like what does the "Q" in John Q. Public stand for ... or should I attend college, and if so, which college and what should I major in? Or should I get married to X? Or what kind of car should I get?
Grand Inquisitor:	*When do people do research?*
Arthur:	All the time.
Grand Inquisitor:	*How do you do research?*
Arthur:	That's the $64,000 question.

❖ SCHOLARLY RESEARCH IS DIFFERENT FROM EVERYDAY RESEARCH

A number of differences between everyday research and scholarly research need to be considered. Scholarly research is, generally speaking, more systematic, more objective, more careful, and more concerned about correctness and truthfulness than everyday research. Notice that I've not said anything about data and numbers and statistics. That's because a great deal of research doesn't involve such matters.

Think, for example, of what historians do. There are, of course, some quantitative historians who do use statistics, but for the most part, historians read various kinds of documents (speeches, letters, diaries, news reports, etc.) and, on the basis of their reading, try to describe what happened and why it happened; they focus on economic, political, and social considerations. Because there's no way to be certain about why things happened (and in some cases even what happened), there are lots of controversies in history, and different historians offer conflicting explanations of, say, the significance of the American Revolution or the causes of the Civil War in the United States.

Or take **cultural studies,** a rather amorphous multidisciplinary field of study that investigates everything from elite fiction to comics, television, films, music, and everyday life. Scholars who write in these fields usually base their analyses on the concepts, ideas, and theories of philosophers, psychologists, social scientists, linguists, and others with a more theoretical bent. Thus, we have scholars who write what we think of as cultural studies, basing their analyses on concepts taken from thinkers such as Marx, Freud, the Russian scholar Bakhtin, and the French scholar Baudrillard.

Because interpretations of these theorists vary and the applications of their ideas vary, we find considerable controversy in cultural studies and in other humanistic disciplines. But we also find controversy in the social sciences, such as economics, sociology, and political science, where a great deal of the research involves numbers. Economics is generally considered the most rigorous of the social sciences as far as gathering hard data is concerned, but we discover that given the same data, economists often differ on how they interpret these data.

❖ NIETZSCHE ON INTERPRETATION

The philosopher Friedrich Nietzsche believed that everything boils down to interpretation. As he wrote in his *Will to Power* (1987),

> Against positivism, which halts at phenomena—There are only *facts.*—I would say: No, facts is precisely what there is not, only interpretations. We cannot establish any fact "in itself": perhaps it is folly to want to do such a thing. (p. 481)

Nietzsche suggested we cannot know facts, only perspectives on things. There is, he said, "no limit to the ways the world can be interpreted." He focused on what he called "perspectivism," a notion that informs much postmodern theory—a topic to be discussed in more detail in Chapter 8. Nietzsche may have overestimated the importance of interpretation, but it is correct to say that, in the final analysis, after social scientists have collected their data, they have to interpret them, and sometimes there is more than one way to interpret these data.

Everyday Research	Scholarly Research
Intuitive	Theory based
Common sense	Structured
Casual	Systematic
Spur of the moment	Planned
Selective (often)	Objective
Magical thinking	Scientific thinking
Flawed thinking at times	Logical to the extent possible
Focus is personal decisions	Focus is knowledge about reality

As the preceding table shows, there is a considerable difference between what I've described as everyday research and scholarly research. In our everyday research, we are often very casual in our methods, and sometimes, when we want to convince ourselves that something we want to do should be done, we are very selective as well. That is, we neglect information that might convince us that a course of action we want to take is wrong. This is known as "selective inattention," which can be understood to mean ignoring information that wouldn't support your research.

Sometimes our everyday research is tied to "magical thinking," which can be defined as believing that "wishing makes it so" or, for example, that we can, through force of will, cause something to happen. Like becoming a movie star.

Our everyday research generally involves personal matters— things we might want to do or products we might want to purchase. In many cases, we make our decisions based on advertising or something else that has an emotional appeal, which colors our decisions. We want to do something and look for information or whatever to support our desire. So the research we do, on the personal level, at times is not a matter of seeking truth but of finding support and justification.

We know, for example, of people who buy a certain brand of car then read advertisements in newspapers to convince themselves that their purchase was the correct one. But the decision to buy that brand or model of car might have been generated by commercials and might be emotional rather than rational.

Scientific thinking is the opposite; it seeks truth and accepts information that runs counter to one's wishes and desires. It is logical and bases its conclusions on rigorous thinking and honesty. Of course, people trying to be scientific and systematic and honest sometimes make mistakes, too, but the emphasis is on honesty, accepting the results one finds, and careful and logical reasoning. Much everyday research exists to justify prior decisions, whereas scientific research is disinterested and honest, accepting what it finds and not stacking the deck to get a desired result.

I can remember reading about some interesting "everyday" research a copy writer named Martin Solow conducted. He was invited to a gathering at a friend's house and asked his hosts about how they decided which products to purchase. Inevitably they told him they paid no attention to advertising and bought most of their products based on what was recommended in *Consumer Reports.* He describes how he conducts his research in his article "The Case of the Closet Target" (originally published in *Madison Avenue* magazine):

I excuse myself and ask, since it is a large house, for a roadmap to the bathroom. Once in the large bathroom, the door safely locked, I open the medicine cabinet and survey the contents: Colgate toothpaste, L'Oreal hairspray; Trac II shaving cream and the new Gilette Trac II razor; Ban Roll-on Deodorant (for him, I guess) and Arid Extra-Dry (for her—or maybe vice-versa); Bayer aspirins. (Solow, 1991, qtd. in A. A. Berger, 2007, p. 71)

The moral of this story is that we often deceive ourselves and think we are making or have made rational decisions about products we buy when, in reality, we've been influenced by the numerous advertisements and commercials to which we've been exposed. When people say "I am aware of advertising but not influenced by it," they are fooling themselves.

❖ THE PROBLEM OF CERTAINTY

Although it is a big generalization, it's fair to say that we seldom (perhaps never) get certainty from our research. Even when we have statistics, the way we interpret these statistics is open to disagreement. This explains why scholarly disciplines are full of disputes and why scholars seem to spend so much time arguing with other scholars (who disagree with their findings or their methodologies or both).

Just because we can't be certain of our interpretations of **data** or of **texts** (the term used in the humanities for works of elite and popular art, such as operas, plays, poems, films, television programs, paintings, and comic books) doesn't mean anything goes and that we can offer interpretations without giving good reasons for these interpretations.

It is our research, I would suggest, that supplies us with the "reasons" we use when we argue about how to interpret a film or a bunch of statistics. It's best to think of academics as spending their careers trying to prove that their way of looking at whatever portion of the world they look at is correct. They do this by writing articles and books, explaining their ideas and theories, and offering support for them.

Thinking doesn't make it so. You have to have some kind of **evidence** that a reasonable person can accept. And that evidence comes from research. How good that research is (that is, is it reliable?) and how well the research is used is another matter.

❖ DIACHRONIC AND SYNCHRONIC RESEARCH

At the heart of all research is the matter of comparisons—in historical studies, we focus on *change over time,* and in comparative studies, we study *change over distance,* to put things in rather simplistic terms. This takes us to de Saussure (1966) and his notion that concepts take their meaning differentially. Saussure used the term *diachronic* for linguistic study that has a historical focus and the term *synchronic* for linguistic research that is comparative in nature.

As de Saussure writes (1966),

> Certainly all sciences would profit by indicating more precisely the co-ordinates along which their subject matter is aligned. Everywhere distinctions should be according to the following illustration, between . . . *the axis of simultaneities* . . . which stands for the relations of coexisting things and from which the intervention of time is excluded; and . . . *the axis of successions* . . . on which only one thing can be considered at a time but upon which are located all the things on the first axis together with their changes. (pp. 79–80)

The axis of simultaneity involves comparison in space, and the axis of successions involves change over time. Those are the two general perspectives on which research tends to locate itself.

In experimental research, the comparison is between a *control* group, to whom nothing is done, and an *experimental* group, to whom something is done. The thing that is done to the experimental group is called an *independent variable.* Then, the two groups are measured to see whether the experimental group was affected by the independent variable.

For example, a study of the impact of televised violence on people would have two groups of people: The experimental group is exposed to televised violence (the independent variable), and the control group is not exposed to televised violence. Then both are tested to see whether the televised violence has had a significant effect.

The following diagram shows the historical and comparative orientations. The horizontal axis is comparative (differences between one place and another), and the vertical axis is historical (change over time).

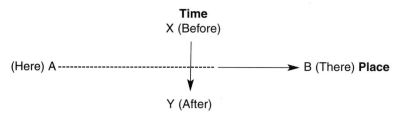

So we usually find that comparisons are at the heart of most research, just as they are at the heart of thinking and communicating, if de Saussure was correct. The A to B axis is comparative at a given moment in time (for example, the way people do things in the United States and the way people do things in some other country), and the X to Y axis is comparative historically, at an earlier time and at a later time (for example, the way we did things earlier and the way we do things now).

We are always asking, one way or another, when we try to make sense of the world and the information we have obtained (because concepts take their meaning differentially) "compared with what?" Another way of putting this is that facts don't speak for themselves; they have to be put into context and their significance explained.

That is where the research report comes in, and the way the report is written plays an important part in how others accept the report. The medium may not be the message, but the way information is conveyed—that is, the quality of your thinking and writing—has a significant impact on how your research is received.

❖ ON THE WAY THE HUMAN MIND WORKS

Let us return to the way people view the world. According to the humorist Robert Benchley, the world is divided into two groups of people: those who divide the world into two groups of people and those who don't. This division is whimsical and doesn't really tell us very much. In part, that is because we are given a statement about a group of people and then a negation.

The human mind, de Saussure argued, makes sense of the world essentially by forming **binary oppositions** such as rich and poor, happy and sad, healthy and ill, and tall and short. These oppositions establish relationships in various areas, and it is through *relationships* that we find meaning.

Facts, by themselves, tell us little. Thus, to say that John Q. Public, who is married and has two children, earns $15,000 a year (a factoid) gives us some information about John Q. Public, but not very much. If we get another fact, that a family of four with an income of $16,000 in America in 1997 is living below the poverty line, then we can see that John Q. Public and his family are living in poverty. We have here some information—how much John Q. Public makes—and a concept—level of poverty—and we can see a relationship between the concept and the information we have.

Saussure's (1966) great insight is that **concepts** are relational. As he wrote in his book *A Course in General Linguistics*, "Concepts are purely differential and defined not by their positive content but negatively by their relations with the other terms of the system. *Their most precise characteristic is in being what the others are not* [italics added]" (p. 117). In other words, as de Saussure put it, "In languages there are only differences" (p. 120) and, more particularly, oppositions. As he explained in his book, language is based on oppositions. Relationships, then, help us make sense of the world, and the most important relationship, de Saussure argued, is that of binary oppositions.

Let me suggest some of the more important binary oppositions that we deal with in our everyday lives and, where appropriate, the thinkers who have made these oppositions part of our fund of knowledge.

Important Binary Oppositions	
Qualitative	Quantitative
The one	The many (Plato)
Active	Passive
Nature	History
Bourgeois	Proletarian (Marx)
Digital	Analog
Gesellschaft	Gemeinschaft (Tonnies)
Raw	Cooked (Lévi-Strauss)
Potentiality	Actuality
I	Thou (Buber)
Ascetic	Hedonistic
Acid	Alkali
Idealism	Materialism
Thesis	Synthesis (Hegel)
Good	Evil
Sacred	Profane (Eliade)
Potentiality	Actuality
Young	Old
Id	Superego (Freud)

(Continued)

(Continued)

Important Binary Oppositions	
Yin	Yang
Existence	Essence (Kierkegaard)
Dionysian	Apollonian (Nietzsche)
Electronic	Mechanical
Rigid	Flexible
Superficial	Profound
Wet	Dry (Lifton)
Classical	Romantic
Ethical	Aesthetic
Free	Enslaved
Democratic	Totalitarian
Hierarchy	Equality
Overt	Covert
Western	Eastern
Free market	Command market
Beginning	End
Capitalism	Communism (Marx)

NOTE: The names in parentheses stand for thinkers who have dealt with these concepts in their work.

These oppositions, and a few dozen others, have shaped our consciousness and profoundly affected our history. In a sense, one can argue that much of history involves confrontations between people believing in one or the other side of certain oppositions in this list and some kind of final resolution of the dialectic between them.

❖ OVERT AND COVERT OPPOSITIONS

In many cases, oppositions are hidden in texts and have to be elicited. Let me offer an example. I will quote the first paragraph from an article by Robert Jay Lifton and then show the bipolar oppositions found in that paragraph.

Lifton's (1974) article "Who Is More Dry? Heroes of Japanese Youth" starts as follows:

> In postwar Japan, especially among young people, it is good to be "dry" (or *durai*) rather than "wet" (or *wetto*). This means—in the original youth language, as expanded by the mass media—to be direct, logical, to the point, pragmatic, casual, self-interested, rather than polite, evasive, sentimental, nostalgic, dedicated to romantic causes, or bound by obligation in human relations; to break out of the world of cherry blossoms, haiku, and moon-viewing into a modern era of bright sunlight, jazz, and Hemingway (who may be said to have been the literary god of dryness). Intellectual youth, of course, disdain these oversimplified categories. But they too have made the words *durai* and *wetto* (typical examples of postwar Japanized English) part of their everyday vocabulary, and they find dry objects of admiration in an interesting place: in American films about cowboys and gunmen. (p. 104)

This passage yields a considerable number of oppositions, which I have listed in the chart that follows.

Dry	Wet
Young people	(Old people)
Direct	Polite
Logical	Evasive
To the point	Sentimental
Pragmatic	Dedicated to romantic causes
Self-interested	Obligated to society
Sunlight loving	Moon viewing
Hemingway	Haiku
Cowboys, gunmen	"Samurai"

I put *old people* in parentheses because they are not mentioned but are logically present, as the "wet" people in Japan, and I put the *samurai* in quotations because they are not mentioned in this paragraph but are dealt with, in some detail, later on in Lifton's (1974) article.

What we see from this little exercise is that de Saussure's (1966) statement about concepts having meaning differentially is correct. Wet is the opposite of dry, and when we see the term *wet*, it has its meaning because of its relationship with its opposition, which is in *not* being its opposite.

Oppositions, I should point out, are different from negations. *Healthy* and *unhealthy* is a negation. *Healthy* and *sick* is an opposition; both terms have meaning, and one term is not simply the negation of the other. (There are some scholars who argue that de Saussure's ideas about the mind finding meaning through polar oppositions is an over-simplification, but their arguments are somewhat arcane, and we need not bother with them.)

❖ ON QUANTITY AND QUALITY IN MEDIA RESEARCH

The stage is now set to discuss the basic opposition in media and communication research (and research of all kinds)—the difference between qualitative and quantitative research. I mentioned some of these oppositions in my introduction, but let us return to them again.

The term *quality* comes from the Latin word *qualitas,* which means "of what kind?" Quality, when it comes to texts carried by one or more of the media, involves matters such as the text's properties, degree of excellence, and distinguishing characteristics. There is an element of evaluation and judgment and taste connected to the term *quality.*

Quantity is a different matter. The term *quantity* comes from the Latin word *quantitas,* meaning "how great" or, for our purposes, "how much" or "how many." When we think of quantitative research in the media and communication, we think of numbers, magnitude, and measurement. Of course, the problem that quantitative researchers often face is that they count only certain things, not everything, and it may be the case that something that cannot be quantified is of great importance in one's research.

Thus, quantitative researchers are sometimes accused of being too narrow, basing their research on what they can count, measure, and observe and neglecting other matters. Qualitative researchers, however, are often accused of "reading into" texts things that are not there or of having opinions or making interpretations that seem odd, excessive, or even idiosyncratic. (The term *idios* means private, and idiosyncratic interpretations of media and texts are highly personal and not defensible.)

Let us look at the two modes of research in terms of the oppositions connected to each of them. These oppositions are somewhat reductionistic (that is, I've oversimplified them to make a point), but they do direct our attention to important elements in the two kinds of research.

Qualitative Research	Quantitative Research
Evaluates	Counts, measures
Uses concepts to explicate	Processes data collected
Focuses on aesthetics in texts	Focuses on incidences of X in texts
Theoretical	Statistical
Interprets	Describes, explains, and predicts
Leads to an evaluation	Leads to a hypothesis or theory
Interpretation can be attacked	Methodology can be attacked

It is instructive to look at the kinds of investigations made by qualitative and quantitative scholars in the media. A number of years ago, I received a flyer from the "Qualitative Studies Division of the Association for Education in Journalism and Mass Communication," the AEJMC, calling for papers for the annual conference. The flyer read (in part) as follows:

> Entries may include studies employing any type of qualitative research approach. Essays, analyses, and literature reviews on topics within the interests of the division are also invited. Subjects falling within the Qualitative Studies Division's interests include, but are not limited to, the following:
>
> Popular Culture
>
> Philosophy of Communication
>
> Literary or Textual Analysis of Communications Context
>
> Performance Studies of Mass Communicators
>
> Mythic/Ideological Studies
>
> Media Criticism
>
> Empirical or Theoretical Work in Cultural Studies
>
> Production/Organization Studies of Mass Media

They listed a number of other topics. I offer this list because it gives a good idea of the range of interests of qualitative methodologists, many of which will be dealt with in this book.

Under quantitative methodologies, I include experiments, content analysis, surveys, and questionnaires—techniques that lend themselves to statistical manipulations to gain information.

❖ MEDIA AND COMMUNICATION

For our purposes, we can focus on five different aspects of **communication.**

1. *Intrapersonal.* This area covers things such as talking to ourselves, thinking about how we will respond to situations we expect to arise, and writing in a journal or diary. We are communicating with ourselves.

2. *Interpersonal.* Here, the communication takes place between ourselves and a relatively small number of people. This area includes matters such as conversations between two people and conversations with friends at dinner parties. There is interaction among all parties involved.

3. *Small group.* In small-group communication, a person might be teaching a class or talking to a relatively small group of people, a group large enough so that ordinary interpersonal communication cannot take place.

4. *Organizational.* This area deals with how organizations communicate to members of the organization and to other interested parties.

5. *Mass media.* Here we are dealing with radio, television, film, and other media. The communication flows from a sender of messages to a large number of receivers of messages. A great deal of the content of the mass media takes the form of texts—narratives or stories found in radio programs, television programs, films, songs, and music videos. We also find narratives in personal conversations and many other areas.

The development of **social media** sites such as Facebook and Twitter and video sites such as YouTube means that individuals now have the capacity to create messages and images that can be seen by huge numbers of people. The fact that most cell phones have decent resolution cameras in them has made everyone with such a camera a potential photojournalist.

Different research methods lend themselves to each of these areas of communication. For example, if you are interested in the narratives carried by the mass media, you will use qualitative or interpretative techniques such as semiotics or ideological analysis, but if you are interested in the effects of the media, you will probably use quantitative techniques such as content analysis or surveys. In some cases, you might wish to use a number of different techniques at the same time.

❖ WHY A BOOK THAT TEACHES BOTH METHODOLOGIES?

There is a logic to teaching both methodologies, for quite often it makes sense to do both a qualitative and a quantitative study research project. Take, for example, a television series about the police. The qualitative researcher might study the metaphors in the dialogue and the narrative structure of the shows in the series, whereas the quantitative researcher might study incidences of violence per minute in the series. It is quite possible that the amount of violence in the series affects the qualitative interpretation of the text or vice versa.

It's reasonable to expect, then, that if a text is so violent it creates psychological distress and a sickening feeling in audiences, quite likely viewers, and perhaps critics, will be rather negative about their aesthetic evaluations. It may be that physiological or ethical considerations will shape evaluations of the text and decisions about whether to look at other episodes.

In some cases, the intensity of the violence in a given scene (a qualitative measure) may be more important than the amount of violence (a quantitative measure) in the text as a whole. So we need to have a repertoire of analytic and measurement techniques so that we can obtain the full array of information we need or want. It's better to have many arrows (that is, techniques one can use in doing research) in one's quiver than just one.

❖ CONSIDERING RESEARCH TOPICS

Here are some things to consider before undertaking a research project:

- Is the problem important enough to bother with?

- Is your hypothesis reasonable and testable?

- Are there ethical problems involved in the research? (Will it violate the privacy of people? If so, should it be done?)

- Do you have the skills to do the research? For example, do you know enough about statistics to be able to deal with your data (if it requires statistical analysis, that is)?

- Is the topic sufficiently narrow and focused so that you can do it in the time you have at your disposal and with limited funds?

- Is your methodology the best one to deal with your hypothesis or subject being investigated?

Does your college or university have resources in the library and in the computer labs that are adequate for your research?

❖ WHAT IS RESEARCH? APPLICATIONS AND EXERCISES

1. Find an article in the *New York Times* that reports on an article that deals with some aspect of research in the social sciences involving media. Analyze the *New York Times* article and answer the following questions:

   a. What methodology was used in the research?
   b. How important is the topic?
   c. What conclusions were reached?
   d. Are the conclusions supported by the data? Are they credible?
   e. Can one generalize from the research?
   f. Does it have any policy implications?

2. Find the scholarly article on which the article in the *New York Times* was based and compare them in terms of how accurate the *New York Times* article conveyed what was in the scholarly article. Did it leave out anything important? Was the report biased in any way?

❖ CONCLUSIONS

If we look at research as an attempt to find out about things and people and the complexities of communication, research becomes fascinating. Because of the way the human mind works, we are, in a sense, always doing research—but not always doing scientific and scholarly research. This book offers an introduction to scientific and scholarly research. It functions as a primer and describes the more commonly used techniques for analyzing media and communication.

A number of years ago, I was asked by a German publisher to write a book—with both a historical and a comparative perspective—on techniques used by women who seduce men. This led to a fascinating search to find material I could use and to a book about women who might be called superstar seductresses, covering everyone from Lilith to Madame de Pompadour, from Cleopatra to Monica Lewinsky.

Who says research can't be fun?

❖ FURTHER READING

Bakhtin, M. M. (1981). *The dialogic imagination: Four essays* (M. Holquist, Ed.; C. Emerson & M. Holquist, Trans.). Austin: University of Texas Press.

Baudrillard, J. (1996). *The system of objects* (J. Benedict, Trans.). London: Verso.

Becker, H. S. (1998). *Tricks of the trade: How to think about your research while you're doing it.* Chicago: University of Chicago Press.

Berger, A. A. (1998). *Media research techniques* (2nd ed.). Thousand Oaks, CA: Sage.

Bernard, H. R. (1994). *Research methods in anthropology: Qualitative and quantitative approaches* (2nd ed.). Walnut Creek, CA: AltaMira.

Creswell, J. W. (2007). *Qualitative inquiry and research design.* Thousand Oaks, CA: Sage.

Flick, U. (2010). *An introduction to qualitative research.* Thousand Oaks, CA: Sage.

Rubin, R. B., Rubin, A. M., & Piele, L. J. (1990). *Communication research: Strategies and sources* (2nd ed.). Belmont, CA: Wadsworth.

Strauss, A., & Corbin, J. (1990). *Basics of qualitative research: Grounded theory procedures and techniques.* Thousand Oaks, CA: Sage.

Surber, J. P. (1998). *Culture critique: An introduction to the critical discourses of cultural studies.* Boulder, CO: Westview.

Wimmer, R. D., & Dominick, J. R. (1983). *Mass media research: An introduction.* Belmont, CA: Wadsworth.

My Illustrious Friend and Joy of My Liver!

The thing you ask of me is both difficult and useless. Although I have passed all my days in this place, I have neither counted the houses nor have I inquired into the number of the inhabitants; and as to what one person loads on his mules and the other stows away in the bottom of his ship, that is no business of mine. But, above all, as to the previous history of this city, God only knows the amount of dirt and confusions that the infidels may have eaten before the coming of the sword of Islam. It were unprofitable for us to inquire into it. O my soul! O my lamb! Seek not after the things which concern thee not. Thou comest to us and we welcomed thee: go in peace.

—Reply of a Turkish official to an
Englishman's questions, quoted in
Austen H. Layard, *Discoveries in the Ruins of Nineveh and Babylon* (London, 1853,
p. 663; see Barzun & Graff, 1957, p. 3)

2

Library Searches

Woody Allen has a wonderful line in one of his standup routines in which the writer F. Scott Fitzgerald brings Allen a book he has just written, *Ivanhoe.* "It's a good book," Allen says to him, "but you didn't have to write it. Sir Walter Scott has already written it." The point of this little story is that it doesn't make sense to reinvent the wheel, to do something that's already been done.

❖ WHY LIBRARY RESEARCH IS SO IMPORTANT

We can find out, if we conduct a good library search, whether or not research we are planning on doing, or research very similar to what we had in mind, has been done. It doesn't make sense to do all the work involved with studying X or Y or Z if someone has done so already— unless, that is, you wish to replicate the research and test whether it was done correctly.

So, generally speaking, scholars do a library search to find out what has already been done. This library search has another value: It sometimes helps our research by leading us to articles and books dealing with research of a similar nature. We can learn, then, from other people's work—and, in some cases, their mistakes.

We generally make library searches to gain as much information as we can about a given subject before narrowing down the focus for our particular research project. Because research demands a good deal of resourcefulness and energy, and in some cases is so difficult, we have to find manageable topics to deal with. Library searches can also be used to help provide readers of your research with background information, with a sense of context.

Sometimes, when doing a library search, if you have the chance to wander around the stacks, you find books that you didn't know existed that can be extremely helpful. That's because the stacks are generally designed so that related subjects are found together, and if you wander up and down the aisles of the stacks, you come across books from related fields—that you may not have discovered when checking through your library's computer system—that are useful. Thus, researchers do library searches for a number of reasons.

A SHORT THEATRICAL PIECE ON LIBRARIES

Grand Inquisitor: *What are all these people doing here? The place is swarming with people of all kinds.*

Arthur: Various things connected to student life.

Grand Inquisitor: *Like what?*

Arthur: Some students are looking for books and journal articles. Some students are doing homework. Some are sleeping. Some are checking databases. Some are making dates. Some students are searching for love . . . looking for a stranger, across a crowded room.

Grand Inquisitor: *Is that what you call a library search? Looking for love? Romance? In a library?*

Arthur: In libraries, in this high-tech era, when students find that "certain someone," we call it a CD-ROMance! Come, let's go to the computer room and play a video game.

❖ SEARCH STRATEGIES

There are two general search strategies:

1. Going from the specific to the general
2. Going from the general to the specific

In the first approach, we have something rather specific in mind for our project, and we search for material of a rather general nature to give us a sense of context and to collect material that might be helpful to us. Thus, if you are doing research on professional wrestling in television, you might investigate topics such as the history of wrestling, sports in society, or media and sports.

In the second approach, we have some area we are interested in studying and look around for information that will help us narrow our subject down to a manageable size—that is, information that will help us to focus. It is particularly important that as a student doing a research project, you find narrow enough subjects to investigate, because your time will be limited (and you probably will have no funds for assistance). If you are interested in violence and television, for example, you have to find a narrower focus, such as the amount of violence on a selected animated cartoon program or violence in professional football, to deal with the subject adequately.

HOW TO READ ANALYTICALLY

Look for important concepts and ideas.
See how they are explained and how they are used.

Look for data, factual material.
How is it used to support theories, arguments (things the authors are trying to prove)?

Look for arguments made by authors.
Why do the authors believe something or don't believe something else?

Look for contrasts and comparisons.
Frequently authors embed these in their texts and do not list them. When you can, make lists of contrasts and comparisons made by authors and see what these lists reveal.

(Continued)

(Continued)

Look at the examples offered.
Are they relevant? Interesting? Useful? Do they support the arguments being made by the authors?

Look for threads.
Find topics and points that keep on coming up repeatedly. What role do these threads play in the argument being made by the authors?

Look for insights.
I define insights as relationships that exist between phenomena that you've never encountered before. Are these insights valuable? Do they have policy implications?

Look for adaptations you can make.
Can you apply the insights you find in work you are doing?

Look at the methodologies employed.
How do the authors attempt to support their arguments? What assumptions do they make? Are the methods they use valid? Are there problems with the way they employ their methodologies? Could other methodologies have been used?

Look at the style of writing, the tone, and related matters.
How does style affect the points being made in an article or book?

Look at the sources they use.
Are their sources up-to-date or dated? Are their sources too narrow?

Remember that people who read what you write will be asking the same questions, so when you write take these matters into consideration.

❖ DOING A LITERATURE REVIEW

A literature review is a particular kind of library search. A literature review summarizes the major findings of scholars and researchers who have conducted research in the area you are interested in investigating. To do a literature search, you search through the library (including databases and the **Internet**) for articles, research reports, journals, and books on your subject, and you offer a summary about what has been done in the particular area you are investigating.

This literature search does two things: First, it offers a sense of context for your readers so that they can see how your research fits into the scheme of things. Second, it shows readers where you got your information and lets them assess how current it is and how reliable it might be.

❖ PRIMARY AND SECONDARY RESEARCH SOURCES

Primary research involves firsthand observation and study by a researcher. For example, you survey a group of people on some topic and then see what the data you have reveal. **Secondary research** uses research performed by others to come to some conclusion about a topic or make some kind of an argument. In essence, this kind of research is a form of editing, in which quotations (and sometimes summaries, paraphrases, and syntheses of the material read) from this scholar and that scholar are collected to produce an essay or article that makes its argument. In primary research, we *do* the actual research; in secondary research, we *use* the research that others have done.

In the *MLA Handbook* (4th ed.), Joseph Gibaldi (1995) describes the difference between primary and secondary research as follows:

> Primary research is the study of a subject through firsthand observation and investigation, such as analyzing a literary or historical text, conducting a survey, or carrying out a laboratory experiment. Primary sources include statistical data, historical documents, and works of literature and art. Secondary research is the examination of studies that other researchers have made of a subject. Examples of secondary research are books and articles about political issues, historical events, scientific debates, or literary works. (p. 2)

Students generally use a good deal of secondary research in their papers and research projects, using ideas and findings of other researchers.

In a sense, what is done in such papers is an appeal to authority; the authority of the "experts" quoted is used to make some argument. At times, quotations from theorists such as Marx, Freud, Aristotle, and Plato can also be used to justify and support contentions. In fields such as literature, media and communication, the arts, and cultural studies in general, many **interpretations** of texts and other phenomena are based on concepts and notions from famous philosophers, thinkers, and scholars that can be applied to whatever is being studied. How well they are applied then becomes the question.

In other cases, arguments are made on the basis of evaluations and interpretations made by scholars and critics about a given work of art or "text." Critics often disagree with one another about how to interpret a particular text, and the researcher has the problem of trying to figure out which critics are correct (and also *when* they are correct) and which are wrong (and *when* they are wrong). I say this because sometime critics are correct about some aspects of a text and wrong about other aspects. In part, the disagreements by critics are tied to the incredible complexity of creative works. In my work, I've had a great deal of fun applying (and maybe, in some cases, misapplying) ideas from Freud and Marx and various philosophers to all kinds of different texts, objects, and practices.

It has been said that there is no disputing taste. We all have the right to our opinions about films, television programs, and other texts, but that doesn't mean that our opinions are always correct or always as good as those of others. It is the quality of the argument you make about a text that counts, not the strength or intensity of your opinion.

❖ SOURCES FOR LIBRARY RESEARCH IN MEDIA AND COMMUNICATION

In libraries now, it is possible to obtain a great deal of primary source material—data of all kinds—from governmental and nongovernmental studies found in articles, scholarly and research journals, books, and other publications. There is also an enormous amount of material available on the Internet.

Let me offer some journals that might be useful to you in doing your library searches. There are, of course, huge numbers of publications and sources, electronic and nonelectronic, that you can use. This listing suggests only some possibilities for you to consider. Many of these journals, incidentally, are covered by *Communication Abstracts,* a bimonthly publication that provides approximately 1,500 abstracts of articles each year.

If you find something in the abstract (a summary of the most important points in an article) that seems useful and interesting, you can then go to the journal and read the entire article.

American Anthropologist	*American Political Science Review*
American Behavioral Scientist	*Canadian Journal of Communication*
American Educational Research Journal	*Central States Speech Journal*
	Communication
American Journal of Psychology	*Communication Education*
American Journalism	*Communication Quarterly*

Communication Research

Communications and the Law

Critical Studies in Mass
   Communication

Human Communications Research

InterMedia

Journal of Advertising

Journal of Applied Communication
   Research

Journal of Broadcasting and
   Electronic Media

Journal of Communication

Journal of Communication Inquiry

Journal of Marketing Research

Journal of Media Law and Practice

Journalism History

Journalism Quarterly

Mass Comm Review

Media, Culture and Society

Political Communication and
   Persuasion

Public Culture

Public Opinion Quarterly

Public Relations Journal

Quarterly Journal of Speech

Reference and Research Book News

Signs: Journal of Women in Culture
   and Society

Telecommunication Journal

Thalia: Studies in Literary Humor

Theory and Society

Western Journal of
   Communication

Written Communication

There are also numerous business or trade periodicals about media, communication, and broadcasting that you can use to get information on topics of interest to you. Many of these trade journals have a great deal of data in them that you can sometimes use or adapt for your own purposes.

❖ OTHER SOURCES OF INFORMATION

Here are some other sources of information that may be of use to you in doing your research:

1. *Computer-based central catalogues* (formerly card catalogues). These list all the books in the library and often tell whether they are available or not. You can also use these catalogues to look for books on particular subjects or books written by an author of interest to you.

2. *Bibliographic databases.* Here, I have in mind resources such as the *Reader's Guide to Periodical Literature,* the *National Newspaper Index,* the *Social Sciences Index,* and the *Business Periodicals Index.*

3. *Indexes to specific periodicals.* The best known of these indexes is probably the *New York Times Index,* which lists articles from the *New York Times.* Because this paper is a newspaper of record, the index can be used to find lengthy articles on many subjects of interest to media and communication researchers. The *New York Times* devotes a great deal of attention to advertising and the media.

4. *Abstracts collections.* Various fields have collections of abstracts, such as *Biological Abstracts, Historical Abstracts, Linguistics and Language Behavior Abstracts, Psychological Abstracts,* and the previously mentioned *Communications Abstracts.*

5. *Guides to Research.* These publications are generally selective and offer what editors consider to be the most important source material in a given area. Some typical guides are *Philosophy: A Guide to the Reference Literature, Guide to Reference Books,* and *A Guide to English and American Literature.*

6. *Dictionaries.* The most authoritative dictionary probably is *The Oxford English Dictionary,* but there are numerous other smaller dictionaries that are useful. And there are dictionaries in specific fields, such as James Watson and Ann Hill's (1997) *A Dictionary of Communication and Media Studies* (4th ed.) and Ellis Cashmore and Chris Rojek's (1999) *Dictionary of Cultural Theorists.*

7. *Encyclopedias.* Many encyclopedias, such as *The Encyclopedia Britannica,* are now available on CD-ROM. There are also encyclopedias, such as Microsoft's *Encarta,* that are only on CD-ROM. Some specialized encyclopedias are devoted to communication, television, and the mass media.

8. *Yearbooks.* Many subjects have yearbooks that often combine important theoretical articles and those with significant new research. The *Communication Yearbook* is such a reference.

9. *Statistical sources.* Every year the federal government publishes a huge volume, *Statistical Abstract of the United States,* and the United Nations publishes two volumes, *Statistical Yearbook* and *Demographic Yearbook.* Private publishers also issue books of statistics on both broad and narrowly focused topics.

10. *The Internet.* The Internet enables students to access mind-bog-
    gling amounts of information using search engines such as
    Google and Yahoo and other sources such as Nexis, Vu-Text,
    and Lexis and other online databases. Some useful Internet
    sources for statistical information include the following:

    http://www.barnesandnoble.com

    http://www.census.gov (Census Bureau)

    http://www.census.gov/stat_abstract (*Statistical Abstract of the
        United States*)

    http://www.fedstats.gov (federal government statistics)

    http://www.demographics.com (*American Demographics Magazine*)

    http://www.amazon.com (Amazon bookstore)

Online bookstores such as amazon.com and barnesandnoble.com are
useful because they can be accessed for information about books on all
kinds of subjects. They sometimes also provide reviews of the books and
links to books on related subjects. As you can see from this list, there are
many sources of statistical data available to researchers. And by using
search engines and other websites, you can obtain all kinds of other information. See Boxes 2.1 and 2.2 for additional useful website addresses.

Libraries, which are increasingly electronic nowadays, generally
have the information people are looking for; the problem is finding this
information. And that's where diligence and ingenuity are needed. It's
also a good idea to use the services of reference librarians, who frequently can be of great help.

For example, if you are looking for information about audiovi-
sual education, you may find material on this subject in a number of
different fields:

Educational media	Radio
Film	Recordings
Graphics	Television
Instructional media	Photography
Multimedia	Visual aids

BOX 2.1   USEFUL INTERNET ADDRESSES

http://www.amazon.com (bookstore)

http://www.barnesandnoble.com (bookstore)

http://www.cios.org (Communication Institute for Online Scholarship—CIOS)

http://www.cios.org/www/afjourn.htm (journals list from CIOS)

http://www.ipl.org (Internet Public Library)

http://www.iTools.com/research-it (research source)

http://www.library.uiuc.edu/cmx (Communications Library, University of Illinois)

http://www.loc.gov (Library of Congress)

http://www.moviedatabase.com (movie database)

http://www.mmds.com/af/fr-bottom.asp (to find the meaning of acronyms)

http://www.nytimes.com (*New York Times*)

http://www.nara.gov (National Archives & Records Administration)

http://www.netlibrary.com (2,000 books, periodicals, journals, and articles)

http://www.onelook.com (dictionaries)

http://www.wsj.com (*Wall Street Journal*)

http://www.wsu.edu/~brians/errors/errors.html (common errors in English)

http://www.Yahoo.com/Reference (research source)

This means you have to exercise some judgment in deciding where to search. The *Library of Congress Subject Headings* is a source that identifies alternative subject headings and may be of help to you with this problem. As you can see, there's a solution for almost every problem you face doing research; you just have to know where to look for it or find the right person to ask for help—such as reference librarians.

BOX 2.2   WEB SEARCH ENGINES

Web search engines keep a catalogue of pages they have investigated, and when you ask about some topic, they scan their catalogue looking for Web pages that are relevant.

Excite   http://www.excite.com

Google   http://www.google.com

Hotbot   http://www.hotbot.com

Info seek   http://www.infoseek.com

WebCrawler http://www.webcrawler.com

Yahoo   http://www.yahoo.com

Web Meta-Search Engines

Meta-search engines send requests for information to a number of search engines simultaneously, which means their searches take more time than regular search engines. They often summarize the data they receive or present only a few matches, and thus they may miss important information.

Dogpile   http://www.dogpile.com

MetaCrawler   http://www.metacrawler.com

SavvySearch   http://www.savvysearch.com

❖ SEARCHING ON THE INTERNET OR THE GAME OF "FIND THE INFO IF YOU CAN!"

Libraries are wonderful places to do research because when you go into the stacks looking for a book, you often find other books of interest. The Internet is also very useful because you can access all kinds of information very quickly. Below I offer some suggestions for searching for material on the Internet. In some cases, you will have to change the wording of your searches to find the information you want.

You might want to think of finding information using the Internet as a game called "Find the Info If You Can." You know the information is out there, somewhere on the Internet; finding it is the problem. It is customary to indicate the location of the information you use and the date you accessed it in papers you write.

1. Use search engines such as Google, Yahoo, and Bing for information on any topic you can think of. You can then click on some of the sites that the search engines provide for more information. The first thing I do when there is something I want

to find out about (and that millions of other people do, every day) is go to Google to see what it has to offer. If you type "media and communication research" in Google, you get 38,200,000 sites on that subject. If you type "media research," you get 172,000,000 sites (accessed February 2, 2010). So you have to learn how to narrow down the topics you search for.

2. Use Google Scholar for academic material. Most of the articles aren't free, but you can find them very quickly on the site and then get them at your library or use your library's electronic access to the journals in which the articles appeared.

3. Use Google Books to read books that they have scanned and which can be accessed on the Internet. You can access 35,000 online books at the University of Pennsylvania's Online Book Page (http:digital.library.upenn.edu/books/) and other online book services.

4. Use Wikipedia for a list of search engines and databases that you can access. It lists many sites that will be helpful to you, such as EBSCO, which lists research databases.

5. Organizations such as the Kaiser Family Foundation (http://www .kff.org) and Pew Research Center (http://pewresearch.org) have a great deal of information about the media, public opinion, and related matters.

6. Amazon.com, Barnes & Noble, and other Internet booksellers have lists of books on most subjects you want to get information about. On Amazon.com, you can look inside many of these books (you can read some passages in the books and look at their indexes, bibliographies, etc.) for more information.

7. Many if not most scholarly journals can be read on the Internet. Your library probably has ways of accessing them, so you can go to scholarly journals related to your search. The advantage of getting information in journals is that the information is much more current than you find in books since it takes around a year to publish a book from the time it is accepted by a publisher.

The most important scholarly journals are "peer reviewed." That means the editor of the journal sends out articles without telling who wrote them to a number of scholars with expertise in the subject of the article. The professors don't know who wrote the article, and the writer(s) of the article don't know to whom it was sent. If the scholars think it should be published, the editor generally will publish it. Sometimes the professors want changes, and other times they think an article isn't worth publishing and explain their decisions in reviews they write about the article. Editors use "peer review" in attempt to make judging articles impartial and ensure that the articles are worth publishing.

❖ ANALYZING METHODOLOGY IN RESEARCH ARTICLES

You can also look at research articles not only in terms of their findings but also in terms of their methodologies. We can learn both from the mistakes in the methods of others and from the ingenious methods described in many research articles. First, however, you have to be able to identify the methodology that was used.

Suppose you were doing research about some subject based on survey research. This methodology, which I will discuss in more detail in Chapter 12, involves giving surveys to gather information from a carefully selected group of people who are thought to be representative of some larger population, such as the audience for television programs in a city or state or country.

In examining journal articles that employ survey research, you should do the following things to evaluate the quality of the research. These items are adapted from materials supplied to me by my colleague Chaim Eyal, who often teaches courses in research in my department.

- Identify the method or methods used in the research.
- Determine the research question(s) or hypothesis(es).
- Identify the independent and dependent variables.
- Consider the sample size. $N = ?$
- Evaluate the sampling method that was used.
- Ask yourself how the survey was conducted.
- Make note of the major results and conclusions.

Just because an article is full of statistics and other data doesn't mean that the research it describes was carried out correctly and that the findings are valid.

In analyzing other kinds of research, we follow a similar routine.

1. What topic was investigated?

2. What methods were used?

3. What were the conclusions or findings?

4. What problems (if any) did you find with the methods used?

5. How valid are the findings, and how useful is the research?

Sometimes we can adapt research methods worked out by someone else to deal with a particular problem for topics we are interested in, so it is always good to look at research articles in terms of both what they say and what methodologies they employ.

❖ LIBRARY SEARCHES: APPLICATIONS AND EXERCISES

1. Using the library's access to scholarly journals, find articles that deal with the following:

   Modernism and postmodernism

   Suicide rates in various countries

   International tourism (how many people go to the top 10 countries)

   Advertising expenditures in the United States, France, Germany, Japan, China, and Brazil

2. Apply Chaim Eyal's list of questions and other things you've learned from this book to ask about research to an article that uses survey research.

❖ CONCLUSIONS

Libraries are wonderful places to go looking for information. They have become extremely high-tech in recent years, and now, with their databases and ties to the Internet, they enable students to access material that it wouldn't have been possible to access only a decade ago. Libraries also have large numbers of popular magazines, scholarly journals, government publications, and books that you can use in your research and, in some cases, for your own reading pleasure. Libraries in universities can be accessed on the Internet now so students don't actually have to be in libraries to use their services.

❖ FURTHER READING

Agosti, M. (Ed.). (2008). *Information access through search engines and digital libraries.* Berlin: Springer.

Fielding, N. D., Lee, R. M., & Blank, G. (Eds.). (2008). *The handbook of online research methods.* London: Sage.

Fink, A. (1998). *Conducting research literature reviews: From paper to the Internet.* Thousand Oaks, CA: Sage.

Gibaldi, J. (2009). *Handbook for writers of research papers* (7th ed.). New York: Modern Language Association.

Gross, R. (Ed.). (1993). *The independent scholar's handbook.* Berkeley, CA: Ten Speed Press.

Hart, C. (1998). *Doing a literature review.* Thousand Oaks, CA: Sage.

Mann, T. (1987). *A guide to library research methods.* New York: Oxford University Press.

Semonche, B. P. (Ed.). (1993). *News media libraries.* Westport, CT: Greenwood.

Weinberg, S. (1996). *The reporter's handbook: An investigator's guide to documents and techniques* (3rd ed.). New York: St. Martin's.

Part II

Methods of
Textual Analysis

❖ ❖ ❖

Language is a system of signs that express ideas, and is therefore comparable to a system of writing, the alphabet of deaf-mutes, military signals, etc. But it is the most important of these systems.

A science that studies the life of signs within society *is conceivable; it would be part of social-psychology and consequently of general psychology; I shall call it semiology (from Greek,* semeion *"sign"). Semiology would show what constitutes signs, what laws govern them. Since the science does not yet exist, no one can say what it would be; but it has a right to existence, a place staked out in advance. . . . By studying rites, customs, etc. as signs, I believe that we shall throw new light on the facts and point up the need for including them in a science of semiology and explaining them by its laws.*

—Ferdinand de Saussure,
Course in General Linguistics (1966, p. 16)

3

Semiotic Analysis

Semiotics—the science of signs—is a vast subject that can, at times, be extremely complicated. Some of the writings of semiotic theorists are quite difficult. Yet it is possible to explain enough of the basic principles of semiotics in this brief chapter (and offer an example or two of applied semiotic analysis) so that you can learn enough about semiotics to make your own semiotic analyses. Those of you who are interested in semiotics can, of course, pursue the matter in greater depth by reading some of the books on semiotics mentioned in the bibliography at the end of this chapter.

You will find that semioticians have analyzed facial expressions, hairstyles and hair colors, teeth, fashions in clothing and eyeglasses and jewelry, body piercing, and just about anything you can think of in terms of how they generate meaning and what they reflect about society and culture. I will analyze several interesting signs later on in this chapter.

A SHORT THEATRICAL PIECE ON SEMIOTICS

Grand Inquisitor: *I've been observing students. Tell me about long hair. What does it mean?*

Arthur: Long hair used to mean counterculture, but now it's lost its meaning. Even squares have long hair now... and earrings, too.

Grand Inquisitor: *What about purple hair and green hair?*

Arthur: That's usually the sign of a punk.

Grand Inquisitor: *What about women with shaved hair? Are they war criminals?*

Arthur: Not now. They're just trying to be cool.

Grand Inquisitor: *But don't their heads get cold in the winter? And why do so many men wear beards all of a sudden? Even baseball players.*

Arthur: American society has become increasingly **desexualized.** Men wear beards to affirm their masculinity. Or to hide weak chins.

Grand Inquisitor: *Do you see that cloud over there? It looks like a camel.*

Arthur: You're right. It does look like a camel.

Grand Inquisitor: *Maybe it's more like a weasel.*

Arthur: It is backed like a weasel.

Grand Inquisitor: *Or like a whale.*

Arthur: Very like a whale.

❖ SAUSSURE'S DIVISION OF SIGNS INTO SIGNIFIERS AND SIGNIFIEDS

The Swiss linguist Ferdinand de Saussure (1857–1913) is the founder of semiology, and the American philosopher Charles Sanders Peirce (1839–1914) is the founder of semiotics—both sciences are involved

This book is one of the foundational texts in the study of signs.

with how to interpret **signs.** In recent years, in part to make life simpler for ourselves, we have taken to using the term *semiotics* to stand for both methods of analyzing signs. But what is a sign? I will explain de Saussure's theories first and then deal with Peirce's.

Ferdinand de Saussure

For de Saussure, the important thing to remember about signs is that they are made up of sounds and **images,** what he called *signifiers*, and the concepts these sounds and images bring to mind, what he called *signifieds*. As he wrote,

I call the combination of a concept and a sound-image a sign, but in current usage the term generally designates only a sound-image, a word, for example . . . I propose to retain the word sign [signe] to designate the whole and to replace concept and sound-image respectively by signified [signifie] and signifier [signifiant]; the last two terms have the advantage of indicating the opposition that separates them from each other and from the whole of which they are parts. As regards sign, if I am satisfied with it, this is simply because I do not know of any word to replace it, the ordinary language suggesting no other. (Saussure, 1966, p. 67)

The relationship de Saussure talked about is shown in the chart that follows:

SIGN	
Signifier	*Signified*
Sound-image	Concept

Example :   Word *tree*   Large stemmed plant . . .

Words are signs, but so are many other things, such as facial expressions, body language, clothes, haircuts—you name it. To a semiotician, *everything* can be taken for a sign. Semiotics is, you will see, an imperialistic science.

One problem with signs, however, is that they can be used to lie. That beautiful blonde woman you see sitting at the bar turns out to be neither a woman nor a blonde but a man, a transvestite who is lying with signs.

Blonde hair (not dyed blonde).

❖ THE SEMIOTICS OF BLONDENESS

Blonde hair is the most popular color used by women who dye their hair. As the saying goes, "Many a blonde dyes by her own hands." In the United States, we think that "blondes have more fun." But there are different ways to interpret what blonde hair means, for it is also associated with coldness or innocence. D. H. Lawrence said that in American novels, blonde women are often portrayed as cold, unobtainable, and frigid while dark haired women are shown as passionate and sexually exciting. Sociologist Charles Winick (1995) informs us, in his book *Desexualization in American Life,* that "for a substantial number of women, the attractiveness in blondeness is less an opportunity to have more fun that the communication of a withdrawal of emotion, a lack of passion" (p. 169). That is why, he suggests, Marilyn Monroe was so popular. It is because, Winick argues, she didn't come across as a temptress but, instead, as innocent. For Winick, a brunette who dies her hair blonde looks like a blonde but thinks like a brunette.

We can cite dyed blonde hair as an example of "lying" with signs.

Umberto Eco (1976), a prominent Italian semiotician (and novelist, the author of *The Name of the Rose*) has explained that if signs can be used to tell the truth, they can also be used to lie:

> Semiotics is concerned with everything that can be taken as a sign. A sign is everything which can be taken as significantly substituting for something else. This something else does not necessarily have to exist or actually be somewhere at the moment in which a sign stands for it. Thus semiotics is in principle the discipline studying everything which can be used in order to lie. If something cannot be used to tell a lie, conversely it cannot be used "to tell" at all. (p. 7)

Think, for examples, of brunettes who dye their hair blonde, of short men wearing elevator shoes, of bald men wearing wigs, and women dressing like men—they are all, semiotically speaking, lying with signs.

Ferdinand de Saussure (1966) said there was something very important to remember about signs: The relation between signifier and signified is based on convention, is arbitrary. The word *tree* and the large stemmed plant for which the word *tree* stands is not natural but historical, tied to conventions and choices that people made. He distinguished symbols from signs by saying that symbols, which he saw as a subcategory of signs, are not completely arbitrary. As he wrote,

> One characteristic of the symbol is that it is never wholly arbitrary; it is not empty, for there is the rudiment of a natural bond between the signifier and the signified. The symbol of justice, a pair of scales, could not be replaced by just any other symbol, such as a chariot. (p. 68)

What is important to remember is that symbols have enormous significance in our lives and play an important role in our thinking and behavior.

❖ SEMIOTICS AND SOCIETY

The fact that the relation that exists between signifiers and signifies is based on conventions has important implications, for it means that we need society and its institutions to teach us how to interpret signifiers. As Jonathan Culler (1986) writes in the revised edition of his book *Ferdinand de Saussure,*

> For human beings, society is a primary reality, not just the sum of individual activities . . . and if one wishes to study human behavior, one must grant that there is a social reality. . . . Since meanings are a social product, explanation must be carried out in social terms. . . . Individual actions and symptoms can be interpreted psychoanalytically because

they are the result of common psychic processes, unconscious defenses occasioned by social taboos and leading to particular types of repression and displacement. Linguist communication is possible because we have assimilated a system of collective norms that organize the world and give meaning to verbal acts. Or again, as Durkheim argued, the reality crucial to the individual is not the physical environment but the social milieu, a system of rules and norms, of collective representations, which makes possible social behavior. (pp. 86, 87)

What semiotic theory tells us, by implication, is that we are social animals and that the way we make sense of the world is connected to the social milieu in which we are brought up. The notion that society doesn't exist and that only individuals exist is something we learn, ironically, from society. We will learn more about this matter shortly in the discussion of **culture codes.**

C. S. Peirce, who gave the study of signs, semiotics, its name.

❖ PEIRCE'S TRICHOTOMY: ICON, INDEX, AND SYMBOL

Peirce had a different system. He believed there were three different kinds of signs: icons, indexes, and symbols. **Icons** signify by resemblance, **indexes** signify by cause and effect, and **symbols** signify on the basis of convention. As Peirce wrote,

Every sign is determined by its objects, either first by partaking in the characters of the object, when I call a sign an *Icon;* secondly, by being really and in its individual existence connected with the individual object, when I call the sign an *Index;* thirdly, by more or less approximate certainty that it will be interpreted as denoting the object, in consequence of a habit (which term I use as including a natural disposition), when I call the sign a *Symbol.* (qtd. in Zeman, 1977, p. 36)

Their relationships are shown in the following chart:

	Icons	Indexes	Symbols
Signify by:	Resemblance	Cause and effect	Convention
Example:	Photograph	Fire and smoke	Cross
Process:	Can see	Can figure out	Must learn

There's a considerable difference, then, between de Saussure's science of signs and Peirce's, although both were interested in signs, and both theories have been very influential. Peirce said a sign "is something which stands to somebody for something in some respect or capacity" (qtd. in Zeman, 1977, p. 27). He also argued that the universe is "perfused with signs, if it is not composed exclusively of signs" (Peirce, epigraph in Sebeok, 1977, p. vi). If everything in the universe is a sign, semiotics is the "master" science!

These two interpretations of signs can be looked on as being at the foundation of the science of semiotics. There are, of course, many other aspects to semiotic thought, but with these two understandings of the sign, we can start making applied semiotic analyses. What they do is enable us to understand how it is that people find meaning in things.

Thus, we can use semiotics to analyze and understand how meaning is generated in print advertisements, television and radio commercials, photographs, buildings, television programs, and films. The media are full of signs, both visual and acoustic, that semioticians can analyze. It can be said that the great filmmakers and creative artists of all kinds are people who subconsciously understand the importance of signs, even if they've never studied semiotics. They've learned about signs the hard way—through their failures and their successes.

❖ ALLIED CONCEPTS

A number of other concepts are useful in making semiotic analyses, the more important of which are explained below.

Denotation. **Denotation** refers to the literal meaning of a term or object. It is basically descriptive. A denotative description of a Big Mac would be that it is a sandwich sold by McDonalds that weighs X number of ounces and comes with certain sauces and so on. Or let's take a Barbie Doll. The denotative meaning of a Barbie Doll is a toy doll, marketed first in 1959, that was 11.5 inches high, 5.25 inches in the bust, 3.0 inches at the waist, and 4.25 inches at the hips.

Connotation. **Connotation** deals with the cultural meanings that become attached to a term. The connotative meaning of a Big Mac is that it stands for certain aspects of American culture—fast foods, uniformity, our lack of time, our lack of interest in cooking, the mechanization of food, and so on. The connotative meanings of a Barbie Doll deal with her significance as a courtesan figure and as a consumer who teaches young girls to be consumers. The following chart shows the differences between denotation and connotation.

Denotation	Connotation
Literal	Figurative
Signifier	Signified
Evident	Inferred
Describes	Suggests meaning

Metaphor. **Metaphor** refers to communicating by analogy. Thus, one might say "My love is a red rose." A great deal of our thinking, as I will shortly point out, is metaphoric.

Simile. **Simile** is a weaker subcategory of metaphor, which uses *like* or *as.* For example, "My love is like a rose." Metaphor is based on identity ("my love = a red rose"), whereas simile is based on similarity ("my love *is like* a red rose").

Metonymy. **Metonymy** deals with communicating by association. We make sense of a lot of things by association, by making connections between things we know about and other things. For example, we learn that Rolls Royce automobiles are very expensive, and this associates Rolls Royces with wealth (and perhaps good taste).

Synecdoche. **Synecdoche** is a subcategory of metonymy in which a part is used to stand for the whole or vice versa. We use, for example, "The White House" to stand for the American presidency and the Pentagon to stand for the American military.

Metaphor and metonymy (and their subcategories) are commonly known as "figures of speech." We encounter them in poetry and other literary works, but they are also found in advertising and many other genres in the media. Metaphors play, it turns out, an important role in our everyday lives. Thus, George Lakoff and Mark Johnson (1980) have argued that metaphor is basic to our thinking:

> Most people think they can get along perfectly well without metaphor. We have found, on the contrary, that metaphor is pervasive in everyday life, not just in language but in thought and action. Our ordinary conceptual system, in terms of which we both think and act, is fundamentally metaphoric in nature. (p. 3)

Sometimes, to make life more complicated, we find that something can function both metaphorically and metonymically. For example, a snake can function metaphorically as a **phallic symbol** and, at the same time, metonymically as suggesting the Garden of Eden.

Intertextuality. **Intertextuality** deals with the relation between texts and is used to show how texts borrow from one another, consciously and sometimes unconsciously. Thus, the famous Macintosh commercial "1984" was intexually related to George Orwell's famous anti-utopian novel, *1984.* Parody, in which a text makes a humorous imitation of another text, is one of the more common examples of intertextuality. Think, for example, of Woody Allen's spoof of science fiction films, *Sleeper.* Many texts borrow stylistic elements from other texts or even use characters from other texts.

Codes. In spy stories, codes refer to ways of interpreting messages that are written in ways that are not easily understood, not easy to "crack." When you know the code, you can "unlock" the meaning in the message. In semiotic thought, we use **codes** to refer to structured behavior and argue that much human behavior can be seen as coded, as having secret or covert structures that are not easily understood.

Culture can be seen as being collections of codes. To understand culture, you have to "decode" the behavior of people in the culture or subculture. Semiotics helps us interpret the meaning of various forms and kinds of communication whose meaning, or in some cases whose most significant meaning, is not evident. For example, as we grow up, we learn certain codes about how to cook meat. We don't boil Porterhouse steaks or pork chops. We also have codes about what starches to eat with steaks: We usually have baked potatoes or French fries, but not boiled potatoes or rice (unless we're Asians). We learn any number of codes but don't think about them because to just about everyone who observes them, they become invisible.

Language and Speaking. Language, from a semiotic standpoint, is a social institution: We learn languages by being raised in a given community (or subculture) where the language is spoken. Saussure (1966) made an important distinction between language and speaking:

> But what is language *[langue]*? It is not to be confused with human speech *[langage]*, of which it is only a definite part, though certainly an essential one. It is both a social product of the faculty of speech and a collection of necessary conventions that have been adopted by a social body to permit individuals to exercise that faculty. (p. 9)

What individuals do, de Saussure calls speaking (*parole*). Thus, we have three different phenomena to consider, which are shown in the following chart:

Langue	Langage	Parole
Language	Speech	Speaking/individual act
Institution (social) rules and conventions	Individual/social act	Individual use of rules

We can use the term *speaking* to also include matters such as haircuts, clothes, facial expression, and other forms of individual communication. Once we understand body language, for example, we can understand what a particular gesture a person makes (turning away from you while you're talking to him or her) means.

❖ CLOTAIRE RAPAILLE ON CULTURE CODES

Let me expand a bit on the discussion of codes. A French scholar and marketing expert, Clotaire Rapaille, deals with codes in his book *The Culture Code: An Ingenious Way to Understand Why People Around the World Live and Buy as They Do* (2006). Rapaille places a great deal of importance of what he calls "imprints," which are combinations of experiences and accompanying emotions. As he explains (2006), "Once an imprint occurs, it strongly conditions our thought processes and shapes our future actions. Each imprint helps make us who we are. The combination of imprints defines us" (p. 6). These imprints, he adds, influence us at the unconscious level. His work, he writes, involved him searching for the search of our imprints so he could decode "elements of our culture to discover the emotions and meanings attached to them" (pp. 10, 11). Most of the imprinting is done by the age of 7 because, he suggests, "Emotion is the central force for children under the age of seven" (p. 21). He went off, he says, searching for the codes "hidden within the unconscious of every culture."

His book deals with the various imprintings and codes found in different cultures. He offers an example of decoding cultures in his discussion of cheese. He writes,

> The French Code for cheese is ALIVE. This makes perfect sense when one considers how the French choose and store cheese. They go to a cheese shop and poke and prod the cheeses, smelling them to learn their ages. When they choose one, they take it home and store it is a cloche (a bell-shape cover with little holes to allow air in and keep insects out). The American Code for cheese, on the other hand, is DEAD. Again, this makes sense in context. Americans "kill" their cheese through pasteurization (unpasteurized cheeses are not allowed into the country), select hunks of cheese that have been prewrapped—mummified if you will—in plastic (like body bags), and store it, still wrapped airtight, in a morgue known as a refrigerator. (p. 25)

Rapaille's choice of language is most telling and amusing. Americans mummify their cheeses and stores them in morgues. The important point that we must keep in mind here is that, from Rapaille's perspective and from a semiotic perspective, cultures can be seen as full of different kinds of codes that the semiotician must learn how to decode.

❖ SEMIOTICS IN SOCIETY: A REPRISE

We are now ready to use these concepts to analyze images, objects, and all kinds of other communication. In a sense, using semiotics seems just like "common sense" except that most of the time, just using common sense to make an analysis doesn't offer as complete and sophisticated an analysis of topics of interest to us. Let me offer two quotations that help explain what semiotics does.

The first, by linguist Jonathan Culler (1986), makes an important point about social and cultural phenomena:

> The notion that linguistics might be useful in studying other cultural phenomena is based on two fundamental insights: first, that social and cultural phenomena are not simply material objects or events but objects or events with meaning and hence signs; and second, that they do not have essences but are defined by a network of relations. (p. 4)

We must learn to see all kinds of different things as signs, and when we do, we must think about relations among these phenomena to understand their meaning. Meaning is based on relationships, to recall de Saussure's notion that concepts are defined differentially.

Maya Pines (1982) makes a similar point about humans as sign-creating and sign-generating creatures. She writes,

> Everything we do sends messages about us in a variety of codes, semiologists contend. We are also on the receiving end of innumerable messages encoded in music, gestures, foods, rituals, books, movies, or advertisements. Yet we seldom realize that we have received such messages, and would have trouble explaining the rules under which they operate. (p. G1)

Thus, semiotics helps us understand how to decipher the messages we are sent and understand better the messages we send, about ourselves, to others. We're often unaware of the messages we're sending and how others are interpreting them.

Pointy teeth are conventionally recognized signifiers of vampires.

I can offer an interesting example here. In a seminar I taught on semiotics, I asked students to bring in some object that "reflected" them somehow. They were to bring these objects in brown paper bags so nobody in the class would know who brought each object. And they were to write down, on a piece of paper, what they thought the object reflected about them and put their list in the bag, as well. One woman brought a large seashell. She listed the attributes of the shell that she thought reflected her: beautiful, delicate, natural, and simple. The other members of the seminar found different attributes in the shell when I showed it to them: empty, sterile, brittle, and vacuous. The point is, we often make mistakes about the messages we think we're sending to others.

❖ THE SYNTAGMATIC ANALYSIS OF TEXTS

We can look at stories, narratives, and tales (that is, "texts") as being similar to sentences, except that they are stretched out and made more complicated. Semioticians use the term **syntagmatic analysis** for interpretation of texts that look at them in terms of the sequence of events that give them meaning—in the same way that the sequence of words we use in a sentence generates meaning. (The term *syntagm* means chain.)

One of the outstanding figures in analyzing narratives was the Russian folklorist Vladimir Propp, author of *Morphology of the Folktale* (1928/1968), a pioneering study of the way narratives generate meaning. The term *morphology* means the study of forms or structures and how the components of something relate to each other and to the whole, of which they are all parts. Propp's book argues that narratives are best understood in terms of the functions of their main characters. He studied a group of Russian fairy tales and tried to make sense of how these tales worked and what they added up to. As he wrote,

> We are undertaking a comparison of the themes of these tales. For the sake of comparison we shall separate the component parts of fairy tales by special methods; and then, we shall make a comparison of the tales according to their components. The result will be a morphology (that is, a description of the tale according to its component parts and the relationship of these components to each other and to the whole). (p. 19)

Propp decided to use a morphological approach because other approaches—looking at the tales in terms of styles or kinds of heroes and other classification approaches—didn't work.

Propp suggested that the basic or minimal unit in narratives was what he called a function, which he explained was "an act of a character, defined from the point of view of its significance for the course of action." He added several other important points:

- Functions of characters serve as stable, constant elements in a tale, independent of how and by whom they are fulfilled. They constitute the fundamental components of a tale.

- The number of functions known to the fairy tale is limited.

- The sequence of functions is always identical.

- All fairytales are of one type in regard to their structure.

There were, Propp argued, 31 functions and an initial situation (in which the hero or heroine and the members of his or her family are introduced). There are many subcategories of each function, ways that the function can be realized.

Propp's ideas can be adapted to analyze contemporary texts, and his functions can be modernized. A list of his functions is shown in Table 3.1 along with his list of principal characters in these Russian fairy tales.

It's quite remarkable how many television programs and films and other narratives can be seen as fairy tales and analyzed using updated and modernized versions of Propp's functions, as long as you don't worry about his rule that the sequence of functions is always identical. For example, you can apply Propp's functions to the James Bond stories quite easily. He is always sent on a mission by M, who has Q give Bond "secret weapons" (what Propp called "magic agents"). Bond is often pursued and captured by a villain, whom he eventually outwits and destroys. And usually he gets to have sex—or so we are led to believe—with some beautiful woman he has rescued from the villain (the equivalent of "the hero is married and ascends the throne").

There is another important method of analyzing narrative texts that needs to be explained—paradigmatic analysis, a search for the oppositions found in texts that help give them meaning.

Table 3.1 Propp's Functions

A	*Initial situation*	Members of family introduced or hero introduced.
B	*Absentation*	One of the members of the family absents self from home.
γ	*Interdiction*	An interdiction addressed to hero.
δ	*Violation*	An interdiction is violated.
ε	*Reconnaissance*	The villain makes attempt at reconnaissance.
ζ	*Delivery*	The villain receives information about his victim.
θ	*Trickery*	The villain attempts to deceive his victim.
η	*Complicity*	The victim submits to deception, unwittingly helps the enemy.
A	*Villainy*	The villain causes harm or injury to a member of a family.
a	*Lack*	One member of a family lacks something or wants something.
B	*Mediation*	Misfortune is made known, hero is dispatched.
C	*Counteraction*	Seekers agree to decide on counteraction.
↑	*Departure*	The hero leaves home.
D	*First function of donor*	Hero tested, receives magical agent or helper.
E	*Hero's reaction*	Hero reacts to actions of the future donor.
F	*Receipt of magic agent*	Hero acquires the use of a magical agent.
G	*Spatial transference*	Hero led to object of search.
H	*Struggle*	Hero and villain join in direct combat.
I	*Victory*	Villain is defeated.
K	*Liquidation*	Initial misfortune or lack is liquidated.
↓	*Return*	Return
Pr	*Pursuit*	A chase: The hero is pursued.
Rs	*Rescue*	Rescue of hero from pursuit.
O	*Unrecognized arrival*	The hero, unrecognized, arrives home or in another country.
L	*Unfounded claims*	A false hero presents unfounded claim.
M	*Difficult task*	A difficult task is proposed to the hero.

N	Solution	The task is resolved.
Q	Recognition	The hero is recognized.
Ex	Exposure	The false hero or villain is exposed.
T	Transfiguration	The hero is given a new appearance.
U	Punishment	The villain is punished.
W	Wedding	The hero is married and ascends the throne.

There are seven dramatis personae in Propp's scheme:		
1	Villain	Fights with hero
2	Donor	Provides hero with magical agent
3	Helper	Aids hero in solving difficult tasks, etc.
4	Princess and her father	Sought-for person. Assigns difficult tasks.
5	Dispatcher	Sends hero on his mission
6	Hero	Searches for something or fights with villain
7	False hero	Claims to be hero but is unmasked

❖ THE PARADIGMATIC ANALYSIS OF TEXTS

Syntagmatic analysis focuses on the sequence of events in a text and how the order of events generates meaning. **Paradigmatic analysis** concerns itself with how oppositions hidden in the text generate meaning; it stems from the work of the French anthropologist Claude Lévi-Strauss and his analysis of myths. As folklorist Alan Dundes (1968, p. xi) writes in his introduction to Propp's *Morphology of the Folktale*, paradigmatic analysis

> seeks to describe the pattern (usually based on an a priori binary principle of opposition) that allegedly underlies the folkloristic text. This pattern is not the same as the sequential structure at all. Rather, the elements are taken out of the "given" order and are regrouped in one or more analytic schema. (p. xi)

We are back now to de Saussure's notion that concepts have meaning differentially. Roman Jakobson, a famous linguist, made the same point—that binary oppositions are the fundamental way the human mind produces meaning. In every text (in addition to concepts), the human mind searches for oppositions that enable it to make sense of things. We do this because that is how language works; concepts are always defined differentially.

❖ HUMPTY DUMPTY: A PARADIGMATIC ANALYSIS

Let me offer a paradigmatic analysis of the poem "Humpty Dumpty" here. The oppositions we will find in the text are either stated or implied.

Humpty Dumpty sat on a wall.

Humpty Dumpty had a great fall.

All the king's horses

And all the king's men

Couldn't put Humpty Dumpty together again.

We can find the following oppositions in this text:

on a wall	on the ground
unsteadiness	stability
danger	safety
liquid in container (egg)	solid object
fragile	hard to break, strong
pieces	wholeness
can't be reconstructed	reconstruction possible

When people read this text or hear it, these polar oppositions give it meaning, even if people aren't consciously making these distinctions, because it is through binary oppositions that we make sense of concepts and texts. We are not told that Humpty Dumpty is an egg, but common knowledge and drawings of Humpty Dumpty provide us with this information.

Some critics argue that paradigmatic analysis does not discover structures but "reads them in" or invents them ("hocus pocus"), whereas others claim that it finds structures (sets of oppositions) that are really there, hidden in the text ("God's truth"), that our minds recognize, even if we don't always bring these oppositions to consciousness.

It is important to remember that there is a difference between negations and oppositions. With oppositions, a different term is used, as, for example, in the case of *happy* and *sad*.

Oppositions	Happy vs. sad
Negation	Happy vs. unhappy

There is always a concept or notion that can be inserted between the pair of opposites. In the case of *happy* and *sad*, it would be something like "mental state." Every text generates meanings two ways, then—first, by the order in which events happen (the syntagmatic structure) and, second, by the hidden oppositions found in the text (the paradigmatic structure).

❖ APPLICATIONS OF SEMIOTIC THEORY

Let's consider how semiotic theory can be applied. I will discuss some "signs" that are all parts of our everyday lives: eyeglasses and teeth. They also have significance in television shows and movies, where they can be used to suggest things about characters. And that is because we all try to "read" faces for clues to personality, character, status, and various other things. This is, of course, a semiotic enterprise— even for those who have never heard of semiotics. Many articles in newspapers and magazines are semiotic in nature in that they attempt to make sense of various objects and phenomena that semioticians would call "signs." (A person may never have heard the term *schizophrenic* but that doesn't prevent him or her from being one!)

I will start with eyeglasses. In 1991, Henry Allen, a reporter for the *Washington Post,* wrote an article titled "Everything You Wanted to Know About Specs" that really is an exercise in applied semiotics. He starts his article as follows: "Eyeglasses are not only optical instruments, but they are also costume, manifesto, clothing for the face, and societal fetish." Allen points out that eyeglasses are a $12 billion a year industry in America and that about 60% of Americans own glasses. He continues, discussing men's glasses from a semiotic perspective:

> Men's glasses got sexy in their own right in the '50s, when intellect, alienation, and flaws became sexy in men. The tortured James Dean was seen in glasses. Buddy Holly wore black plastic rims that said, I wear glasses, I don't care if you think I'm handsome or not.

Allen then offers interpretations of the meaning of various styles of glasses, which I will offer in the form of a chart:

Signifier	Signified
KIND OF GLASSES	MEANING
Small glasses	Earnest intensity
Small glasses in wire	Industry and fierce modesty
Big glasses	Not embarrassed to wear glasses
Round glasses	Tradition, authenticity, intellect
Squared-off glasses	Technology, can-do, engineering
Aviator (teardrop)	Masculine adventure
Eye high in frame	Introspection
Eye low in frame	Optimism, action
Silver wire	Mechanical practicality
Black wire	Solid state electronics, minimalist art
Heavy plastic frames	Big ego, big bucks
Colored rims	Playful, creative, eccentric
Rimless	Cool, modest, denying one has glasses
Tinted	Mysterious

These interpretations are semiotic, and the author, Allen, is aware of the science, for he concludes his article with a discussion of General Douglas MacArthur, the famous general in World War II, who was seen as a great strategist by some and a great self-promoter by others.

At the heart of the **aesthetics** of glasses, from deliberate contradiction to preempting of stereotype, is coyness.

Contradiction: General Douglas MacArthur decorated his face with aviator sunglasses, symbol of technological daring, and a corncob pipe, symbol of primitive wisdom—one of the semiotic masterstrokes of the century (Allen, 1991).

Thus, we can see that eyeglasses are used for many purposes—not only to allow us to see more clearly.

Teeth would seem an unlikely candidate for semiotic analysis, but according to a dentist, they are important signs and may have a great deal to do with our love lives and success in the business world. We all know, of course, what a couple of sharp and pointy teeth sticking out of the mouth of a pale and tired-looking man mean—he's a vampire. This is a convention we've learned from films.

But teeth have other meanings as well. A San Francisco cosmetic dentist named Jeff Morley caught the attention of the *Wall Street Journal* a number of years ago by arguing that people unconsciously "read" teeth. Because of this, Morley argues that people have to make sure their teeth convey the right messages and have to make sure their teeth are perfect.

An advertisement by Morley and an associate tells the story:

> Your smile says a lot about you. The alignment, shape, color and condition of your teeth are powerful communicators to friends, family and business associates. They may also have a lot to do with your self esteem.

As Morley explained, in an interview with a reporter from the *Wall Street Journal*,

> What it comes down to is this: Buck teeth imply people are dumb. Large canines imply aggressiveness. Weak chins imply passivity, while strong chins imply a macho, study personality—I don't know who made these up, but the fact is, they're cultural standards. (Chase, 1982, p. 1)

Thus, our eyeglasses and our teeth function as signs that people interpret to gain information about us. We are always sending messages, then, even if we don't say a word—and it is the task of semiotics to help us determine how to "read" the messages others are sending us and make sure that the messages we are sending are the ones we want to send.

❖ PAUL EKMAN ON FACIAL EXPRESSION

Paul Ekman, probably the foremost authority on **facial expression,** did extensive research and found that there are seven universal facial expressions and one "neutral" state that doesn't show any emotion. They are, in alphabetical order:

Anger	Neutral (no particular emotion)
Determination	Pouting
Disgust	Sadness
Fear	Surprise

In a classroom exercise, I showed photographs of Ekman demonstrating these emotions to my students and found they could not correctly identify most of the emotions (see Figure 3.1).

Figure 3.1   Five Facial Expression Images

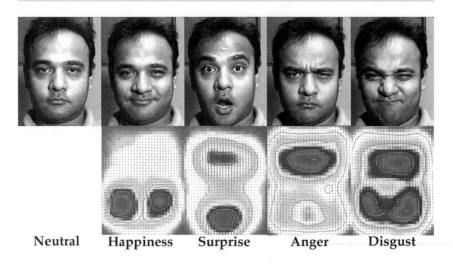

These images reflect five emotions reflected in facial expressions. The images below them shows the energy expended for each facial expression going from neutral to the expression. Courtesy of Irfan Essa. © Irfan Essa.

Ekman developed a Facial Action Coding System, which states that there are 43 muscles in the human face that in different combinations show our emotions. Sometimes an emotion lasts for just a fragment of a second on our faces and we aren't aware of having had it. In a report to the National Science Foundation, *Facial Expression Understanding* (1992), co-written with Terrence J. Sejnowski, we find the following information about facial expressions:

- they provide information about our emotions and our moods;

- they reflect cognitive activity like perplexity, concentration, and boredom;

- they reveal truthfulness and lying; and

- they offer diagnostic information about depression, mania, and schizophrenia and about our responses to treatment for these afflictions.

The report adds that "the technological means are now in hand to develop automated systems for monitoring facial expressions and animating artificial models. . . . Face technology . . . could revolutionize fields as diverse as medicine, law, communications, and education." So faces can reveal a great deal to the trained observer.

❖ SEMIOTIC ANALYSIS: APPLICATIONS AND EXERCISES

1. Find an advertisement that has both metaphor and metonymy in it and explain how they function to sell the product. Study the facial expressions of the people in the advertisement. What do you think they reveal? On what basis do you come to your conclusions?

2. Find articles that use semiotics to analyze hairstyles and hair color for women, men, or both. What insights did they offer? How convincing are the articles?

3. Write a 1,000-word semiotic analysis of *Avatar*. Start your paper with an Applications Chart (see Figure 3.2) on a separate page. To make the chart, you list semiotic concepts on the left-hand side of the page and the applications of the concept to events and dialogue in the film on the right-hand side of the page. In your paper, you amplify and explain your applications.

Note: Use Applications Charts for all your analyses of texts.

Figure 3.2   Sample Applications Chart

Arthur Asa Berger
Sample Concepts/Appications Chart for "Arrival"

Semiotic Concepts	Applications to "Arrival"	
1. Signifier/Signified	Filing Cabinets The Village Numbers Blonde housekeeper	Bureaucracy Small Town Prisoners Innocence
2. Syntagmatic Analysis	See chart in essay.	
3. Paradigmatic Analysis	See chart in essay.	
4. Metaphor	One important metaphor in this text is that the village is a prison.	
5. Synecdoche	Rover stands for the authority of Number Two and the administration.	
6. Icons	Some of the more important icons were the photographs of Number Six and the statues found in the village.	
7. Indexes	The smoke that poured into the agent's room, while he was packing, was a gas that knocked him out and enabled people to bring him to the village.	
8. Symbols	The helicopter was a symbol for escape and the pawns on the chessboard symbolized the villagers.	
9. Intertextuality	*The Prisoner* is related to a program that McGoohan was on earlier, *Danger Man,* and to spy and science fiction genres in general.	
10. Codes	One important code is the smaller the number, the greater the power. Another is duplicity: nobody can be trusted. Another is lack of privacy: Number Six and others are always being monitored.	

4. Using semiotic methods, write a 1,000-word analysis of "The Schizoid Man" episode of *The Prisoner* (available free on the Internet). Use the Application Chart format described above.

Note: Free videos of *The Prisoner* can be found at http://www.amctv .com.

❖ CONCLUSIONS

Semiotics, then, is a valuable tool for understanding how people find meaning in life—in objects, in rituals, in texts of all kinds. When you see the world as "perfused with signs, if not made up entirely of them," and know something about how signs communicate, you have an extremely useful research tool that can be used to analyze texts found in the mass media as well as communication in everyday life.

❖ FURTHER READING

Barthes, R. (1973). *Mythologies* (A. Lavers, Trans.). New York: Hill & Wang.

Berger, A. A. (1992). *Reading matter: Multidisciplinary perspectives on material culture.* New Brunswick, NJ: Transaction Books.

Berger, A. A. (1997). *Bloom's morning: Coffee, comforters and the secret meaning of everyday life.* Boulder, CO: Westview/HarperCollins.

Berger, A. A. (1999). *Signs in contemporary culture: An introduction to semiotics* (2nd ed.). Salem, WI: Sheffield.

Berger, A. A. (2009). *What objects mean: An introduction to material culture.* Walnut Creek, CA: Left Coast Press.

Bignell, J. (2002). *Media semiotics: An introduction* (2nd ed.). Manchester, England: Manchester University Press.

Blonsky, M. (1992). *American mythologies.* New York: Oxford University Press.

Danesi, M. (1995). *Interpreting advertisements: A semiotic guide.* Toronto: Legas.

Danesi, M. (1999). *Of cigarettes, high heels, and other interesting things: An introduction to semiotics.* Basingstoke, UK: Macmillan.

Eco, U. (1984). *The role of the reader: Explorations in the semiotics of texts.* Bloomington: Indiana University Press.

Gottdiener, M. (1995). *Postmodern semiotics: Material culture and the forms of postmodern life.* Cambridge, MA: Blackwell.

Leeds-Hurwitz, W. (1993). *Semiotics and communication: Signs, codes, cultures.* Mahwah, NJ: Lawrence Erlbaum.

Rapaille, C. (2006). *The culture code.* New York: Broadway Books.

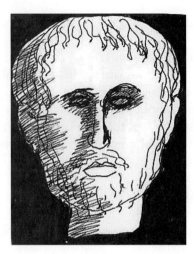

Aristotle.

If all good art has no rhetorical dimension, as so many have argued, then the "rhetoric" is left to those who will use it for the devil's purposes. . . . How much better it would be if we could develop a way of understanding how great literature and drama does in fact work rhetorically to build and strengthen communities. Reading War and Peace *or seeing* King Lear *does change the mind, just as reading* Justine *or taking a daily dose of TV fare changes minds. A movie like* The Graduate *both depends on commonplaces shared much more widely than our slogans of fragmentation and alienation would allow for, and strengthens the sharing of those commonplaces; like* The Midnight Cowboy *or* Easy Rider, *it can be said to make a public as well as finding one already made. All of them work very hard to appear nonrhetorical; there are no speeches by anyone defending the graduate's or the cowboy's values against the "adult" world that both movies reject so vigorously. But the selection from all possible worlds is such that only the most hard-bitten or critical-minded viewer under forty is likely to resist sympathy for the outcasts and total contempt for the hypocritical aging knaves and fools that surround them. If sheer quantity and strength of pressure on our lives is the measure, the rhetoric of such works, though less obvious, is more in need of study than the open aggressive rhetoric of groups like* The Living Theatre.

—Wayne Booth, "The Scope of Rhetoric Today"
in *The Prospect of Rhetoric Today* (1971; qtd. in
Medhurst & Benson, 1984, p. 102)

4

Rhetorical Analysis

❖ ❖ ❖

Retorical analysis used to be confined to speech and written materials, but with the explosive development of the mass media, rhetorical theory is now also being used to interpret works found on radio, television, and film—that is, what we now call mass-mediated culture. Wayne Booth, a well-known critic from the University of Chicago, was one of the first to point out the need for rhetoricians to pay attention to the mass media. And his call has been heeded, for now rhetoricians have become increasingly interested in the mass media.

❖ ARISTOTLE ON RHETORIC

Aristotle's *Rhetoric* was the most influential rhetorical text for thousands of years. Aristotle was endlessly cited by rhetoricians as the authority on matters rhetorical. He divided **rhetoric** into two general areas—public speaking and logical discussion—and explained that although every field of thought has its own means of persuasion, *rhetoric* is the term for means of persuasion useful in all fields. He writes,

Rhetoric may be defined as the faculty of observing in any given case the available means of persuasion. This is not a function of any other art. Every other art can instruct or persuade about its own particular subject-matter; for instance, medicine about what is healthy and unhealthy, geometry about the properties of magnitudes, arithmetic about numbers, and the same is true of the other arts and sciences. But rhetoric we look upon as the power of observing the means of persuasion on almost any subject presented to us; and that is why we say that, in its technical character, it is not concerned with any special or definite class of subjects. (qtd. in McKeon, 1941, p. 1329)

Aristotle adds that there are three modes of persuasion speakers can use: first, *ethos,* based on the personal character of the speaker—that is, his or her credibility; second, *pathos,* based on putting the members of the audience into a certain frame of mind—that is, stirring their emotions; and third, *logos,* based on the proof or apparent proof generated by the words in the speech itself—that is, the arguments made in the speech or text.

Aristotle wrote another book, *Poetics,* about tragedy and comedy, the nature of plots and related matters, but for our purposes, we can think of poetics as being part of rhetoric (although some scholars would not agree with this, I should point out). Our focus will not be limited to argumentation, per se (as in debates), but will also be on persuasion in a broader sense—that is, on how creators of texts achieve their ends. That involves things such as how advertising agencies "convince" us to buy the products and try the services they advertise, how novelists "move" us, and how filmmakers and playwrights create characters with whom we can empathize.

Numerous classifications and subclassifications have been made by rhetorical theorists. For example, Aristotle argued that there are three branches to rhetoric—or, more precisely, three kinds of oratory:

Kind	Area	Function
Deliberative	Legislative	Exhorts or dissuades
Judicial	Forensic	Accuses or defends
Panegyric	Ceremonial	Commemorates or blames

Marcus Tullius Cicero (106–43 BC), a famous Roman orator, statesman, and rhetorician, suggested that rhetoric had five parts:

ethos - ethics/character
pathos - emotions
logos - logic/proof

Chapter 4   Rhetorical Analysis   75

Since all the activity and ability of an orator falls into five divisions, . . . he must first hit upon what to say; then manage and marshall his discoveries, not merely in an orderly fashion, but with a discriminating eye for the exact weight as it were of each argument; next go on to array them in the adornments of style; after that keep them guarded in his memory; and in the end deliver them with effect and charm.

—Cicero, *De Oratore,* I xxxi, pp. 142–143

Rhetoric, for Cicero, breaks down into the following five parts:

Term	In Latin	In Greek
Invention	*Inventio*	*Heuresis*
Arrangement	*Dispositio*	*Taxis*
Style	*Elocutio*	*Lexis*
Memory	*Memoria*	*Mneme*
Delivery	*Actio*	*Hypocrisis*

Even though these terms were originally used for oratory, they also have relevance to conversations (a form of interactive oratory, if you think about it) and the rhetorical analysis of mass-mediated culture. The term *mneme* is the root of a field known as *mnemonics* (it has a silent "m" and is pronounced nem-onics)—ways of remembering material, using all kinds of different strategies to achieve its ends.

❖ RHETORIC AND THE MASS MEDIA

In the preface to Martin J. Medhurst and Thomas W. Benson's (1984) *Rhetorical Dimensions in Media: A Critical Casebook,* we find a rationale for applying rhetoric to the mass media. They point out that the Greeks and Romans considered rhetoric a very important subject because it played a role in enabling men and women to live together in society. They write,

> With rhetoric—*the attempt by one person or a group to influence another through strategically selected and stylized speech,* a society could perpetuate itself, debate its internal problems, and decide which norms and values it would follow without resorting to violence. (p. vii)

In the present day, as they point out, human speech is still the basic means we have of influencing one another:

> The study of how people choose *what to say* in a given situation, *how to arrange or order* their thoughts, *select the specific terminology* to employ, and decide precisely *how they are going to deliver their message* is the central focus of rhetorical studies. (p. vii)

If you look at this passage, you can see it draws directly on Cicero's five ways of communicating.

A SHORT THEATRICAL PIECE ON RHETORIC

Grand Inquisitor:	*What are the ways?*
Arthur:	When I was in the Army (yes, it's true—I'm a *trained killer*) I was told that there were three ways: the right way, the wrong way, and the Army way.
Grand Inquisitor:	*Are there any other ways?*
Arthur:	Yes! For media students, there's the segue.
Grand Inquisitor:	*Is that the last way?*
Arthur:	Not at all. Now that we live in a multicultural world, there's also the Zimbabwe! And the Amway!
Grand Inquisitor:	*Did anyone ever tell you that you're "far out"?*
Arthur:	No, I'm not far out. Your problem is that you're "far in"!
Grand Inquisitor:	*Is that what being a foreigner means?*
Arthur:	I'm supposed to be the one making the puns!

What is important to recognize, the authors add, is that platform oratory—the delivery of formal speeches—is no longer the crucial element in exchanging communication. We live in an age of mass media, and we can use rhetoric to analyze this mass-mediated communication. Medhurst and Benson (1984) mention two important rhetoricians,

Kenneth Burke and Wayne Booth, who suggest that all symbolic communication is inherently rhetorical because it is intended to communicate, and rhetorical criticism is concerned with how symbols communicate.

I should mention, in passing, that some of the terms found in semiotic thought are also found in rhetorical thought. Saussure, one of the founders of semiotics, was a linguist, we must remember. Who lays claim to these terms is not particularly important for our concerns.

In the preface to *Rhetorical Dimensions in Media* (Medhurst & Benson, 1984), the authors list nine understandings of the term *rhetoric* as it applies to media. The list that follows is an adaptation of their list:

1. Intentional persuasion

2. Social values and effects of symbolic forms found in texts (whether intentionally placed in them or not)

3. Techniques by which the arts communicate to audiences

4. Persuasion techniques used by characters on one another in dramatic or narrative works

5. Cicero's five rhetorical practices found in texts

6. Study of **genres** or types of texts

7. Implicit theories about human symbolic interaction implied by authors of symbolic works

8. An ideal for the conduct of communication among humans

9. Study of what makes form effective (known as pragmatics)

Medhurst and Benson offer this list as a guide for their readers who may wonder what the authors of the articles in the book are doing. We can also use them when we make our own rhetorical analyses of texts such as print advertisements, radio and television commercials, television shows, films, MTV, and other forms of mass-mediated entertainment.

The term *entertainment* deserves a bit of explanation. Many people assume that entertainments are trivial and have no significance. We now recognize that our entertainments—television programs, films, commercials, music videos, songs—play an important role in shaping our consciousness, as the quote from Booth at the beginning of the chapter suggests.

❖ A BRIEF NOTE ON THE COMMUNICATION PROCESS

It is useful to clarify, at this point, who is communicating what to whom. I will use a well-known model for the communication process by the linguist Roman Jakobson. I will also discuss an equally well-known one by Harold Lasswell and tie it to one I have developed that deals with the five **focal points** in communication: the **artist** (creator), the work of art, the **audience,** the **medium** used by the artist, and America (or any society).

Jakobson's (see McQuail & Windahl, 1993) model is shown below:

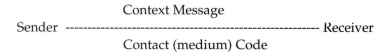

Let me explain this model. Whatever kind of communication we are dealing with involves a message that someone (the sender) sends to someone else (the receiver). The message is delivered through a contact (medium), is given in a code (such as the English language), and is affected by the context in which it is given. Thus, the message "pass the syringe" means one thing in a dark alley and another thing in a hospital, so context plays an important role in the communication process.

Jakobson suggests that messages can have a number of different functions:

1. The **referential function,** involving the surroundings in which senders find themselves

2. The **emotive function,** involving the emotions expressed by senders

3. The **poetic function,** involving the use of literary devices such as metaphor and metonymy by senders

Lasswell (see McQuail & Windahl, 1993), a political scientist, offered perhaps the most famous phrase in communication research, when he said communication researchers should ask the following:

Who?

Says what?

In which channel?

To whom?

With what effect?

I have dealt with more or less the same concerns with my five focal points—although when I elaborated them, I didn't realize that they correspond with Lasswell's famous question or dictum.

We can see this if we line up the Lasswell formulation with my focal points and with Jakobson's model as shown in Table 4.1. In essence, all of these **models** contain the same fundamental elements, and communication researchers tend to focus on some relationship among these elements when doing their research.

Table 4.1   Theories of Communication

Lasswell	Focal Points	Jakobson
Who	Artist	Sender
Says what?	Artwork (text)	Message
In which channel?	Medium	Contact
To whom?	Audience	Receiver
With what effect?	America (society)	Meaning

There are problems in communication at all levels arising from things such as the differences between the way senders encode their messages and the way receivers decode these messages. That is why Umberto Eco (1976), the distinguished Italian semiotician, suggested that when dealing with the mass media, we often find **aberrant decoding** as audiences decode messages (that is, interpret dialogue and events in television programs, for instance) differently from the way the writers expect them to. But the same thing often happens in personal conversations. We say something, and the person we are talking to takes it "the wrong way," by which we mean he or she didn't interpret what we said the way we meant it.

Eco - aberrant decoding - decoders interpretation is different than sender's preferred meaning.

❖ MICHEL DE CERTEAU ON SUBVERSIONS BY READERS AND VIEWERS

In his book *The Practice of Everyday Life*, the French scholar Michel de Certeau suggests that we must pay more attention to the uses people make of media and that those who are members of the audiences of the media put their own interpretations on what they see and hear, and their responses are not always the ones the senders of messages expect. He writes, discussing the impact of the media,

> To a rationalized, expansionist and at the same time centralized, clamorous, and spectacular production [of media] corresponds *another* production, called "consumption." The latter is devious, it is dispersed, but it insinuates itself everywhere, silently and almost invisibly, because it does not manifest itself through its own products, but rather though its *ways of using* the products imposed by a dominant economic order. (de Certeau, 1984, pp. xii, xiii)

He offers an example of the way Indians reacted to their Spanish conquerors. The Indians, he explains, seemed to be submissive and consenting, but they subverted the various rituals and laws imposed upon them in various ways for their own purposes. Certeau suggests that audiences of modern mass media do the same thing and, using various tactics, subvert the messages imposed on them by dominant elites in contemporary societies. Certeau's point is that we cannot assume that everyone is affected the same way by the messages to which they are exposed in the media and that people reinterpret the texts to which they are exposed in ways that suit their needs.

❖ APPLIED RHETORICAL ANALYSIS

Rhetoricians are particularly interested in one element of the communication process, the matter of persuasion (covered in the models in rather general ways by terms such as *effects* or *impact on society*). This stems, in part, from Aristotle's definition of rhetoric as being the art of persuasion. Thus, in his book *The Rhetorics of Popular Culture: Advertising, Advocacy, and Entertainment,* Robert L. Root Jr. (1987) offers a description of how he will conduct his analyses:

> In every case I will attempt to apply rhetorical analysis to a specific aspect of popular culture and repeatedly ask the same questions about them: What is the mode of presentation? How does the mode affect the presentation? What is the purpose of the discourse? Who is the audience for the discourse? How is the discourse directed at that audience? What person is created, how is it created, and why is it

created? What is the argument of the discourse? How is it arranged? Upon what is it based? Generally these are questions of rhetoric which can be asked of any discourse. (p. 21)

Root, drawing on Aristotle, suggests that there are certain universal elements of rhetorical analysis: ethos, pathos, logos, aim, and mode. Let me offer brief definitions of these terms in the following chart:

Term	Definition
Ethos	Character of speaker helps convince
Pathos	Appeal to emotions in listener (audience)
Logos	Proof based on reason, logical argument
Aim	Purpose of discourse
Mode	Medium used (talk, radio, TV, film, etc.)

These are the concerns Root has and that, he suggests, rhetorical critics should have, regardless of what kind of communication it is that they are researching.

These terms are somewhat general and abstract. When you are actually doing research, it is necessary to use concepts that are lower down on the ladder of abstraction. Thus, for example, if you are analyzing print advertisements and radio and television commercials, you would consider the arguments found in these texts and the methods used to convince people to buy products and services such as the following:

Be first on your block to have one. . . . Others will be jealous.

Buy one and you'll find the lover of your dreams.

Buy one and make your lover happy.

Buy one and you will keep your lover and not lose him or her.

Show everyone you're a quality person with good taste and buy one.

This or that celebrity has one or uses one; shouldn't you?

One could go on and on about the appeals found in advertising and the way ads and commercials attempt to manipulate people: to attract attention, stimulate desire, and lead to a desired action.

You might also consider some of the specific rhetorical devices or means that copywriters use, such as alliteration, rhyme, rhythm, definition, metaphor and metonymy (discussed in detail in Chapter 3 on semiotics), comparison, exemplification, and irony. Various dictionaries and handbooks of rhetorical terms list hundreds of technical terms, generally with Latin names, used by rhetoricians. I will define some of the more common rhetorical devices below.

❖ A MINIGLOSSARY OF COMMON RHETORICAL DEVICES

Allegory. Allegories are narratives in which abstract ethical and philosophical beliefs are represented by characters and events—that is, made concrete. One of the most famous television allegories is the Kafkaesque British cult series *The Prisoner,* starring Patrick McGoohan, which was **broadcast** in the late 1960s. (Reruns of it are shown constantly, and there are numerous books about it, as well.) Allegories can be seen as extended metaphors in which the meanings of events in a text lie outside of the text itself, and the characters can be seen as personifications of abstract ideas.

Alliteration. Generally, using a number of words in a passage that start with the same letter or that repeat some vowel. Let me offer an example:

"Magazines Move Millions. One Mind at a Time."

(This was the headline in an advertisement in a number of newspapers by Magazine Publishers of America.) Alliteration has a certain playfulness to it and also helps people remember messages better. I used alliteration in my model of the focal points of communication: artist, artwork, audience, America (or society), and medium.

Comparison. As I explained earlier, when I quoted de Saussure (1966), meaning arises out of comparisons. "Comparisons are odious," it has been said. We can see, then, that speakers and writers use comparisons to reinforce the arguments they are making. For example, in the 1970s, my book *The TV-Guided American* was reviewed in the *New York Times Book Review.* The reviewer concluded his review with the following statement: "Berger is to the study of television what Idi Amin is to tourism in Uganda."

Definition. There are a number of different kinds of definitions. There are *lexical* or dictionary definitions, which refer to the way words are conventionally used. There are also *stimulative* definitions, which refer to a definition given for the purpose of argument. And there are *operational* definitions, which do not rely on words but offer a list of operations to perform that will lead to an understanding of what is being defined.

Encomium. An encomium praises a thing (or a person) by dealing with its various inherent qualities. This is a widely used technique in advertising. The advertising slogan "tastes good, less filling" is an encomium.

Exemplification. We often use examples to support our position in some argument. We must be careful, of course, that we don't allow selective perception to blind us to examples that would cast doubt on our argument or to overgeneralize from examples. For example, I once mentioned in a class that smoking is bad for people, and one of my students told me about an uncle of his who smoked two packs of cigarettes a day and was 85. My student's uncle, I would suggest, is not representative of the American **public.**

Irony. Verbal irony involves using words to convey the opposite of what they literally mean. One problem with irony is that many people do not recognize that a statement is meant to be seen as ironic and take it at face value. This can lead to all kinds of misunderstandings. An example of verbal irony in humor is illustrated by the following joke:

> A man named Katzman decided to change his name to a French name so people wouldn't be able to recognize that he was Jewish. He went to a judge for help. "French, you say," said the judge. "Well, the French word for cat is 'chat' and the French word for man is 'l'homme,' so we'll change your name to Chat-l'homme."

The irony in this joke is that Chat-l'homme is pronounced "shalom," the Hebrew word for "hello," so the man ended up with a more Jewish name than his original name was.

There are other kinds of irony: dramatic irony, in which the fates lead to a resolution that is the opposite of what a character intended, and Socratic irony, which involves pretending to be ignorant. A stronger and more insulting form of irony is sarcasm, which means, literally, "tearing the flesh."

Metaphor. Metaphor uses analogy to generate meaning. Metaphor means equivalence as in "My love *is* a red rose." (These terms are also discussed in Chapter 3 on semiotics.)

Metonymy. Metonymy uses association to generate meaning. Advertisers who want to inform their readers or viewers that someone is very wealthy can use big mansions and Rolls Royce automobiles to convey this information. Metonymy is one of the most commonly used techniques used by advertisers because it builds on information that audiences already have and thus is very economical. (Metonymy is also dealt with in Chapter 3 on semiotics.)

Rhyme. The repetitive use of words with similar terminal sounds is a commonly used device to attract people's attention and help them remember things. It is found in much poetry, as in

> I think that I shall never see
> A billboard lovely as a flea . . .

but also in other forms of communication, such as advertising. Let me offer a classic example of a rhymed jingle from my younger days:

> Pepsi Cola hits the spot
> Twelve full ounces, that's a lot
> Twice as much for your money, too . . .
> Pepsi Cola is the drink for you.

Rhyme has the power to stick in our minds, which explains why it is often used in advertising jingles.

Rhythm. Rhythm refers to patterned and recurring alternations, at various intervals, of sound or speech elements. Another term for rhythm is *beat.* If you look at the lyrics of rock and roll songs, they look idiotic, but that's because the printed versions of the lyrics don't convey the beat at which they are sung or the melody of the song.

Simile. A weaker form of metaphor, which uses *like* or *as.* Metaphor is based on equivalence, but simile is based on similarity. "My love is *like* a red rose." (Similes are dealt with in Chapter 3 on semiotics.)

Synecdoche. A weaker form of metonymy in which part is used to stand for the whole or vice versa. For example, we use the Pentagon to stand for the entire American military establishment or the White House to stand for the American presidency. (Synecdoche is dealt with in Chapter 3 on semiotics.)

❖ OTHER CONSIDERATIONS WHEN MAKING RHETORICAL ANALYSES

In addition to the spoken language, there are other considerations when doing rhetorical analysis of texts in the mass media. In film and television, we might consider matters such as the use of sound effects, the way actors and actresses speak and use body language and facial expressions, the use of music, the way these texts are edited, and the use of keyed-in written material. Analyzing a television commercial or MTV video from a rhetorical perspective, it is easy to see, can be an extremely complicated matter.

❖ A SAMPLE RHETORICAL ANALYSIS: A SATURN ADVERTISEMENT

I will use rhetorical concepts to analyze a Saturn advertisement. I will number each sentence to make it easier to follow my analysis. The advertisement is on two pages that face one another (a double-truck in printing lingo).

1. Is handling the way a car responds to you, or the way you respond to a car?

2. "After I drove it the first time, everyone was asking me, 'What are you smiling about?'"

3. That's how Anna Lang, a vehicle auditor at Saturn, describes her first experience behind the wheel of a Saturn.

4. After testing the ride and performance of one of the first Saturn cars ever built, she had a decision to make.

5. "I was surprised at how solid the car felt."

6. "It just hugged the road."

7. "I mean, this car's about the size of a Toyota Celica, and small cars aren't supposed to be so smooth."

8. "To be honest, I was a little nervous before I drove it."

9. "I've put too much into the company to build a car I didn't like."

10. "And a lot of people here feel that way."

11. "Fortunately, I got to tell everyone how nice it was to step out of the car wanting to buy one."

12. Saturn. A different kind of company.

13. A different kind of car.

I will analyze this advertisement using some of the concepts discussed in my glossary.

Definition. In Sentence 1, we have a somewhat convoluted definition, involving the term *handling.* The sentence plays with the term, asking whether handling means how the car responds to the driver or the driver responds to the car. There's an element of antithesis involved here, also.

Metonymy. In Sentence 2, we find that the woman is asked by everyone what she is smiling about. Here, we have an association between smiling and her having driven the car, which suggests that the Saturn was the source of her happiness. The smile symbolizes the happiness the woman feels.

Exemplification. Sentence 3 tells us how Anna Lang "describes her first experience behind the wheel of a Saturn." We are offered a testimonial (from a company employee, we must remember) about the car.

Metonymy. In Sentence 6, we read that the Saturn "hugged" the road, which calls to mind experiences we have of hugging people we like, associations that are positive, warm, and pleasant.

Comparison. In Sentence 7, she compares Saturns with Toyota Celicas, which are considerably more expensive. "This car's about the size of a Toyota Celica," she says. The comparison works to the benefit of the Saturn, because it is less expensive. In the reader's mind, the two are made more or less equal. There may be an element of what is called a "halo effect" in this comparison in that the Saturn is, it is suggested, equal to the Celica.

Alliteration. The alliteration is not obvious, but it is in the text. I'm talk-ing about all the S sounds we have in this sentence fragment: . . . this car's about the size of a Toyota Celica, and small cars aren't supposed to be so smooth.

We find S sounds in the following words: *car's, size, Celica, small, cars, supposed, so,* and *smooth.* And it just happens that Saturn also starts with an S.

Allegory. We can look at Anna Lang's adventure as somewhat allegorical in nature. At the end of this little tale, there is a happy ending. She tells us, "I got to tell everyone how nice it was to step out of the car wanting to buy one." Notice the pitch in the last two words, which suggests an action that readers should do, also—"buy one." She represents a person who tests a car and finds it is one she can purchase with confidence. She had been nervous but now realizes that her involvement with Saturn was worthwhile. As she says in Sentence 9, "I've put too much into this company to build a car I didn't like." And she's like her other workers, described in Sentence 10. "A lot of people here feel that way." We can see from this story that Saturn has dedicated workers who build a really great car.

Comparison. That's why Saturn is, as Sentence 12 puts it, "A different kind of company" that builds, as Sentence 13 informs us, "A different kind of car." We have a comparison between Saturn, a company full of dedicated workers who build cars that hug the road and are smooth and, implicitly, other car companies that have workers who, in the **stereotype** we have of people who make automobiles, don't really give a damn about the cars they assemble. That's why folklore tells us not to purchase cars assembled on Mondays (when the autoworkers are supposedly recovering from being drunk over the weekend) and Fridays (when the autoworkers aren't able to concentrate on what they are doing).

As you can see, the copywriters for Saturn cars used a number of rhetorical devices in this advertisement. In this analysis, I've not dealt with a paragraph in the advertisement, in small type, about the kind of engine the Saturn has, its wheels and tires, and other matters that are rather technical in nature. Nor have I dealt with the two images—one of the car and another of a windy road (easily handled, we are led to assume, by the smooth-driving, road-hugging Saturn)—or with the Saturn logo or with the kind and size of the typefaces used. All of these elements might also be analyzed.

Other matters could also be discussed, such as the choice of language in the textual material in this advertisement. Terms such as *respond, auditor, performance, honest,* and *fortunately* all have rather positive connotations that give readers an image of the Saturn that the company wishes people to have. In technical terms, we have both *ethos* in which the persuader's character and credibility are established (she's an auditor, and she had a decision to make, which she made based on the performance of the Saturn) and *logos* (she tested the Saturn and found that it is smooth riding and that it hugs the road), so her decision to buy one strikes us as rational.

❖ RHETORICAL ANALYSIS: APPLICATIONS AND EXERCISES

1. Using the terms in the miniglossary of common rhetorical devices and the analysis of the Saturn advertisement as a model, make a 1,000-word rhetorical analysis of an advertisement that has a large number of words and many rhetorical devices in it. Use the Applications Chart format to list the concepts and their applications to the advertisement on the first page. Turn in the advertisement with your paper.

2. Make a rhetorical analysis of the passage from Robert Musil's (1965) *The Man Without Qualities* that is found on page **xviii.** Use as many terms from the miniglossary as you can. Use the Applications Chart format described above. List rhetorical concepts on the left-hand side of the chart and their applications to the passage on the right-hand side of the chart.

3. How would you characterize Musil's "style" of writing? Do you like his style? Explain your answer.

4. Make a rhetorical analysis of the lyrics of a popular song. Use an Application Chart in our analysis.

❖ CONCLUSIONS

The more you know, the more you see and understand. It is our conceptual knowledge that enables us to move beyond simple descriptions and make sense of what we are seeing. Thus, in media and communication research, rhetoric plays an important role because it gives us a large number of concepts that enable us to understand how a text generates meaning and helps shape people's emotions and their behavior.

❖ FURTHER READING

Bal, M. (1985). *Narratology: Introduction to the theory of narrative* (C. van Boheemen, Trans). Toronto: University of Toronto Press.

Berger, A. A. (1992). *Popular culture genres: Theories and texts.* Newbury Park, CA: Sage.

Berger, A. A. (1997). *Narratives in popular culture, media and everyday life.* Thousand Oaks, CA: Sage.

Berger, A. A. (2005). *Media analysis techniques* (3rd ed.). Thousand Oaks, CA: Sage.

Booth, W. (1961). *The rhetoric of fiction.* Chicago: University of Chicago Press.

Brooke, C. G. (2009). *Lingua franca: Toward a rhetoric of new media.* Creskill, NJ: Hampton.

Chatman, S. (1978). *Story and discourse: Narrative structure in fiction and film.* Ithaca, NY: Cornell University Press.

Esslin, M. (1982). *The age of television.* San Francisco: W. H. Freeman.

Foss, S. K. (2008). *Rhetorical criticism.* Long Grove, IL: Waveland.

Jowett, G., & O'Donnell, V. (1999). *Propaganda and persuasion* (3rd ed.). Thousand Oaks, CA: Sage.

Lakoff, G., & Johnson, M. (1980). *Metaphors we live by.* Chicago: University of Chicago Press.

Lanham, R. A. (1991). *A handlist of rhetorical terms* (2nd ed.). Berkeley: University of California Press.

Rice, J. (2007). *The rhetoric of cool: Composition studies and new media.* Carbondale: Southern Illinois University Press.

Root, R. L., Jr. (1987). *The rhetorics of popular culture: Advertising, advocacy, and entertainment.* New York: Greenwood.

Karl Marx.

We begin with real, active men, and from their real life-process show the development of the ideological reflexes and echoes of this life-process. The phantoms of the human brain are also necessary sublimates of men's material life-process, which can be empirically established and which is bound to material preconditions. Morality, religion, metaphysics and other ideologies, and their corresponding forms of consciousness, no longer retain therefore their appearance of an autonomous existence. They have no history, no development; it is men, who, in developing their material production and their material intercourse, change, along with this their real existence, their thinking and the products of their thinking. Life is not determined by consciousness, but consciousness by life.

—Karl Marx, *Selected Writings in Sociology and Social Philosophy* (1964, p. 75)

5

Ideological Criticism

W hat is ideological criticism and why is it important? The matter is complicated by the fact that **ideology** is a difficult and complex concept. By ideological criticism, I refer to any kind of criticism that bases its evaluation of texts or other phenomena being discussed on issues, generally of a political or socioeconomic nature, that are of consuming interest to a particular group of people. Traditionally, the term *ideology* refers to a systematic and all-inclusive sociopolitical explanation of what goes on in a society.

In this chapter, I will be dealing mostly with Marxist criticism, but I will also consider feminist criticism and the work of political scientist Aaron Wildavsky (see Wildavsky, 1982) on political cultures. His work suggests that all democratic societies have four **political cultures** in them that compete for **power.** One of them, what he calls Egalitarians, is very similar in its value structure to **Marxism.**

❖ MANNHEIM'S *IDEOLOGY AND UTOPIA*

In one of the classic studies of ideological thinking, Karl Mannheim's (1936) *Ideology and Utopia,* we find an interesting analysis of ideology. Mannheim writes,

The concept "ideology" reflects the one discovery which has emerged from political conflict, namely, that ruling groups can in their thinking become so intensively interest-bound to a situation that they are simply no longer able to see certain facts which would undermine their sense of domination. There is implicit in the word "ideology" the insight that in certain situations the collective unconscious of certain groups obscures the real condition of society both to itself and to others and thereby stabilizes it. (p. 40)

In opposition to the ideologists, Mannheim argues, are Utopians who come from various repressed subcultures and other groups and see only the negative aspects of the societies in which they find themselves. Mannheim's ideologists see no evil in their societies, and his Utopians see no good; both, of course, are deluded.

❖ DEFINING IDEOLOGY

Claude Mueller (1973), in his book *The Politics of Communication,* defines ideology in the following manner: "Ideologies are . . . integrated belief systems which provide explanations for political reality and establish the collective goals of a class or group" (pp. 101–102). The term *ideology* is often found in the writings of Marxist critics. They argue that the media and other forms of communication are used in capitalist nations, dominated by a bourgeois ruling class, to generate false consciousness in the masses, or in Marxist terms, the proletariat. Just because people are not aware that they hold ideological beliefs does not mean they don't hold them. They haven't brought them to consciousness and may not be able to articulate the ideological beliefs they have, but from a Marxist perspective, everyone has ideological beliefs.

A SHORT THEATRICAL PIECE ON IDEOLOGICAL CRITICISM

Grand Inquisitor:	*Are you a Marxist?*
Arthur:	I'm a double Marxist! The two philosophers who have shaped my thinking most are Karl Marx and Groucho Marx!

> **Grand Inquisitor:**   *Karl Marx wrote about alienation and the heartlessness of bourgeois (boo-jwah) capitalist consumer societies. He argued that we needed a revolution to liberate the proletarian from oppression. How was Groucho Marx political?*
>
> **Arthur:**   Groucho was a poet of anarchy. With his brothers, he waged war on WASPish snobbishness as personified by the long-suffering Margaret Dumont, who starred in many of his films. His famous line, "Either you're dead or my watch has stopped" is, when you think about it, as devastating an attack on the bourgeoisie (boo-jwah-zee) as anything Karl Marx wrote.
>
> **Grand Inquisitor:**   *I don't know why I pay any attention to you. Sometimes I think I'm my own worst enemy.*
>
> **Arthur:**   Not as long as I'm alive! (Stolen from Groucho Marx)

❖ MARXIST CRITICISM

It is the task of Marxist critics (and all ideological critics, of whatever persuasion) to point out the hidden ideological messages in mediated and other forms of communication. These hidden messages, the argument goes, shape the consciousness of those who receive the messages. Even more insidious, Marxist critics argue, many people in the media, for example, do not recognize the extent to which their messages contain ideological content.

Donald Lazere (1977), a Marxist critic, explains how Marxists interpret cultural messages of all kinds:

> Applied to any aspect of culture, Marxist method seems to explicate the manifest and latent or coded reflections of modes of material production, ideological value, class relations and structures of social power racial or sexual as well as politico economic or the state of consciousness of people in a precise historical or socio-economic situation. . . . The Marxist method, recently in varying degrees of combination with structuralism and semiology, has provided an incisive analytic tool for studying the political signification in every facet of contemporary culture, including popular entertainment in TV and films, music, mass circulation books, newspaper and magazine features, comics, fashion, tourism, sports and games, as well as such acculturating institutions as education, religion, the family and child

rearing, social and sexual relations between men and women all the patterns of work, play, and other customs of everyday life. . . . The most frequent theme in Marxist cultural criticism is the way the prevalent mode of production and ideology of the ruling class in any society dominate every phase of culture, and at present, the way capitalist production and ideology dominate American culture, along with that of the rest of the world that American business and culture have colonized. (pp. 755–756)

There is, then, for Marxists, if Lazere is correct, political significance to everything in culture. And it is the job of Marxist critics to point out the ideological content "latent" or hidden in whatever Marxist critics choose to analyze whether it be mass-mediated texts, artifacts, or forms of collective behavior such as fashion.

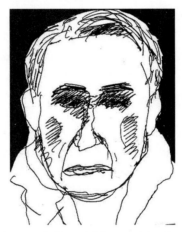

Roland Barthes, an influential French Marxist semiotician.

❖ ROLAND BARTHES ON *MYTHOLOGIES*

The French Marxist semiotician Roland Barthes was one of the most important critics of media, **popular culture,** and everyday life. His book *Mythologies,* published in France in 1957 and translated into English in 1972, is one of the most influential semiotically informed Marxist analyses of media and popular culture. Barthes writes, in his preface to the 1970 edition of his book,

This book has a double theoretical framework: on the one hand, an ideological critique bearing on the language of so-called mass-culture; on the other, a first attempt to analyze semiologically the mechanics of this language. I had just read Saussure and as a result acquired the conviction that by treating "collective representations" as sign-systems, one might hope to go further than the pious show of unmasking them and account in detail for the mystification which transforms petit-bourgeois culture into a universal nature. (Barthes, 1972, p. 9)

The book has two parts. The first part of the book consists of 28 short essays in which Barthes deals with topics such as "The World of Wrestling," "The Romans in Films," "Soap-Powders and Detergents," "Operation Margarine," "The Face of Garbo," "Striptease," "The New Citroen," "Photography and Electoral Appeal," and "Plastic." The second part of the book, "Myth Today," deals with Barthes's theories about myth and its relationship to bourgeois culture and society.

Barthes's essay "The World of Wrestling," the first essay in the section on "mythologies" and the longest one as well, is a good example of Barthes's writings. He offers a number of insights about wrestling as "theater" such as the following:

The quality of light in wrestling generates extreme emotions.

Wrestling is not a sport but a spectacle.

Wrestling is "an excessive portrayal of suffering."

Wrestling is full of excessive gestures.

Each sign in wrestling is "endowed with absolute clarity."

The bodies of wrestlers are signs about the way they wrestle.

Wrestling provides the image of passion, not passion itself.

"In America wrestling represents a sort of mythological fight between Good and Evil."

Mythologies is a slender volume; it is only 158 pages long. But its impact has been enormous, and it is commonly held to be one of the seminal books for semioticians, Marxists, and cultural theorists interested in media and communication analysis.

❖ THE PROBLEM OF HEGEMONY

Since, according to Marxists, there is an ideological content to every-thing, it becomes impossible to see this domination because we have nothing to compare it to, no way of isolating it. The term *hegemony,* made popular by the Italian Marxist thinker Antonio Gramsci (1891–1937), refers to the notion that ideological domination is invisible because it is all-pervasive. The situation is made worse because, Marxists argue, the forces contending against this domination, if any exist at all, are relatively weak and powerless.

In essence, the media are used to manipulate the masses into accepting the status quo economically and in many other areas as well, although many Marxists argue that the term *manipulation* is too simplistic and even too old-fashioned. Manipulation suggests that people who do the manipulating, the petty bourgeois types who run the newspapers and television stations and make the films, actually recognize what they are doing, but this is not the case, say the Marxists. That is because the petty bourgeoisie believes the ideology it is peddling and so does not recognize it as ideology.

❖ THE BASE AND THE SUPERSTRUCTURE AND THE "SELF-MADE MAN AND WOMAN"

There have been many developments in Marxist thought since Marx, of course, but the essence of his argument is still generally accepted—namely, that the base, the economic relations found in a society, shape (but do not determine) the cultural institutions in that society, and they in turn shape the consciousness of individuals who are brought up in that society. (The notion that the base determines the superstructure is known as "vulgar Marxism" and is not in vogue and hasn't been for many years.) This process of ideological indoctrination is subtle and invisible; people do not recognize the extent to which their consciousness has been shaped by forces external to them. People are full of illusions about themselves and their possibilities.

In the United States, for example, many people embrace the notion of the "self-made man and woman." This belief means that we downgrade the significance of social, economic, and political matters and place too much importance on individual psychology and personality, the will to succeed, personal resolution, and the ability to "market" oneself. We are, one could argue, "prisoners of psychology," in that we don't see society as important—only ourselves, our willpower, our personality. Like Margaret Thatcher, former prime minister of England, we believe that only individuals exist; society is just an abstraction. If only individuals count, psychology is the master science!

This notion of being self-made is of great use, Marxists argue, to the bourgeoisie, that element in society or, more to the point, that class that owns and controls the mode of production. Anyone who does not "make it" (whatever that means) has only himself or herself to blame and has failed, logic tells us, because of some deficiency in willpower, resolution, or character. Success is purely personal, and so is failure.

The Marxist attacks this notion as ideological, as justifying the status quo, which is just what the ruling class desires. The concept of the self-made man or woman puts the blame for failure or poverty, or what Marxists would describe as a social ill, on individuals and turns everyone's attention away from the ruling classes and socioeconomic matters.

❖ POST-SOVIET MARXIST CRITICISM

The downfall of Soviet Communism has led Marxist critics to pull in their horns, but many Marxist critics didn't approve (to put it mildly) of what was going on in Russia and didn't regret, by any means, seeing the totalitarian government in Russia disappear. In countries such as the United States, Marxist critics focus their attention now on the following:

- The inequality that exists in the United States and all problems that stem from it

- The way the wealthy are able to dominate the political agenda

- The extent to which the media are becoming more and more centralized and function as tools of the ruling classes

The wealthy classes own the media and thus, Marxist critics argue, are able to use the media to maintain their dominance. "He who pays the piper calls the tune," as the saying goes. And the forces of globalization are now, Marxist critics suggest, spreading bourgeois capitalist ideology all over the world. This is because the media are increasingly becoming controlled by gigantic multinational corporations in the United States (and other First World nations) whose films and television programs and other kinds of media are now seen all over the world.

One of the things the media spread is consumer lust, a desire for consumer goods instilled in people by films, television programs, newspapers, and other forms of **mass communication,** especially the institution of advertising. Bourgeois societies are consumer cultures and need to be, Marxists argue, because bourgeois societies generate alienation, a sense of estrangement from oneself and from others, and use consumer lust to assuage the pangs of alienation felt in people. Marxists argue that everyone in bourgeois societies is alienated—the wealthy as well as the poor. The capitalist classes use ideological persuasion when they can do so and, when necessary, use force.

❖ BASIC IDEAS IN MARXIST CRITICISM

Let me summarize the points I have made about Marxist ideological criticism:

- In all countries, the base, or mode of economic relations, shapes the superstructure of the institutions such as art, religion, and education that shape the consciousness of individuals.

- There are different classes in bourgeois societies. The bourgeoisie are the ruling class; the proletariat is the working class. And there is also a class of people, the petty bourgeoisie, who run the factories and make the television shows and do various tasks for the bourgeoisie. For Marxists, class conflict is a basic force in history.

- The bourgeoisie maintains its dominance over the proletarian class by generating in it a **false consciousness,** which takes a number of forms, such as the idea that the relationships in a given society are natural, that success is a function of willpower (and those who are successful deserve their success), and that those who fail have only themselves to blame.

- Bourgeois societies generate alienation, which is assuaged by consumer lust or commodity fetishism, but only partially and temporarily. All classes in bourgeois societies suffer from alienation, which means, literally, no connections or ties with others.

- Consumer cultures reinforce privatism and the sense that community and social classes are not important.

- The globalization of the media and economic institutions allows the ruling classes to spread their bourgeois ideology and export problems they may be facing to the Third World. The Marxists call this phenomenon "cultural imperialism."

This is a very brief, highly schematic picture of Marxist ideological thought, or perhaps "classical Marxist thought" would be a better term. For like any group, or entity, or party, there are a number of different kinds of Marxism, each of which emphasizes different things in Marxist thought.

Now that I've explained some of the basic elements of Marxist theory, I will apply some concepts from this theory to a very interesting text an advertisement for Fidji perfume, shown in Figure 5.1.

❖ A MARXIST INTERPRETATION OF THE FIDJI "SNAKE" ADVERTISEMENT

One point a Marxist critic would make about this advertisement is that it reflects, in graphic manner, the exploitation of people of the Third World, the world of people of color, by people in the First World. This exploitation is done by First World bourgeois capitalist

Figure 5.1   Fidji Perfume "Snake" Advertisement

Fidji de Guy Laroche.

A fascinating ad for Fidji perfume.

SOURCE: Fidji Perfume "Snake" Advertisement.

societies—the kind that are full of corporations such as Guy Laroche. According to Marxist theory, capitalism has survived by exporting its problems, and thus the woman in the Fidji advertisement is really an advertisement not only for perfume but also a reflection of capitalist cultural imperialism.

She is alone; we see and we don't even see all of her face. She's one more anonymous figure in the Third World, who has nothing but her First World fantasy, as represented by the bottle of Fidji perfume she holds in her hands. We, in the First World, are invited to her world to have our fantasy of uninhibited sex with an innocent and "natural" woman like her. But is she a natural woman? In some respects, yes. But although the flower in her hair and the snake suggest some kind of Edenic, primitive innocence, that bottle of perfume she holds in her hands in such a curious way suggests that she has been captured by a fantasy manufactured by our bourgeois capitalist system of indoctrination. What city, after all, is more "civilized" and more bourgeois than Paris?

The Fidji advertisement is also a classic example, Marxist critics would argue, of the excesses of bourgeois consumer culture, which has come to dominate every aspect of our lives, especially our sexuality. Our sexuality can be used "against us" by the ruling classes to encourage us to ever-greater wasteful expenditures in the name of a spurious value, glamour.

Advertising is, then, one of the central institutions of contemporary bourgeois cultures and is not to be thought of as merely a form of product entertainment. The price we pay for our so-called free media is much higher than we can possibly imagine. Advertising exists to sell products, but it also has a political mission—distracting us from the breakdown of our civic cultures and focusing our attention on private expenditures and on personal fantasies. We revel in our personal luxuries, Marxists argue, as our society disintegrates around us into chaos and we take refuge in gated communities to escape from the dangers of the social disorganization and pathology our **lifestyles** have generated.

What advertisements such as this one for Fidji perfume demonstrate is that alienation is very **functional,** by which I mean useful, for those who own the means of production. We attempt to assuage our alienation by creating consumer cultures and by continually purchasing things, which creates greater and greater profits for those who own the instruments of production and distribution. That is, alienation generates consumption. And because, in recent years, bourgeois capitalist societies have even "sexualized" the act of consumption, there are even stronger inducements now for people to participate in consumer cultures.

The bottle of Fidji perfume that the maiden holds so lovingly in her hands might be construed to represent, symbolically, the domination of bourgeois capitalist cultures over Second and Third World cultures. That is, this advertisement might be seen as a reflection of the **cultural imperialism** that we find in contemporary society.

Because the cost of making media texts is so high, Third World countries import most of the programs they show on their television stations and most of the films they show on television and in their theaters. The "cultural imperialism" argument made by Marxists and others is that this First World media are destroying the native cultures found in the Third World, leading to an eventual homogenization of culture. This culture will, of course, be dominated by capitalist bourgeois values that are hidden in the texts that Third World cultures import and work so perniciously on people who watch First World television programs and films, listen to First World music, and play First World video games.

One problem with the Marxist analysis of this advertisement and of advertising and consumer cultures is that it is so doctrinaire, so predetermined by Marxist theory. The "party line" covers advertising and just about every other aspect of capitalist societies and knows what it is going to find before it looks at any text. In addition, Marxism, politically speaking, has imploded, and former Soviet-dominated societies are now feverishly obsessed with consuming, trying, it would seem, to make up for lost time. It has even been suggested that the consumer cultures are what caused Marxist regimes in Eastern Europe and Russia to lose power.

And although the critique that Marxists offer of bourgeois societies may be logical and even correct in some respects, we face many problems when looking at communist societies. Studies have shown that Communist Party members and members of the political elite in previously communist societies exploited people terribly and consumed enormous amounts of food and goods in proportion to their numbers.

Thus, Marxist criticism faces many problems. Although it often reveals inequities and other troubling aspects of capitalist societies, it turns a blind eye to similar problems in communist societies. Furthermore, there are few communist societies around anymore as Marxism and communism have been discredited in some countries and abandoned in others. It has been suggested that a large percentage of the Marxist critics you find nowadays are teaching in American universities. There's a certain amount of truth to this notion.

❖ JOHN BERGER ON GLAMOUR

The British Marxist writer John Berger offers some interesting insights into the nature of glamour. In his book, *Ways of Seeing,* he deals with the role of advertising (he uses the term *publicity* to stand for advertising) in the creation of a sense of glamour. He writes,

> Publicity is usually explained and justified as a competitive medium which ultimately benefits the public (the consumer) and the most efficient manufacturers—and thus the national economy. It is closely related to certain ideas about freedom: freedom of choice for the purchaser: freedom of enterprise for the manufacturer . . . It is true that in publicity one brand of manufacture, one firm, competes with another; but it is also true that every publicity image confirms and enhances every other. Publicity is not merely an assembly of competing messages: it is a language itself which is always being used to make the same general proposal. . . . It proposes to each of us that we transform ourselves, or our lives, by buying something more. . . . Publicity persuades us of such a transformation by showing people who have apparently been transformed and are, as a result, enviable. The state of being envied is what constitutes glamour, and publicity is the process of manufacturing glamour. (J. Berger, 1972, pp. 130–131)

Advertising/publicity works, he adds, because it feeds on our natural desire for pleasure, and advertising, in the final analysis, is about pleasure and not the products it tries to sell us.

Advertising works, J. Berger (1972) writes, by offering us an image of ourselves made glamorous by using the products it sells us, which means that advertising is really about social relations and the promise of happiness and not about things that we purchase. Advertising uses the power of envy to motivate us—the envy we have of ourselves and that others have of us after we've been transformed by purchasing this or that product. This envy by others justifies our loving ourselves. Publicity images work, he asserts, by stealing our love of ourselves as we are and offering it back to us for the price of whatever it is we purchase.

A French literary scholar, René Girard, has a theory that is relevant here. He argues in his book, *A Theater of Envy: William Shakespeare* (1991), that Shakespeare's characters and people in general are all motivated what he calls **mimetic desire.** Mimesis means imitation, and Girard believes that imitation plays a major role in social relationships. What we do, when we purchases goods and services, is imitate the desire of celebrities and others who we see in advertisements and commercials using various products. In essence, our envy leads us to imitate the desire of those we see in advertisements and commercials and, in some case, our everyday lives.

❖ IDENTITY POLITICS

Even though Marxist thought and political philosophy is not widespread in the United States, the influence of a coherent ideological critique of American culture and society by the Marxists has had important consequences. One consequence is the spread of what is called identity politics, the all-consuming passion that various groups have about their situations, their problems, and their needs. This kind of thinking is very close to what Mannheim (1936) called Utopian thought.

Some groups focus mostly on their particular desires and their ideological critique of American culture and society, and others do the same thing but are also concerned with social justice. Thus, we have movements such as queer (gay and lesbian) theory, as well as politics based on racial and ethnic groups, many of which are absorbed in their own particular concerns but others of which argue that the solution to their difficulties lies in creating a more just society.

There is a famous joke that points to this phenomenon:

> Mordecai Goldberg, a little Jewish boy, comes running in one day to his grandfather and says, "Grandpa, Babe Ruth just hit his 60th home run!" "Very interesting," says the old man, who doesn't know who Babe Ruth is or perhaps even what a home run is. "But tell me, this home run . . . is it good for the Jews?"

In identity politics, perhaps pushing things to an extreme, we can say that different groups react to any news about social, economic, or political matters, or whatever, by asking a similar question: "Is it good for women?" "Is it good for lesbians and gays?" "Is it good for African Americans" "Is it good for the Italian Americans?" "For Polish Americans?" (You can substitute any racial or religious or ethnic group here.) "Is it good for children or the elderly?"

Some groups, however, argue these questions but look outward as well. They argue that it is necessary to make major changes in society for their goals to be met. I will discuss this matter in terms of feminist media and communication theory.

❖ FEMINIST CRITICISM OF MEDIA AND COMMUNICATION

Feminist criticism of media and communication is concerned with a number of issues:

- The roles women are given in texts and the roles they have in everyday life

- The exploitation of women in the media and in everyday life as sexual objects, objects of male desire, and lust

- The exploitation of women in the workplace and the domination of women in various areas of life, including sexual relationships

- The need for women to develop a consciousness of their situation and to do something about it

These two advertisements for Tanqueray and an "Authentically Brazilian" drink (Figures 5.2 and 5.3) are examples of the way women are used as sexual objects in advertising. Note the way the untanned portions of each of the women and their poses are used to send messages about their sexuality and to arouse viewers. The folds in the body of the woman in the Brazilian ad also have a sexual content.

In speaking of feminists, it is important to note that, as within any group, be it a family, a church, or a baseball team, not every group member thinks the same way as every other member. In an article titled "Class and Gender in Prime-Time Television Entertainment: Observations From a Socialist Feminist Perspective," by H. Leslie Steeves and Marilyn Crafton Smith (1987), we find a distinction made between liberal and socialist feminists. They write,

> In contrast to liberal feminists, socialist feminists, as Marxists, assume that the class system under capitalism is fundamentally responsible for women's oppression. At the same time they agree with radical feminists

Figure 5.2   Advertisement for Tanqueray

Notice how by using untanned portions of her body, this
woman's body is turned into an advertisement for Tanqueray.

Figure 5.3   Advertisement for Cabana, an "Authentically Brazilian" Drink

What it is that makes this photograph of a woman's legs so erotic? Note the way
the untanned portion of the woman's body leads our eyes toward her vagina.

that "patriarchy" (gender oppression) is fundamental in its own right and certainly existed long before capitalism. Thus, most socialist feminists argue that patriarchy and capitalism must be simultaneously addressed, largely via the eradication of divided labor by both gender and class. . . . Also, in contrast to liberal feminists' focus on how media affects individual attitudes and behaviors, socialist feminists emphasize the centrality of media (and other communication processes, such as language, education and art) in actually constructing ideology, including the ideology of women's secondary status. (pp. 43–44)

According to the authors, then, writing as Marxists, capitalism is the core of the problem and has to be dealt with along with the specific problems women face. And Marxist feminists are concerned with how the media portray or represent women and how the media and communication affect society as a whole rather than this or that woman.

I'm not sure this is a fair characterization of what the authors describe as "radical" feminism, because many radical feminists concern themselves with the way media affect U.S. culture and society. For example, in the same issue of the journal (which is devoted to feminism and communication) in which the Steeves and Smith article appears, we find Kathryn Cirksena (1987) offering her understanding of feminist criticism:

Three facets of a radical feminist critique that I consider pertinent to communication processes include: the social construction of knowledge and information, especially those assumptions concerning gender; the role of language in supporting gender-based inequities; and conceptions of "difference" as they challenge masculinist philosophers' assertions about the universality of the human condition and related methodological and political positions. (p. 20)

There is a considerable difference, let me point out, between the socialist conception that capitalism is at the root of women's subordination (and every other group's problems, as well) and the social conception of knowledge.

❖ THE SOCIAL CONCEPTION OF KNOWLEDGE

The social conception of knowledge recognizes that education, the media, our families, and other parts of society play a major role in giving people the ideas they hold. The idea, for example, that only individuals are important and that society is irrelevant is, ironically, socially transmitted—learned by individuals from reading, talking with others, being exposed to the media, and so on. One of the classic statements about the social origin of knowledge is found in Karl Mannheim's (1936) book *Ideology and Utopia:*

> Strictly speaking it is incorrect to say that the single individual thinks. Rather it is more correct to insist that he participates in thinking further what other men have thought before him. He finds himself in an inherited situation with patterns of thought which are appropriate to this situation and attempts to elaborate further in inherited modes of response or to substitute others for them in order to deal more adequately with the new challenges which have arisen out of shifts and changes in his situation. Every individual is therefore in a two-fold sense predetermined by the fact of growing up in a society: on the one hand he finds a ready-made situation and on the other he finds in that situation preformed patterns of thought and conduct. (p. 3)

There is a problem with this analysis; namely, it becomes difficult to see how new ideas come into being. One solution to this is to suggest that new ideas (and even the possibility of a critique of existing society) are the result of what might be described as the imperfect **socialization** of individuals and also from **subcultures** that reject many of the basic norms of the societies in which they find themselves. Mannheim's "utopians" reject much of what they find in their societies. Feminists, from this perspective, can be understood as being "utopians." We turn now to another aspect of feminist thought: the notion that male power is phallocentric.

❖ PHALLOCENTRIC THEORY: THE PHYSICAL BASIS OF MALE DOMINATION

Some feminists locate the source of male domination not in the class system and capitalism but in the bodies of men, specifically in their genitals, and talk about patriarchal "phallocentric" domination. According to **phallocentric theory,** men assume that the power relationships they find in society (in which men are dominant) are natural and are unable to recognize the fact that women are subordinated, treated unfairly, and so on.

The institutions found in societies, the roles played by men in these societies, and the representations of women in the arts and media are all shaped, ultimately, by male sexuality and, in particular, the power of the male phallus. Men, of course, do not recognize this and react with shock and often with laughter and ridicule (reflecting their sense of power and dominance) when feminists make this argument.

Feminists also talk about phenomena such as the "male gaze" in which men look at women as sexual objects. Women, of course, are frequently portrayed in mass-mediated texts as sexual objects or objects of desire, and what is worse, many women in real life, taking their cues from the media, present themselves as sexual objects.

The reason we have so many different critical approaches to mediated texts is that these texts are so complicated and contain so much information and data that they are susceptible to many kinds of analysis and, some would argue, require a multidisciplinary form of analysis, one that considers, for example, political, economic, social, psychological, and other matters.

I have taken feminism, one of the more important ideological approaches to media and communication, as a case study representing other oppressed groups. And, of course, it is possible to have combinations of oppressed groups such as Islamic feminists or gay and lesbian African Americans. Let me suggest another approach to understanding the political aspects of media and communication that offers valuable insights and puts things in perspective, an approach that deals with political cultures in American society.

❖ POLITICAL CULTURES, THE MEDIA, AND COMMUNICATION

This analysis draws upon the work of Mary Douglas, an English social anthropologist, and Aaron Wildavsky, an American political scientist. Douglas developed what she called **Grid-Group theory.** Her theory is described in Michael Thompson, Richard Ellis, and Aaron Wildavsky's *Cultural Theory* (1990):

> She argues that the variability of an individual's involvement in social life can be adequately captured by two dimensions of sociality: group and grid. Group refers to the extent of which an individual is incorporated into bounded units. The greater the incorporation, the more individual choice is subject to group determination.
>
> Grid denotes the degree to which an individual's life is circumscribed by externally imposed prescriptions. The more binding

and extensive the scope of prescriptions, the less of life that is open to individual negotiation. (p. 5)

Wildavsky argued that focusing on interest groups in politics was not useful because these groups can't determine where their interests lie. He suggested that the best way to understand politics is to recognize the importance of political cultures, which are tied to people's values and shape a great deal of the decision making and voting by individuals who often know little about the issues they vote on.

As Wildavsky (1982) wrote in *Conditions for a Pluralist Democracy or Cultural Pluralism Means More Than One Political Culture in a Country,*

> What matters to people is how they should live with other people. The great questions of social life are "Who am I?" (To what kind of a group do I belong?) and What should I do? (Are there many or few prescriptions I am expected to obey?). Groups are strong or weak according to whether they have boundaries separating them from others. Decisions are taken either for the group as a whole (strong boundaries) or for individuals or families (weak boundaries). Prescriptions are few or many indicating the individual internalizes a large or a small number of behavioral norms to which he or she is bound. By combining boundaries with prescriptions . . . the most general answers to the questions of social life can be combined to form four different political cultures. (p. 7)

See the following figure, which shows how these four political cultures are related to one another.

		Group Boundaries	
		Weak	*Strong*
Rules &	*Numerous*	Fatalists	Hierarchical elitists
Prescriptions	*Few*	Individualists	Egalitarians

Wildavsky's Four Political Cultures

Wildavsky slightly changed the names he used for these four political cultures over the years. I will use terms that offer the easiest understanding of them. The four political cultures form on the basis of group boundaries (weak or strong) and prescriptions (few or numerous):

1. *Fatalists:* Group boundaries weak, prescriptions numerous

2. *Individualists:* Group boundaries weak, prescriptions few

3. *Elitists:* Group boundaries strong, prescriptions numerous

4. *Egalitarians:* Group boundaries strong, prescriptions few

Wildavsky described these four different political cultures as follows:

> Strong groups with numerous prescriptions that vary with social roles combine to form hierarchical collectivism. Strong groups whose members follow few prescriptions form an egalitarian culture, a shared life of voluntary consent, without coercion or inequality. Competitive individualism joins few prescriptions with weak boundaries, thereby encouraging ever new combinations. When groups are weak and prescriptions strong, so that decisions are made for them by people on the outside, the controlled culture is fatalistic. (qtd. in A. A. Berger, 1990, p. 6)

These four cultures, found in all democratic societies, can be described in terms of some basic beliefs.

Individualists believe in free competition and as little government involvement in things as possible; government should maintain a level playing field and protect private property. Hierarchical elitists believe that stratification and hierarchy are necessary and correct, but they have a sense of obligation toward those beneath them. Egalitarians focus their attention on the fact that everyone has certain needs that should be looked after (thus, they try to raise up the fatalists) and criticize elitists and individualists. Egalitarians tend to be in opposition to mainstream American political thought. And the fatalists believe they are victims of bad luck and tend to be apolitical. The combination of elitists and individualists represents the dominant belief system in America and in democratic societies, but you need all four for democracy to flourish. All the groups need one another, and none is viable without the others.

One of the values of Wildavsky's analysis of political cultures is that it shows how each of them responds to certain problems, such as how to deal with envy, leadership, who to blame when things go wrong, what to do about risk, and related matters.

The responses of each culture to these and other matters are dealt with in Table 5.1, which shows the attributes of the four political cultures. In later years, Wildavsky changed some of his terms, and thus we find him writing about hierarchical elitists instead of hierarchical collectivists, for example. We see from Table 5.1 that the four political

Table 5.1   Attributes of Wildavsky's Four Political Cultures

	Individualist	Hierarchical	Egalitarian	Fatalist
Leadership	Each own leader	Authority valid	Rejects	Led by others
Envy	Differences OK	Not a problem	Big problem	No envy
Blame	Personal	Deviants	System blame	Fate
Fairness	Chance to compete	Treat all according to station	Treat all equally	Life not fair
Wealth	Create more, keep more	Collective sacrifice	Equality of condition basic	Luck
Risk	Opportunity to create new wealth	Short-run dangers	System inequality basic	Luck
Control	By results	Process basic	Consensual decisions	Avoidance
Ostentation	OK due to need to build networks	Public events only	Little display of	Hide
Equality	Equal chance to compete	Before law	Equality of result basic	Inequality inevitable
Scarcity	Use resources while valuable	Bureaucratic control to allocate	System exploits nature	Natural

cultures deal with matters such as equality, ostentation, scarcity, and control in different ways. (Wildavsky spells out these matters in considerable detail in his writings.)

I should add that people (except for fatalists, that is) can move from one political culture to another one if they are not getting what they consider to be "payoff" from the political culture they identify with. Let me offer an example. A neighbor of mine who was a pilot for a major airline was what Wildavsky would describe as a competitive individualist. But in the late 1980s, when the airline started doing things that my neighbor considered to be unfair, such as cutting his salary and assigning him tasks that he considered beneath him, he switched his allegiances and became very pro-union (and thus much more of an egalitarian).

❖ POP CULTURAL AND MEDIA PREFERENCES OF THE FOUR POLITICAL CULTURES

These four political cultures can also be used to deal with popular culture and the mass media. Let us assume two things:

1. People wish to reinforce their beliefs and thus tend to choose films, television programs, songs, books, and other similar materials that are congruent with their beliefs that support their values.

2. People wish to avoid dissonance and thus tend to avoid films, television shows, and other forms of mass-mediated culture that challenge their belief systems.

If the desire for reinforcement of their presently held beliefs and the desire to avoid challenges to their beliefs and values (**cognitive dissonance**) are operative, it suggests that there are, in reality, four different audiences or taste and value publics in the United States (and in any other democratic country), each of these being one of the four political cultures that Wildavsky discusses.

What this means, then, is that we can look at specific television programs, songs, films, books, sports, and so on in terms of which of these four political cultures or taste publics to which it would most likely appeal. Most of the decisions that people make about which television shows to watch, books to read, and films to see are not made, consciously that is, on the basis of the political culture one belongs to. In part, that's because most people do not recognize that they are, in fact, a member of one of Wildavsky's political cultures. But they are.

Being a member of a political culture enables people to make decisions about politics (who to vote for, what party to join, and so on) with relatively little information. All one has to know is "he's one of us" or "this issue is one we believe in." As Wildavsky put it, "Culture is the India rubber man of politics, for it permits preferences to be formed from the slimmest clue" (qtd. in A. A. Berger, 1989a, p. 40). It is conceivable, then, that it is the fundamental values and beliefs connected to one's political culture that may be at work, secretly, in our decision making about what television shows to watch.

If you ask people why they watch television, they say they want to be entertained. But why is it that one person watches televised wrestling and another watches a situation comedy and a third watches a nature documentary at a given hour? In Table 5.2, I offer a number of examples of specific songs, films, television programs, and other forms of popular culture according to the degree to which they reflect a given political culture. This table stems from classroom discussions in my media criticism courses and reflects the consensus of my students. Many new films, books, television programs, and so on could be substituted for the ones mentioned in the table.

If people were consistent, their choices would all (or mostly) fall under one of the four political cultures; of course, we know that they aren't. In the same light, one could simply list all of the films and television shows, books, magazines, and other media or texts found in the table and ask people which of them they like. If they formed a pattern, one could argue that these people, whether they recognized it or not, belonged to one of the four political cultures. If they were strongly ideological, there would be a distinctive pattern found of texts that were egalitarian, elitist, individualist, or fatalist.

Table 5.2 Political Cultures and Popular Culture

Topic Analyzed	Hierarchical Elitist	Competitive Individualist	Egalitarian	Fatalism
Songs	"God Save the Queen"	"I Did It My Way"	"We Are the World"	"Anarchy in the UK"
TV shows	*PBS Newshour*	*Dynasty*	*The Equalizer*	*A-Team*
Films	*Top Gun*	*Color of Money*	*Woodstock*	*Rambo*
Magazines	*Architectural Digest*	*Money*	*Mother Jones*	*Soldier of Fortune*
Books	*The Prince*	*Looking Out for Number One*	*I'm Okay, You're Okay*	*1984*
Heroes	Reagan	Iacocca	Gandhi	Jim Jones
Heroines	Queen Elizabeth	Ayn Rand	Mother Teresa	Madonna
Games	Chess	Monopoly	New games	Russian roulette
Sports	Polo	Tennis	Frisbee	Roller derby
Fashion	Uniforms	Three-piece suit	Jeans	Thrift store

One thing that Wildavsky's work on the four political cultures offers us, as researchers, is a means of gaining information about people's politics indirectly, by studying their taste in media and popular culture. We can use survey research about people's preferences for particular texts in media and popular culture to find out about which political culture they belong to, and this may lead to interesting insights into their past or future behavior.

It may also be that we can generalize, although it is risky, and move from individuals to societies as a whole, by looking at bestsellers, successful television programs, and films that attract huge audiences. We can study the basic values found in such texts to see which of the four political cultures they belong to, and if we find that the same values and beliefs of one particular political culture seem to be growing stronger or weakening, we can infer that there may be significant changes going on in that society. What we discover should be used in conjunction with other ways of studying society to see whether our research about mediated texts and political cultures agrees with findings in other studies.

❖ IDEOLOGICAL CRITICISM: APPLICATIONS AND EXERCISES

1. You are appointed media critic for the Marxist journal *Arts/Comrade*. Using the most important concepts from Marxist theory, write a 1,000-word Marxist interpretation of the film *Avatar* or one that your instructor assigns. Use the Applications Chart format described earlier. Which of the four political cultures does *Avatar* or the film you review appeal to most? Explain your answer.

2. Using Marxist concepts, write a 1,000-word analysis for *Arts/Comrade* of "The General" episode of *The Prisoner*. You can find this episode on the Internet and see it at no cost. Use an Application Chart format described earlier. Would a psychoanalytic or semiotic analysis of this episode have been a better approach?

❖ CONCLUSIONS

One of the things we look at when we examine media and popular culture is the ideological content of particular films, television shows, songs, and advertisements—whatever. People with different ideological positions see different things in a given text, which is why qualitative media research is often so complicated. That is because works of art are enormously complex and rich and often are susceptible to many different modes of analysis and interpretation. As the Russian critic Yuri Lotman (1977) explains,

> Since it can concentrate a tremendous amount of information into the "area" of a very small text (cf. the length of a short story by Chekhov or a psychology textbook) an artistic text manifests yet another feature: it transmits different information to different readers in proportion to each one's comprehension: it provides the reader with a language in which each successive portion of information may be assimilated with repeated readings. It behaves as a kind of living organism which has a feedback channel to the reader and thereby instructs him [or her]. (p. 23)

Lotman also argues that everything in an artistic text is meaningful, which makes interpreting them even more complicated. The works carried by the media may not be great works of art, from an aesthetic point of view, but their influence and significance is, if Marxist and other ideological critics are correct, of great importance.

❖ FURTHER READING

Barthes, R. (1972). *Mythologies* (A. Lavers, Trans.). New York: Hill & Wang.

Berger, A. A. (1990). *Agitpop: Political culture and communication theory.* New Brunswick, NJ: Transaction Books.

Dorfman, A. (1983). *The empire's old clothes: What the Lone Ranger, Babar, and other innocent heroes do to our minds.* New York: Pantheon.

Gramsci, A. (1971). *Selections from the prison notebooks* (Q. Hoare & G. N. Smith, Eds. & Trans.). New York: International Publishers.

Hammer, R., & Kellner, D. (Eds.). (2009). *Media/cultural studies: Critical approaches.* New York: Peter Lang.

Haug, W. F. (1986). *Critique of commodity aesthetics: Appearance, sexuality, and advertising in capitalist society.* Minneapolis: University of Minnesota Press.

Jameson, F. (1991). *Postmodernism; or, The cultural logic of late capitalism.* Durham, NC: Duke University Press.

Kellner, D. (2003). *Media spectacle.* London: Routledge.

Lefebvre, H. (1984). *Everyday life in the modern world.* New Brunswick, NJ: Transaction Books.

Lotman, J. M. (1977). *The structure of the artistic text.* Ann Arbor: Michigan Slavic Contributions.

Tomlinson, J. (1991). *Cultural imperialism: A critical introduction.* Baltimore: Johns Hopkins University Press.

Wayne, M. (2003). *Marxism and media studies: Key concepts and contemporary trends.* London: Pluto Press.

It was a triumph for the interpretive art of psychoanalysis when it succeeded in demonstrating that certain common mental acts of normal people, for which no one had hitherto attempted to put forward a psychological explanation, were to be regarded in the same light as the symptoms of neurotics: that is to say, they had a meaning, which was unknown to the subject but which could easily be discovered by analytic means. The phenomena in question were such events as the temporary forgetting of familiar words and names, forgetting to carry out prescribed tasks, everyday slips of the tongue or pen, misreadings, losses and mislaying of objects, certain mistakes, instances of apparently accidental self-injury, and finally habitual movements carried out seemingly without intention or in play, tunes hummed "thoughtlessly," and so on. All of these were shorn of their physiological explanation, if any such had ever been attempted, and were shown to be strictly determined and were revealed as an expression of the subject's suppressed intentions or as a result of a clash between two intentions one of which was permanently or temporarily unconscious. . . .

Finally, a class of material was brought to light which is calculated better than any others to stimulate a belief in the existence of unconscious mental acts even in people to whom the hypothesis of something at once mental and unconscious seems strange and even absurd.

—Sigmund Freud, *Character and Culture*
(Vol. 9 of Collected Papers, edited by Philip Rieff,
1910/1963b, pp. 235, 236)

6

Psychoanalytic Criticism

On the cover of *TIME Magazine*'s issue dealing with the century's greatest minds (March 29, 1999), who should we find but Sigmund Freud (listening to Alfred Einstein, who is lying on a couch, talking about his mother, no doubt). In the article about him, we find Freud's impact characterized as follows:

> For good or ill, Sigmund Freud, more than any other explorer of the psyche, has shaped the mind of the 20th century. The very fierceness and persistence of his detractors are a wry tribute to the staying power of Freud's ideas. (p. 66)

Freud's ideas have always been controversial, and Freud is continually being relegated to the ash heap of history. But it seems every time you turn around, you see Freud's theories, and those of his followers, being used to help people deal with their problems (psychotherapy) and to help make sense of people's behavior, in real life and in the arts (psychoanalytic theory).

Freud was born in 1856 and died in 1939. He earned a medical degree in 1881 and published his masterpiece, *The Interpretation of Dreams*, in 1900, when he was 43 years old. His ideas have been with us, then, for around 100 years, and they are still controversial and influential.

Psychoanalytic theory applies the insights of Sigmund Freud and other thinkers, such as Carl Jung, to texts of all kinds—works of serious literature as well as mass-mediated texts. My focus will be on Freud's ideas, but I will also discuss some important concepts from Carl Jung, whose ideas are also very useful for psychoanalytic criticism. They both had theories about how the human mind functions, theories that can be used to interpret matters such as the creative process and the motivations of characters in stories in all media.

Sigmund Freud, the father of modern psychoanalytic theory.

❖ FREUD'S CONTRIBUTION

The Unconscious

Psychoanalytic theory tells us that the human psyche is divided into three spheres: consciousness, preconsciousness, and the unconscious. Although Freud might not have discovered the unconscious, it is fair to say that he was aware of its significance and used it in his work to an unprecedented degree. He offers a classic description of the unconscious in his essay, "One of the Difficulties of Psychoanalysis":

> You believe that you are informed of all that goes on in your mind if
> it is of any importance at all, because your consciousness then gives
> news of it. And if you have heard nothing of any particular thing in

your mind you confidently assume that it does not exist there. Indeed, you go so far as to regard "the mind" as coextensive with "consciousness," that is, with what is known to you. . . . Come, let yourself be taught something on this one point. What is in your mind is not identified with what you are conscious of; whether something is going on in your mind and whether you hear of it, are two different things. (Freud, 1910/1963b, pp. 188, 189)

It was then, and still is, difficult for many people to recognize that there can be contents of their minds of which they are unaware.

The three levels of the psyche (Freud's topographic hypothesis) can be represented by an iceberg. The top of the iceberg, which we can all see, is consciousness. The part of the iceberg five or six feet below the waterline, which we can dimly make out, is the preconscious. And the part of the iceberg, below that line, that cannot be seen is the unconscious. It makes up most of the iceberg and, it is important to recognize, the human psyche.

According to Freud, all of our experiences are stored in the unconscious and have an effect on our minds and behavior. Psychoanalytic criticism suggests that works of art resonate with this unconscious material in our minds. It is likely, psychoanalytic critics suggest, that works of art send messages, in hidden and rather mysterious ways, from the unconscious of creative artists to the unconscious of people who are the audience for their works.

The Oedipus Complex

If people found the idea of an unconscious difficult, they found Freud's notion of the Oedipus complex outrageous. And it still is a very controversial matter as scholars in many fields argue about whether it exists or was just a fantastic notion of Freud's. He believed that we all experience, when we are young children (around the age of 3), Oedipal strivings. That is, we all desire to have the undivided attention and love of our parent of the opposite sex. Freud called this phenomenon the Oedipus complex because it resembled in important ways the myth of Oedipus, the Greek hero who unwittingly killed his father and married his mother.

Most people, Freud suggested, resolve these oedipal strivings, which are always unconscious, so they do not cause trouble. But some people do not resolve them, and oedipal strivings have a major impact on their lives. These hidden oedipal strivings, Freud suggests, explain why people are so moved when they see Sophocles's play *Oedipus Rex*, which is based on the Oedipus myth. The same applies to other works where the connection is not as obvious, such as Shakespeare's *Hamlet.*

Freud wrote a famous letter (October 15, 1897) to his friend Wilhelm Fleiss:

> The Greek myth seizes on a compulsion which everyone recognizes because he has felt traces of it in himself. Every member of the audience was once a budding Oedipus in fantasy, and the dream-fulfillment played out in reality causes everyone to recoil in horror, with the full measure of repression which separates his infantile from his present state. The idea has passed through my head that the same thing may lie at the root of *Hamlet.* I am not thinking of Shakespeare's conscious intentions, but supposing rather that he was impelled to write by a real event because his own unconscious understood that of his hero. (qtd. in Grotjahn, 1957, pp. 84–85)

Although this theory is very controversial, it is interesting to notice how useful it is in dealing with works of art. The Oedipus complex has been used by critics to interpret everything from *King Kong* to the James Bond stories and films.

Let me offer an example. Mark Rubinstein writes in his article, "The Fascinating King Named Kong,"

> It should be clearer now, at least to those who have seen the movie of 1933, why the story of King Kong has the power to move us the way it does. It not only retells certain basic myths of human society and

religion, but it also recounts stories of our childhood passions and development. (qtd. in A. A. Berger, 1991, p. 189)

He is referring to King Kong, here, as a "father" figure and the battle that occurs between him and a small, puny, ordinary-sized human being (symbolically a "child" figure) for a woman (symbolically the "mother" figure). We might also think of the relationship between Luke Skywalker and Darth Vader, Luke's father (we discover), in *Star Wars.* James Bond, the hero of numerous books and films, deals with villains who are usually fixated on controlling the world; they tend to be older and very powerful men who capture Bond and torture him but are ultimately defeated by Bond, who then makes love to a beautiful woman. The oedipal aspects of these relationships are obvious.

Human Sexuality

Freud used the term *libido* for the "force by which the sexual instinct is represented in the mind." Freud suggested that all human beings pass through four stages in their sexual development. These stages— the oral, the anal, the phallic, and the genital—are described in the *Encyclopedia of Psychoanalysis* (Eidelberg, 1968) in the following manner:

> The mouth represents an erotogenic zone for the infant. Sucking and later eating represent the gratification of oral needs. The fact that the infant often sucks a pacifier indicates that he is not only concerned with the incorporation of calories. When the infant begins to have teeth, the need to bite expresses his sadistic desires. The second stage of development is usually referred to as the sadistic-anal, and is characterized by the infant's interest in excreting or retaining his stools. Finally, the third stage is referred to as the phallic, in which the boy is interested in his penis and the girl in her clitoris. The boy's interest in his penis appears to be responsible for his positive Oedipus complex, which is finally dissolved by the fear of castration. The girl reacts with penis envy, if she considers her clitoris to be an inferior organ to the penis.
>
> Freud pointed out that the stages are not clear-cut, and that the fourth stage, the genital phase, is achieved only with puberty. (pp. 210–211)

Thus, according to Freud, our sexual life during infancy is rich, but it is unfocused and not directed at others. That happens only with puberty.

Conscious
Preconscious
Unconscious

The Id, Ego, and Superego

Freud developed a second theory about the psyche as his thought evolved. This theory, known as Freud's "structural" hypothesis, suggests that the psyche has three parts: the id, the ego, and the superego. Freud suggested that an unconscious conflict goes on in all people between the id and superego aspects of their personalities. Freud described the id as "chaos, a cauldron of seething excitement" and said it is characterized by impulse and the desire for gratification of various kinds. When we think of the id, we should focus on matters such as sexual desire, lust, passion, and desire. Opposed to the id we find the superego, which represents parental influence, conscience, and restraint. The superego, according to Brenner (1974), in his book, *An Elementary Textbook of Psychoanalysis,* can be characterized as follows:

> 1. the approval or disapproval of actions and wishes on the grounds of rectitude. 2. critical self-observation. 3. self-punishment. 4. the demand for reparation or repentance of wrong-doing. 5. self-praise or self-love as a reward for virtuous or desirable thoughts and actions. Contrary to the ordinary meaning of "conscience," however, we understand the functions of the superego are often largely or completely unconscious. (pp. 111–112)

The **id** says "I want it all and I want it now," and the **superego** says "Don't do it or you'll be sorry." The id provides energy and is necessary, but if it is not restrained, we cannot accomplish anything. The superego provides restraint, but if not controlled would overwhelm us all with guilt. All of these forces operate, generally speaking, at the unconscious level.

The **ego** mediates between the id and superego. It is that agency in the human psyche that Freud says "stands for reason and good sense."

The ego is charged with helping us relate to the environment and helping us preserve ourselves. If the ego can maintain a decent balance between id and superego forces, all is well, and we are able to avoid becoming neurotic. However, if either the id or superego becomes dominant, all kinds of problems follow.

We can use these three components of the psyche in criticism by finding characters in texts who tend to be essentially (that is, not always purely) "id" or "ego" or "superego" characters. For example, in *Star Trek*, it is possible to see the three main characters are follows:

Id	Ego	Superego
McCoy	Spock	Kirk
Emotion	Rationality	Commands

I'm not suggesting that the creators of the television series or films consciously intended to create characters that represent a component of the psyche. We must remember that what we are conscious of represents but a small portion of our psyches, and that applies to creative artists, too. It is interesting to note that Kirk means "church" in German, which would give added support to my suggestion that he is a superego figure.

We can use the id/ego/superego **typology,** roughly speaking, to understand other media texts and kinds of texts as the chart below shows.

Topic	Id	Ego	Superego
Books	Romances, vampire novels	Textbooks	Bible, Koran
Magazines	*Playboy*	*National Geographic*	Religious publications
Films	*Twilight*	*Agora*	*The Girl Who Played with Fire*
Television shows	Dance shows, romantic comedies	Nature shows	Religious shows
Cities	Las Vegas	Boston area (Harvard)	Rome (Vatican City)
Heroes (fictional)	Don Juan	Sherlock Holmes, Mr. Spock	Superman, Batman, Spiderman

Cities are important because they give people ideas about what kind of actions to expect in films and other kinds of texts. People are not aware of the id, ego, or superego aspects of the characters they follow in mass-mediated texts, but we can say that there are strong elements from the typology in all the media.

It is also possible to suggest that certain genres can be analyzed in terms of Freud's structural hypothesis. Thus, news programs would be ego texts, cop shows and religious programs would be superego texts, and soap operas, pornographic films, and many music videos would be id texts.

A SHORT THEATRICAL PIECE ON PSYCHOANALYTIC CRITICISM

Grand Inquisitor: *Psychoanalytic thought is mostly nonsense! Don't you agree?*

Arthur: You mean you don't believe in repression, condensation, displacement, regression, or symbolization? In the id, the ego, and the superego? In the Oedipus complex? In the unconscious?

Grand Inquisitor: *I like the superego, best of all. I'm big on guilt! There's nothing personal in it, mind you. We must control the id! Where there is id, let there be superego.*

Arthur: Don't you sometimes deal with unconscious heretics—people who think they are believers but, without recognizing what they are doing, hold heretical beliefs?

Grand Inquisitor: *Of course I do. They're a major problem. "Sometimes a cigar is only a cigar," and sometimes a person who thinks he's a true believer is really a heretic. These unconscious heretics . . . they really burn me up!*

Arthur: That's odd. I thought it was you who burnt them up!

Defense Mechanisms

Freud suggested that the ego uses a number of **defense mechanisms** to help people ward off anxieties and maintain psychological equilibrium. The following lists a number of the more important defense mechanisms:

Ambivalence: A simultaneous feeling of opposite emotions, such as love and hate, toward the same person or object.

Avoidance: Refusing to deal with subjects that distress or perturb us because they are connected to our unconscious aggressive or sexual impulses.

Denial: Unwillingness to recognize the reality of subjects that are distressing to us and generate anxiety in us by blocking them from consciousness or becoming involved in a wish-fulfilling fantasy.

Fixation: An obsessive attachment or preoccupation with something or someone, usually as the result of a traumatic experience.

Identification: The desire to become "like" someone or something in some aspect of thought or behavior.

Projection: Denying some negative or hostile feelings by attributing them to someone else.

Rationalization: Offering seemingly rational reasons or excuses for behavior generated by unconscious and irrational forces. (This term was introduced to psychoanalytic theory by Ernest Jones.)

Reaction formation: Suppressing one element of an ambivalent attitude (and keeping it in our unconscious) and maximizing and overemphasizing the other (its opposite).

Regression: Returning to an earlier stage of development when confronted by an anxiety-producing or stressful situation or event.

Repression: Unconsciously barring instinctual desires from consciousness; generally considered the most basic defense mechanism.

Suppression: Consciously deciding to put something out of mind. This is the second most basic defense mechanism. Because suppression is voluntary, suppressed material can be brought back to consciousness without too much difficulty. That is not the case with repression, which unconsciously bars material from consciousness.

It is useful for critics to know these defense mechanisms because in making a psychoanalytic interpretation of a text, we can see the characters using a number of them. When we recognize them, we are able to understand better the motives of the characters and also gain some insight into why these texts are so important to their readers and viewers.

Symbols

Perhaps no aspect of Freudian thought seems more far-fetched and absurd than his writings on symbolization. Symbols play a very important role in psychoanalytic thought. They are defined by Hinsie and Campbell (1970) in the *Psychiatric Dictionary* as follows:

> The act or process of representing an order or idea by a substitute object, sign, or signal. In psychiatry, symbolism is of particular importance since it can serve as a defense mechanism of the ego, as where unconscious (or forbidden) aggressive or sexual impulses come to expression through symbolic expression and thus are able to avoid censorship. (p. 734)

Symbols enable us to mask or disguise unconscious aggressive or sexual desires and thus avoid the feeling of guilt that would be generated by the superego if it recognized what we were doing.

Freud (1953) explained that in our dreams, the id uses symbols to trick the superego and obtain desired gratification. He writes,

> The male genital organ is symbolically represented in dreams in many different ways. . . . Its more conspicuous and, to both sexes, more interesting part, the penis, is symbolized primarily by objects which resemble it in form, being long and upstanding, such as *sticks, umbrellas, poles, trees,* and the like; also by objects which, like the thing symbolized, have the property of penetration, and consequently of injuring the body—that is to say pointed weapons of all sorts: *knives, daggers, lances, sabres;* firearms are similarly used: *guns, pistols and revolvers.* (pp. 161–162)

Freud adds other items that also function as phallic symbols— objects from which water flows and objects that can raise themselves up, mirroring erections in males. All of these symbols, Freud explained, are tied to wish fulfillment and the desire of men to be with women.

If men are symbolized by penetrating objects and those that resemble the penis functionally, women are represented by incorporative objects. Freud (1953) writes,

The female genitals are symbolically represented by all such objects as share with them the property of enclosing a space or are capable of acting as receptacles: such as *pits, hollows and caves,* and also *jars and bottles,* and *boxes* of all sorts and sizes, *chests, coffers, pockets,* and so forth. *Ships,* too, come into this category. Many symbols refer rather to the uterus than to the other genital organs: thus *cupboards, stoves* and above all, *rooms.* Room symbolism here links up with that of houses, whilst *doors and gates* represent the genital opening. (pp. 163–164)

Freud adds other phenomena such as woods and thickets (symbols of pubic hair) and jewel cases.

Freud's theory of symbolization actually is close in many respects to semiotic theory. He is, from a semiotic perspective, talking about icons when he discusses phallic symbols being long and thin, like sticks, snakes, or cigars, which resemble the penis. Freud, of course, realized that it was possible to take his theory of symbols and push it to extremes. He is reported to have said, "Sometimes a cigar is just a cigar." This has been used by his critics to attack his theory, for even Freud recognized that a cigar is not always a phallic symbol. But we must recall that if "sometimes a cigar is just a cigar," it means that sometimes a cigar isn't just a cigar!

❖ JUNGIAN THEORY

After Freud, Carl Jung (1875–1961) is probably the most important psychoanalytic theorist for our purposes—criticism of texts in the media and popular culture. Jung was originally associated with Freud, who thought Jung might be his disciple. They met for the first time in 1907 in Vienna. But Jung broke away from Freud in 1913 and created his own school of "analytic psychology." Jung developed a number of concepts and theories that led to different methods of helping people. His theories also are of great help to us in analyzing societies and interpreting texts. I will list and briefly discuss some of his most widely known concepts.

Archetypes

According to Jung, there are universal themes found in dreams, myths, religions, and works of art. These universal themes, which he called **archetypes,** exist independent of the personal unconscious of individuals. The archetypes are connected, Jung suggested, to past history and to what Jung asserted was a collective unconscious found in all people. These archetypes are unconscious, Jungians argue. We become aware of them only as the result of images that come to us in our dreams, in works of art, or in everyday emotional experiences we have that connect us to them in ways that, suddenly, somehow, we recognize.

As Jung (1968) explains,

> What we properly call instincts are physiological urges, and are perceived by the senses. But at the same time, they also manifest themselves in fantasies and often reveal their presence only by symbolic images. These manifestations are what I call archetypes. They are without known origin; and they reproduce themselves in any time or in any part of the world—even where transmission by direct descent or "cross fertilization" through migration must be ruled out. (p. 58)

Jung suggests that "the hero figure is an archetype, which has existed from time immemorial" and so the same applies to the myth of Paradise or of a past Golden Age, where people lived in peace and abundance. Heroes and heroines, of course, play a major role in mass-mediated texts. Whether the archetypes are "hardwired" in people is a matter of considerable debate.

The Collective Unconscious

These archetypes are found, Jung tells us, in what he described as the collective unconscious. Jung (1968) makes an analogy with instincts in explaining the collective unconscious:

> We do not assume that each new-born animal creates its own instincts as an individual acquisition, and we must not suppose that human individuals invent their specific human ways with every new birth. Like the instincts, the collective thought patterns of the human mind are innate and are inherited. They function, when the occasion arises, in more or less the same way in all of us. (p. 64)

Their instinct-like origin explains, Jungians argue, why myths are universal. They also explain why certain themes and motifs are, so Jungians assert, found in works of art all through history and everywhere in the world. Jung's notions about archetypes, the collective unconscious, and the universality of myths, I should add, are extremely controversial, and many psychologists and other kinds of social scientists take issue with them. There is no way to demonstrate, for instance, that the Jungian collective unconscious actually exists.

The Myth of the Hero

Heroes, according to Jung, are the most important kind of archetypes and are manifestations of the collective unconscious. As such, they play a crucial role in Jungian thought. Joseph L. Henderson (in Jung, 1968), a Jungian, writes,

> The myth of the hero is the most common and the best known myth in the world. We find it in the classical mythology of Greece and Rome, in the Middle Ages, in the Far East, and among contemporary primitive tribes. It also appears in our dreams. . . .
>
> These hero myths vary enormously in detail, but the more closely one examines them the more one sees that structurally they are very similar. They have, that is to say, a universal pattern, even though they were developed by groups or individuals without any direct cultural contact with each other. . . . Over and over again one hears a tale describing a hero's miraculous but humble birth, his early proof of superhuman strength, his rapid rise to prominence or power, his triumphant struggle with the forces of evil, his fallibility to the sin of pride (*hybris*), and his fall through betrayal or heroic sacrifice that ends in his death. (p. 101)

Henderson's description deals with tragic heroes. Most heroes, especially those found in the mass media, generally don't succumb to the sin of pride. Instead, they survive to fight new villains, in endless succession, who keep appearing with incredible regularity. According to Henderson, the myth of the hero has an important role—it has the function of helping individuals develop their ego consciousness. This enables them to deal with the many trials and problems they will face as they grow older. Heroes (and now we add heroines) help people with one of the biggest problems they face—separation and individuation from their parents and other tutelary figures. That explains why heroes and heroines are found all through history and why they are so important.

The Anima and the Animus

In Jungian thought, the anima represents the female element found in all males, and the animus represents the male element found in all females. This duality, according to Jungians, is symbolized in hermaphrodites (people with sexual organs from both sexes) and in witches, priestesses, medicine men, and shamans. A Jungian theorist, M.-L. von Franz (in Jung, 1968), discusses the anima and animus in terms of their impact on personality, the arts, and related phenomena:

> The most frequent manifestations of the anima takes the form of erotic fantasy. Men may be driven to nurse their fantasies by looking at films and strip-tease shows, or by day-dreaming over pornographic material. This is a crude, primitive aspect of the anima, which becomes compulsive only when a man does not sufficiently cultivate his feeling relationships—when his feeling attitude toward his life has remained infantile. (p. 191)

Franz points out that the anima also has a positive side; it enables us to do things such as find the right marriage partner and explore our inner **values,** leading to deeper and more profound insights into our psyches. The animus, according to Franz, functions in much the same way for women. The animus is formed, she suggests, essentially by the woman's father and can have positive and negative influences. It can, on one hand, lead to coldness, obstinacy, and hypercritical behavior. However, on the other hand, the anima can help women develop an enterprising approach to life, inner strength, and learn how to relate to men in positive ways.

The Shadow Element in the Psyche

The **shadow,** for Jungians, refers to the dark side of the human psyche—the side that we generally keep hidden from our consciousness. But we must recognize and deal with our shadow if we are to escape neurosis. Henderson (in Jung, 1968) explains Jung's concept of the shadow:

> Dr. Jung has pointed out that the shadow cast by the conscious mind on the individual contains the hidden, repressed and unfavorable (or nefarious) aspects of the personality. But this darkness is not just the simple converse of the conscious ego. Just as the ego contains unfavorable and destructive attitudes, so the shadow has good qualities—normal instincts and creative impulses. Ego and shadow, indeed, although separate, are inextricably linked together in much the same way that thought and feeling are related to one another. (p. 110)

According to Jungians, a battle for deliverance occurs in the psyche between the shadow and the ego. Heroes provide the means by which the ego symbolically "liberates the mature man from a regressive longing to return to a blissful state of infancy in a world dominated by his mother" (Henderson, in Jung, 1968, p. 111).

Freudians do not have the shadow concept, but it is easy to see that the battle between the shadow and the ego that Jungians talk about is vaguely analogous to what Freudians describe as going on in the psyche. The struggle for dominance between the shadow and the ego is similar to the battle that Freudians assert goes on between the id and the superego—a battle that the ego tries to mediate. Although Jung's shadow seems to be more negative than Freud's id, both the shadow and the id are, it turns out, the source of creative activity.

❖ PSYCHOANALYTIC CRITICISM: APPLICATIONS AND EXERCISES

1. You are appointed media critic of *Psyche* magazine. Write a psychoanalytic interpretation of *Avatar* (or some other film or an episode from some television show chosen by your instructor).

Use an Applications Chart to make your analysis.

2. Write a 1,000-word psychoanalytic interpretation, for *Psyche* magazine, of the "A, B, and C" episode of *The Prisoner*. Use an Applications Chart for the first page of your paper.

3. Find an advertisement that uses sexuality to sell some product. Write a 1,000- to 1,500-word psychoanalytic interpretation of the symbolism, language, and other matters for *Psyche* magazine. Use an Applications Chart for the first page of your analysis. Turn in the advertisement with your paper.

❖ CONCLUSIONS

As we might expect from a theory that was developed many years ago, there have been many new developments in psychoanalytic theory. Stephen A. Mitchell and Margaret J. Black (1996) deal with this topic in their book *Freud and Beyond: A History of Modern Psychoanalytic Thought*. They write,

> Very little of the way Freud understood and practiced psychoanalysis has remained simply intact. The major pillars of his theorizing— instinctual drives, the centrality of the Oedipus complex, the motivational primacy of sex and aggression—have all been challenged

and fundamentally transformed in contemporary psychoanalytic thought. And Freud's basic technical principles—analytic neutrality, the systematic frustration of the patient's wishes, a regression of an infantile neurosis—have likewise been reconceptualized, revised, and transformed by current clinicians. (p. xvii)

There have been many reconceptualizations and transformations in psychoanalytic theory, but Freud's ideas and discoveries still remain at the heart of the enterprise.

Psychoanalytic criticism rests on the assumption that we are not always aware of all that is in our minds and that often we are governed by forces and motivations beyond our consciousness. Freud's goal was a noble one; he wished to rescue people from being dominated by their unconscious id forces, which often function in destructive ways. Freud summed this up in his famous statement, "Where Id was, there Ego shall be." Freud and his one-time collaborator Jung developed psychoanalytic theories that have been used, with extremely interesting results, by sociologists, historians, anthropologists, and critics of both "elite" literature and the mass media.

❖ FURTHER READING

Bettelheim, B. (1977). *The uses of enchantment: The meaning and importance of fairy tales.* New York: Vintage.

Brenner, Charles. (1974). *An elementary textbook of psychoanalysis.* Garden City, NY: Doubleday.

Freud, S. (1963). *Character and culture: Vol. 9. The collected works* (P. Rieff, Ed.). New York: Collier. (Original work published 1910)

Freud, S. (1965). *The interpretation of dreams.* New York: Avon. (Original work published 1900)

Fromm, E. (1951). *The forgotten language: An introduction to the understanding of dreams, fairy tales and myths.* New York: Grove.

Jung, C. G. (with von Franz, M.-L., Henderson, J. L., Jacobi, J., & Jaffe, A. (1968). *Man and his symbols.* Garden City, NY: Doubleday.

Jung, C. G. (2009). *The red book.* New York: Norton.

Mitchell, S. A., & Black, M. J. (1996). *Freud and beyond: A history of modern psychoanalytic thought.* New York: Basic Books.

Rutherford, P. (2007). *World made sexy: Freud to Madonna.* Toronto: University of Toronto Press.

TIME Magazine. (1999, March 29).

Zaltman, G. (2003). *How customers think: Essential insights into the mind of the market.* Cambridge, MA: Harvard University Business School Press.

Part III

Qualitative Research
Methods

An investigator sits with pages of tape-recorded stories, snips away at the flow of talk to make it fit between the covers of a book, and tries to create sense and dramatic tension. There are decisions about form, ordering, style of presentation, and how the fragments of lives that have been given in interviews will be housed. The anticipated response to the work inevitably shapes what gets included and excluded. In the end, the analyst creates a metastory about what happened by telling what the interview narratives signify, editing and reshaping what was told, and turning it into a hybrid story—Values, politics, and theoretical commitments enter once again. Although a kind of betrayal . . . it is also necessary and productive; no matter how talented the original storyteller was, a life story told in conversation certainly does not come ready-made as a book . . . an article, or a dissertation. The stop-and-start of oral stories of personal experience gets pasted together into something different.

—Catherine Kohler Riessman,
Narrative Analysis (1993, pp. 13, 14)

7

Interviews

Interviews are one of the most widely used and most fundamental research techniques—and for a very good reason. They enable researchers to obtain information that they cannot gain by observation alone. That is why one sees so many studies by researchers involving interviews.

❖ WHAT IS AN INTERVIEW?

Perhaps the simplest way to describe an interview is to say that it is a conversation between a *researcher* (someone who wishes to gain information about a subject) and an *informant* (someone who presumably has information of interest on the subject).

We most commonly think of interviews as involving jobs, and most of us have, at one time or another, been interviewed for a job by one or more members of a company we wanted to work for. The goal of these interviews is similar to the goal of interviews conducted by all researchers—to obtain information.

The term *interview* is related to the French term *entrevue,* which means "to see one another or meet." This points out an important element of interviewing—usually there is a face-to-face relationship.

But not always. Some interviews are conducted by telephone or other electronic means, such as the Internet.

❖ FOUR KINDS OF RESEARCH INTERVIEWS

There are four kinds of interviews found in scholarly research.

Informal Interviews. There are few controls in these interviews; they just take place, are not organized or focused, and are generally used to introduce researchers to those being studied. Informal interviews are, in essence, conversations that serve the purpose of helping the researcher gain the confidence of his or her informant. An informant is a person (often a member of some group being studied) who conveys information to a researcher. That is, informants are people who have (it is hoped) important knowledge and who are willing to tell interviewers what they know.

Unstructured Interviews. In these interviews, the researcher is focused and is trying to gain information, but he or she exercises relatively little control over the responses of the informant.

Semistructured Interviews. Here, the interviewer usually has a written list of questions to ask the informant but tries, to the extent possible, to maintain the casual quality found in unstructured interviews. **Focus groups,** which are widely used in market research, are considered to be semistructured interviews.

A NOTE ON PROBLEMS WITH FOCUS GROUPS

Focus groups are free-form discussions by a group of people, usually between 6 and 12 individuals, led by a moderator, designed to obtain information about some topic. Focus groups are commonly used by advertising agencies and other organizations to get an idea about how people feel about some product or service—or, during elections, some politician or campaign issue.

Gerald Zaltman, a professor at the Harvard Business School, discusses the weaknesses of focus groups in his book *How Customers Think: Essential Insights Into the Mind of the Market* (2003). He argues that focus groups are overrated and that one-on-one interviews are much more efficient and reliable. He writes,

Focus groups are easy and affordable to implement. Like every research method, focus groups do have a place in the research toolbox. For example, they can provide feedback on the attractiveness of an existing product design and ease of product use. Contrary to conventional wisdom, they are not effective when developing or evaluating new product ideas, testing ads, or evaluating brand images. Nor do they get at deeper thoughts and feelings among consumers. In fact, focus groups fail an important test for any method: Is the method based on well-founded insights from the biological and social sciences and the humanities? (p. 122)

He points out that if focus group leaders have 5 or 10 topics and eight people, the focus group leaders can devote only a couple of minutes on each topic with each person. Focus groups also can be skewed by matters such as social dominance (some people in the group doing most of the talking), the eagerness to please by members of the group, anxieties of members of the group about their privacy, and so on. The best way to get information, Zaltman argues, is to use one-on-one interviews, which enable skilled interviewers to get beyond superficial opinions and get at the deeper meanings that people hold, generally below their level of awareness, about things.

Structured Interviews. In this kind of interview, the researcher uses an interview schedule—a specific set of instructions that guide those who ask respondents for answers to questions. For example, the instructions might tell what follow-up questions to ask if a question is answered in a certain way. Questionnaires that are self-administered are also classified as structured interviews. (Interviewing techniques are also an important element of survey research, a methodology discussed in Chapter 12.)

❖ WHY WE USE INTERVIEWS

As I mentioned above, there are a number of ways of getting information about people: first, observing what they do; second, asking them about what they are doing; and third, analyzing texts and artifacts produced by people, which is done when we make content analyses (discussed in Chapter 11). Unless we have the chance to observe people for a long period of time, we cannot know much about their past activities, their history. But we can discover this information by asking them about it.

We also can find out about people's ideas, their thoughts, their opinions, their **attitudes,** and what motivates them by talking to them and asking the right questions. Let me suggest some basic differences between observation and interviewing in the following chart.

Observation	Interviewing
Present	Past and present
Actions	Attitudes
Context	Motivations
Seeing	Hearing and probing

In many cases, when possible, we use the two approaches together, but this is not always practical. Observation does give us a sense of context, which often helps explain what people do. But it doesn't help us get inside people to understand why they do things, what motivates them, and what anxieties they have.

One advantage of interviews is that one can generally record interviews and thus have a written record that can be analyzed in detail. In some cases, it is possible to use videotape when doing research and capture visual information, but videotaping is much more difficult to do.

In this chapter, I will focus on unstructured interviews. Interviews, as I suggested earlier, are widely used in research because they provide us with information that we cannot obtain any other way. You can observe a person (for example, if you are doing some participant observation research in a gymnasium or video game parlor or bar), but you can't know what the people you are observing think about what they are doing or what they know from just observing them.

In some respects, an interview (and remember, I will be talking about unstructured interviews when I use the term in this chapter) is like a psychoanalytic consultation. The interviewer is probing for information that the informant presumably has but may not be conscious or aware of or may not consider important.

❖ HOW TO INTERVIEW PEOPLE

There's an art to interviewing people, and it takes time for researchers to become good interviewers. Let me offer a list of some important considerations to keep in mind when interviewing people.

Guarantee Anonymity. Explain to your informants or respondents that what they tell you will be anonymous and that nobody (except you) will know who provided the information you obtained. Generally speaking, a distinction is made between *informants* (people you've gotten to know and who you will have a chance to interview a number of times) and *respondents* (people who will be interviewed only once).

Make Sure You're Accurate. You should tape-record your interviews to ensure that you'll have accurate information. If this is not possible, you'll have to jot down notes as you proceed with the interview. If it is not possible to take notes, write down what you remember immediately after the interview. Make certain you always record the following:

The date of the interview

Where it is taking place or took place

Who you interviewed

Also, be sure that you have extra batteries (even if you can plug your tape recorder into a socket) and clean tapes and that your tape recorder is functioning properly. Some researchers take two tape recorders in case something happens to one of them. It is best to use high-quality 60-minute cassettes with screws in them (in case you have to take the cassettes apart); longer ones have very thin tape that often breaks or stretches.

Avoid Leading Questions. When you ask questions of your informants, don't offer leading questions, which more or less push your respondent toward an answer. For example, let's imagine you are interviewing a student about a class she's taking and she says her teacher is unfair. You can respond to this statement several ways:

Leading question: "Is that because your teacher favors men over women?"

Asking for definitions: "What do you mean by unfair?"

This suggests our next point.

Have Your Informants Define Terms. If your informants use terms that you are unfamiliar with or that you think need some attention, ask them to define the terms, to tell you what they mean by the terms. Make them give their own definition of a term; don't ask them if your understanding of a term is correct.

Stay Focused. Once your informants have started talking, make sure your questions don't get off the track; focus on getting more details about what your informants are saying. In conversations, there is often a tendency to wander about on all kinds of side issues. You must resist this and stay "on target."

Make Sure Your Questions Are Clear. If you ask unclear questions, you'll get ambiguous and relatively useless answers. Your respondents may be trying to answer your questions as accurately as possible, but if they don't understand your questions or your questions are "fuzzy," informants won't be able to supply the information you are seeking.

Ask for Amplifications and Examples. When you are talking with your informants, keep in mind some ways of getting more details about the subject being discussed. One useful response to a statement by an informant is this:

1. And then what happened?

Some other responses and requests for amplifications are these:

2. Who was involved?

3. When did it happen?

4. Why did it happen?

5. Where did it happen?

6. What was the result?

7. How do you feel about it?

You can also ask for examples of things informants talk about—anything to get more information and more details, as long as it is related to the subject being investigated and does not lead you off on a tangent.

❖ QUESTIONS INVESTIGATIVE REPORTERS ASK

We can learn something from the questions that investigative reporters, who are experts in conducting research, in general, ask themselves. Let's consider a situation in which an investigative reporter is asked to do a story about a trial of someone accused of running a Ponzi scheme and defrauding stockholders. Here are some questions reporters might want to find out about:

WHO: Who is involved in the case? Who has been accused of running the Ponzi scheme and who were the victims? Who is the judge? Who are the suspect's lawyers? Who first discovered what was going on?

WHAT: What is a Ponzi scheme? What are the facts about the case? What are law enforcement officials doing? What do the suspect's lawyers have to say?

WHEN: When did the accused person start running the Ponzi scheme? When was it discovered?

WHERE: Where was the accused person located? Where were the victims located?

WHY: Why did the Ponzi schemer engage in illegal activities?

HOW: How did he or she get away with it? How was the scheme discovered?

All researchers must deal with these questions, because these questions are at the heart of all inquiries that they make. These questions require investigators to offer descriptions, explanations, narratives, and interpretations.

Sometimes, instead of just asking a general question such as "where?" you can ask for more detail and say something like, "Could you tell me some places where?" to obtain more information from the informant. "Where?" suggests one place while "some places where" asks for more information.

Prepare Some Questions Before the Interviews. Even though you don't use a prepared list of questions in unstructured interviews, you should do some thinking about the topic you are dealing with and do what you can to stay focused on that topic and avoid going off on tangents.

Some researchers suggest that a research protocol be developed to guarantee uniformity and accuracy. A typical interview protocol contains material such as the following:

A title or heading for the interview

Instructions for the interviewer to follow

A list of key questions to be asked

Follow-up questions (or probes) once the key questions have been asked

Comments and notes by the interviewer relative to the interview

Be Nonjudgmental. This is absolutely imperative. You should never suggest, by the questions you ask, the tone of your voice, your facial expression, or your body language, how you feel about the information you are given by your informant. If you show any signs of being judgmental, either positively or negatively, this will have a profound impact on your informant and will color the information you are given.

Use "Uh-huh" and Other Phatic Communications. In some cases, just saying "uh-huh" or "I see" is sufficient to continue the interview. This phatic (literally, *phatic* means just making noises) communication is a commonly recognized cue to the informant to keep talking. It is a form of acknowledgment that means, in effect, "I hear what you are saying . . . please continue."

Take Notes About Other Matters. Take notes, while conducting the interview, about matters that strike your attention; for example, was the informant nervous or relaxed, were there interruptions, were there distracting noises or music, and so on.

Be a Good Listener. Don't interrupt your informants or complete their sentences. Make sure your mind doesn't wander when you are listening.

❖ THE STRUCTURE OF CONVERSATIONS AND INTERVIEWS

Conversations (extremely informal interviews) and unstructured interviews (conversations with a defined purpose) share a common structure. This structure is shown as follows:

Q&A Q&A Q&A Q&A Q&A Q&A Q&A

That is, typically a conversation involves questions and answers and turn taking between those talking. (The turn taking is represented by the regular and boldface type in the example shown above.) Conversations seldom take the form of simple declarative statements by themselves. Frequently, questions are used as transitional devices to keep a conversation going. In an ordinary everyday conversation, the answers are usually considerably longer than the questions.

It might be useful to think of the kind of interrogations one finds in trials as a metaphor for interviewing, except that in interviewing, the questions are not asked with a hostile intention. But the goal is the same—to gain detailed information, to obtain "the truth, the whole truth, and nothing but the truth."

A SHORT THEATRICAL PIECE ON INTERVIEWS

Grand Inquisitor: *Being a Grand Inquisitor is very hard! I seem to have lost my touch in recent years.*

Arthur: What do you mean by "touch"?

Grand Inquisitor: *I used to put people on the rack with a certain amount of flair. I yielded a wicked knout and was renowned for my skill in pouring hot lead down the throats of heretics.*

Arthur: When did all this happen?

Grand Inquisitor: *About a thousand years ago, give or take a few centuries.*

(Continued)

(Continued)

Arthur: Why did the Inquisition occur?

Grand Inquisitor: *We had so many heretics that we had to do something.*
                      The worst cases were the people who thought they were
                      believers but were really unconscious heretics.

Arthur: Sounds vaguely Freudian. Fortunately, there's no more
                      Inquisition and no torturing to speak of nowadays.

Grand Inquisitor: *Ha! Ever hear of adolescents? And adolescence? Or*
                      freshman composition?

One thing we learn from seeing films about trials and television programs of trials (think of the O. J. Simpson trial or President Clinton's impeachment hearings) is that witnesses sometimes contradict themselves and sometimes lie and that different witnesses frequently offer different accounts of the same event. (The classic movie about different accounts of the same event is the Japanese masterpiece *Rashōmon.*) But the fact remains that in interviewing informants and respondents—as in trials—every word is potentially important.

The reason the O. J. Simpson trial was so fascinating to viewers was that it became a narrative—a story with dramatic qualities to it, which means, according to Aristotle, a story with a beginning, a middle, and an end. Viewers and listeners kept asking themselves questions as the trial progressed: Who is telling the truth? Who is lying? What do the jurors believe? What will the verdict be?

Researchers who study how people construct conversations, such as W. Labov and J. Waletzky (cited in Riessman, 1993), suggest that conversations or "personal narratives" about some event of significance have the following properties (the material that follows is adapted from Catherine Kohler Riessman's [1993] *Narrative Analysis*):

Symbol	Property	Function
A	An abstract	Summary of the narrative's content
O	Orientation	Time, place, situation, those involved
CA	Complicating action	Sequence of events
E	Evaluation	Significance and meaning of the action
R	Resolution	How things turned out
C	Coda	Returns the discussion to the present

What Labov and Waletzky are suggesting is that when informants discuss things with interviewers, researchers can generally find the functions listed above in a given segment of conversation. Interviewers must be especially mindful of judgments, criticisms, and evaluations made by the informants, for they point to important attitudes and beliefs.

In principle, most every segment of the interview can be classified as having a particular function and can be labeled by one of the symbols. This helps researchers interpret what was said by informants because it shows what the function of a particular statement was.

❖ TRANSCRIBING TAPES

The tapes you've made of your interviews have to be transcribed. Generally, this is done with a transcription machine, which costs a few hundred dollars or so. These machines enable you to use a foot pedal to operate the machine—to start it, move backward and forward, and even slow down the machine. It may be possible to use word recognition software to do transcriptions. You play the tape recorder into the microphone of a computer and have the program transcribe the material. (It is also possible to bring a portable computer with the software program on it and have the interview directly recorded and transcribed by the program, but that is too risky, because there may be some important words that the word recognition program misses.) Some of these software programs claim 95% accuracy, and that may be enough to speed up the process of transcribing tapes.

Because it takes something like 7 or 8 hours to transcribe an hour's tape, using the new software programs may save you an enormous amount of time—if you can get them to work. But even with these programs, you'll have to go over the material and fix errors, so the process will consume a considerable amount of time whatever method you use.

❖ MAKING SENSE OF THE INFORMATION ON TRANSCRIBED INTERVIEWS

When you have the interviews transcribed and have checked them for accuracy, the next step is to make sense of it as best you can. One thing you must do is look for information that will be useful to you. What "facts" did you learn? What information about people, practices, ideas, beliefs, and so on did you get? (And how reliable is it?)

Another thing is to classify and categorize the material in the transcripts. I have already suggested one way of classifying this material—using the functions in the Labov and Waletzky chart and determining whether a given passage functions as an abstract, an orientation, a sequence of action, an evaluation, or a resolution.

But there are other procedures to consider. For example, we should see how our informant categorizes things. How are *old* and *young* and *good* and *bad* defined by the informant? What kinds of groups are mentioned? How does the respondent categorize people—by age, by membership in a group, by **gender,** by occupation, by status?

I sometimes ask students in my classes to talk about their high schools (this is, in effect, a group interview), and generally, I get lists of different groups or subcultures found in their high schools: preppies, greasers, skaters, surfers, white punks on dope, jocks, cheerleaders, nerds, geeks, creeps, and so on. That is, when young people are asked about high schools, they often respond by categorizing their fellow students into various interest groupings. This offers an insight into how they think about their high school experiences.

The purpose of looking for classifications and categories used by informants is to get a sense of how their minds work, how they make sense of the world. We assume that these usages are culturally conditioned, so finding out how informants think offers important clues about their culture or subculture or group. This process of determining categories and classification systems is done by coding.

❖ CODING

When you have your transcriptions of the interviews you've conducted, you have to find ways of making sense of the material you have, and this is done, as suggested above, by looking for patterns, classifications, themes, and categories in this material. There are no absolute rules about how coding is done; a great deal depends on the nature of the material being coded.

The list that follows is drawn from John W. Creswell's (1994) *Research Design: Qualitative and Quantitative Approaches.* It is a general guide to the process of coding:

1. Read the material over as a whole and get an overview of it.

2. Pick one transcript and examine it carefully, looking for topics covered.

3. Do this for several transcripts and make a list of all the topics that were covered.

4. Make abbreviations for each topic and go through the transcripts, putting down the appropriate abbreviation beside each example of a given topic. If your topics list doesn't cover all the material, see if you can think up new topics that will help you do the job.

5. Turn your topics into categories. Make sure that the categories cover all your transcripts and don't duplicate one another.

6. Decide on a final set of abbreviations for your categories and alphabetize them. You now have an alphabetical list of codes in the transcripts.

7. Assemble all the material found under each category in one place and analyze it to see what you find.

8. See whether you can refine your coding and get fewer and more-descriptive categories.

Creswell deals with the ideas of R. C. Bogdan and S. K. Biklen (1992, pp. 167–172), who suggest using abstract coding categories as topics. They propose that researchers look for the following kinds of codes:

Setting and context codes

Perspectives held by subjects

Subjects' ways of thinking about people and objects

Process codes

Activity codes

Strategy codes

Relationship and social structure codes

Preassigned coding schemes

There are also computer software programs that help researchers find ways of coding their transcripts and catch coding errors. Coding is an attempt by researchers to see if any common themes and topics inform the interview transcripts; these common themes will help researchers see what is important to informants and what is secondary.

A number of years ago, I did some research on humor. I was looking specifically for the techniques that humorists used in creating humor.

I examined a wide range of materials, including joke books, folklore books, comic books, books on humor, humorous plays, humorous short stories, and comic novels.

From this research, I elicited 45 techniques that, I believe, are the building blocks of all humor and that are used, in various permutations and combinations, by all humorists. When I got my list, I started examining it and discovered that each of the techniques fit into one of four different and mutually exclusive categories—humor of logic, humor of identity, linguistic humor, and visual or action humor (see Table 7.1).

Any example of humor contains, my argument goes, one or more of these techniques. It took a considerable amount of thinking and speculation before I became aware of the categories "hidden" in the 45 techniques. My point, then, is that finding categories is not always an easy task.

Table 7.1   Techniques of Humor According to Category

Language	Logic	Identity	Action
Allusion	Absurdity	Before/after	Chase
Bombast	Accident	Burlesque	Slapstick
Definition	Analogy	Caricature	Speed
Exaggeration	Catalogue	Eccentricity	
Facetiousness	Coincidence	Embarrassment	
Infantilism	Comparison	Exposure	
Insults	Disappointment	Grotesque	
Irony	Ignorance	Imitation	
Misunderstanding	Mistakes	Impersonation	
Overliteralness	Repetition	Mimicry	
Puns/wordplay	Reversal	Parody	
Repartee	Rigidity	Scale	
Ridicule	Theme and variation	Stereotype	
Sarcasm	Unmasking		
Satire			

❖ PROBLEMS WITH INTERVIEW MATERIAL

One question about interviews that is debated is whether what interviewers are looking for are data, information, and factual matters, or whether it is the way informants speak and how they organize their information that is most important. That is, should researchers focus on what people are doing and have done or on the way they express themselves about what they've done and are doing? Which is most important and yields the most interesting information, *what* informants say or *how* they say it?

There is a link between the two matters, or maybe it is best to suggest that the two are connected (two sides of a coin) because the analysis of expression is also the analysis of thought and thinking. It is useful to keep in mind what E. W. Said (1978) wrote in *Orientalism,*

> [The] real issue is whether indeed there can be a true representation of anything, or whether any and all representations, because they are representations, are embedded first in the language and then in the culture, institutions, and political ambiance of the representator. If the latter alternative is the correct one (as I believe it is), then we must be prepared to accept the fact that a representation is *eo ipso* implicated, embedded, interwoven with a great many other things besides the "truth," which is itself a representation. (pp. 272–273)

Said's point is that we must consider the extent to which a culture shapes the way people talk and give information (that is, give a "representation"), so we must always be cautious about accepting what people tell us as being the truth. Is the information respondents give "the truth" or "their truths?"

Just because a person agrees to be an informant and tell you something about some group or entity that the person has been involved with doesn't mean that you'll be getting "the truth, the whole truth, and nothing but the truth" from your informant. Let me suggest some of the problems that researchers face in dealing with informants and respondents (which apply to all other forms of research, such as focus groups, questionnaires, and surveys).

1. *People don't always tell the truth.* People want to put their best foot forward, want to appear nobler and better than they actually are, and so they often lie or distort things. Sometimes they actually have convinced themselves that their accounts are not lies but are the truth.

2. *People don't always remember things accurately.* Even if people want to tell the truth, sometimes their memory lets them down, and without recognizing what they are doing, they fabricate the truth—that is, they make up things.

3. *People don't always have useful information.* They may think they do and may feel important because they are being interviewed, but in reality, they have little to say of interest.

4. *People sometimes tell you what they think you want to hear.* In some cases, informants tailor their responses to questions in terms of their perceptions of what will best satisfy the interviewer. They do this be cause they like you and want to give you material that will be helpful, they are bored and want to get through the interview as soon as they can, or they want to impress you.

5. *People use language in different ways.* The problem is one of communicating and interpreting meaning. The intended meaning may not be the communicated or articulated meaning, and most important, the meaning received or gained by the interviewer may be different from the meaning intended by the interviewee. Thus, it is important to be an efficient and active listener who seeks clarifications and uses feedback techniques to ascertain that the meaning received is the meaning intended.

It is a good idea to ask several informants about the same thing to see whether there's any consistency. You can also see, sometimes, whether there's a difference between what people say and what people do. You want to get accounts from your informants and respondents that are true, reliable, and complete.

You must remember that your respondent's point of view is not a reliable explanation of behavior. Some of the reasons for this are given above and are due to the way we represent ourselves to others and to the illusions we all have about ourselves. People tend to justify their actions to themselves and others, so you have to be careful about accepting anyone's point of view as being accurate, correct, and unbiased.

The material you get in interviews can be understood in terms of the figure/ground metaphor. An informant's interview should be seen as a figure against a ground of everything from the actual interview itself to some event in or aspect about the culture or subculture that the informant is providing information about. The background has an effect on the figure; context makes a great deal of difference.

❖ INTERVIEWS: APPLICATIONS AND EXERCISES

1. A person (he, she, or it) arrives from Mars in a spaceship. You are a reporter for a major television news show. Prepare a list of key interview questions to ask the Martian and a list of follow-up questions. Explain your rationale for asking each question. What problems did you face in making your list of interview questions? How do your questions solve these problems? You can practice interviewing this Martian with someone in your class to get a sense of the difficulties one faces in conducting an interview.

2. The President of the United States grants you an interview but says you can ask only 10 questions. What questions would you ask him or her? How did you decide on your questions?

Compare your list of questions with those asked by other members of your class. Are there any questions that everyone asked? Any surprising questions? Any important questions that should have been asked?

3. Tape an interview on some television interview program and analyze it in terms of the questions the interviewer asked, questions that should have been asked, and other topics dealt with in this chapter.

Observe things such as facial expressions, body language, the tone of the interview, and the relationship that existed between the interviewer and person being interviewed.

❖ CONCLUSIONS

Interviews are one of the most fundamental techniques researchers use to get information. But interviews are difficult to do and involve a great deal of work (recording them, transcribing them, coding them), and the information gained is always suspect. So one must proceed with caution when generalizing from interviews, but they are unique in allowing researchers to get inside the minds of people and to gain access to material of considerable importance. Like many high-risk activities, they are also high-gain ones.

❖ FURTHER READING

Atkinson, R. (1998). *The life story interview*. Thousand Oaks, CA: Sage.

Fetterman, D. M. (1998). *Ethnography: Step-by-step*. Thousand Oaks, CA: Sage.

Gilham, B. (2005). *Research interviewing: The range of techniques*. London: Open University Press.

Kvale, S. (1996). *Interviews: An introduction to qualitative research interviewing*. Thousand Oaks, CA: Sage.

Kvale, S., & Brinkman, S. (2008). *Interviews: Learning the craft of qualitative research interviewing* (2nd ed.). Thousand Oaks, CA: Sage.

Laver, J., & Hutcheson, S. (1972). *Communication in face to face interaction: Selected readings*. Baltimore: Penguin.

Psathas, G. (1994). *Conversation analysis: The study of tale-in-interaction*. Thousand Oaks, CA: Sage.

Rubin, H. J., & Rubin, I. S. (1995). *Qualitative interviewing: The art of hearing data*. Thousand Oaks, CA: Sage.

Seidman, I. (2006). *Interviewing as qualitative research: A guide for researchers in education and the social sciences* (3rd ed.). New York: Teachers College Press.

Stewart, C. I., & Cash, W. B. (2008). *Interviewing: Principles and practices* (12th ed.). New York: McGraw-Hill.

Weingraf, T. (2001). *Qualitative research interviewing: Semi-structured, biographical and narrative methods*. London: Sage.

Zaltman, G. (2003). *How customers think: Essential insights into the mind of the market*. Cambridge, MA: Harvard University Business School Press.

The pastiche is a quintessential postmodern art form.

The co-existence of the upper and lower levels forces upon the historian an illuminating dialectic. How can one understand the towns without understanding the countryside, money without barter, the varieties of poverty without the varieties of luxury, the white bread of the rich without the black bread of the poor?

It remains for me to justify one last choice: that of introducing everyday life, no more no less, into the domain of history. Was this useful? Or necessary? Everyday life consists of the little things one hardly notices in time and space. The more we reduce our vision, the more likely we are to find ourselves in the environment of material life: the broad sweep usually corresponds to History with a capital letter, to distant trade routes, and the networks of national or urban economies. If we reduce the length of time observed, we either have the event or the everyday happening. *The event is, or is taken to be, unique; the everyday happening is repeated, and the more often it is repeated, the more likely it is to become a generality or rather a structure. It pervades society at all levels, and characterizes ways of being and behaving which are perpetuated through endless ages. . . . Through little details, travellers' notes, a society stands revealed. The ways people eat, dress, or lodge, at the different levels of that society,* are *never a matter of indifference. And these snapshots can also point out contrasts and disparities between* one *society and another which are not all superficial.*

—Fernand Braudel, *The Structures of
Everyday Life: Civilization and Capitalism,
15th–18th Century* (1981, p. 29)

8

Historical Analysis

What is history and what should historians do? Who should write what? Who can do research and write historical studies with authority? The first question I will discuss in this chapter on historical method deals with what history is and how it is traditionally defined.

❖ WHAT IS HISTORY?

This is not an easy question to answer, but let me deal with some of the more common understandings of the term. First, when we think of history, we think of studies of the past, and in that respect, history is about the past. That means we have to rely on documents and other materials. If we are dealing with the relatively recent past, we can interview people and get firsthand information that way. If we are dealing with the distant past, we have to confine ourselves to the materials that historians typically use to make sense of the past: books, articles, records of one sort or another, works of art, objects, and whatever else can be used to gain information.

A problem arises here. From the immense amount of material available to historians, they have to select relevant and important sources. How do they do this? The answer is that historians always have some concept or **theory** that guides them. As Robert F. Berkhofer Jr. (1969) explains in his book, *A Behavioral Approach to Historical Analysis,*

> Historians do not recapture or reconstruct the past when they analyze history; they interpret it according to surviving evidence and conceptual frameworks. All of past reality can never be known to them because not all evidence remains. Furthermore, historians do not choose to deal even with all the facts derivable from the available evidence. They confine their interest to man's past, but not even all of that concerns them, for they further select from these data those parts that can be organized according to some interpretation or theory. Thus an historical synthesis is a highly selective account of a postulated past reality. Theory in the most general sense is crucial to every phase of historiography. (p. 23)

That is, all historians have some theory or conceptual framework that guides them and helps them select materials to use in writing history. Berkhofer (1969) then explains that because views of and theories about people and society continually keep changing, historical interpretations of any given subject also keep changing. He writes,

> It should now be evident why history must be and is rewritten constantly in terms of the historians' own times. Every step of producing history presumes theoretical models of man and society, which in turn seem to change in terms of the shifting conceptions of man and society occurring in the historian's own society. (p. 24)

For example, were Berkhofer writing today, he quite likely would have added the words "and woman's" to his sentence "They confine their interest to man's past" and ended up with the following sentence: "They confine their interest to man's *and woman's* past." And that is because of the influence of feminist thought on contemporary historians and other scholars. There is also the matter of how historians are trained and what kind of background historians need.

A SHORT THEATRICAL PIECE ON HISTORICAL ANALYSIS

Grand Inquisitor: *Things are going to hell. I've not tortured anyone or put anyone on the rack for a thousand years! I particularly liked burning witches!*

Arthur: You miss the good old days, eh?

Grand Inquisitor:	*We did wonderful research during the Inquisition. We discovered a lot of people who didn't recognize that they were heretics. Research is so important.*
Arthur:	With you and your colleagues, one could say "heretic today, gone tomorrow!"
Grand Inquisitor:	*Are you mocking me? Dostoevsky never treated me like this. In* The Brothers Karamazov, *I had, at least, a certain amount of gravitas.*
Arthur:	A thousand pardons to someone who I imagine gave none. But you were doing your work, you must keep in mind, before Newton discovered the law of gravitas.

❖ HISTORY AS METADISCIPLINE OR SPECIALIZED SUBJECT

Can historians study anything they want? Is history, like rhetoric, an overarching metadiscipline that studies the past and change over time and is applicable to all subjects? Or is history tied to specific subjects? If the latter is the case, it would mean the history of philosophy should be written by philosophers, the history of science should be written by scientists, the history of **political theory** should be written by political theorists, and so on.

A different way to put this dilemma is to ask the following question about training historians: Do we teach students who wish to be historians a certain methodology and let them specialize in whatever they wish, or do we take specialists and teach them historical methods? This is a problem because our understanding of what history is has changed over the years, and history now is much broader than the way it once was defined, "the study of past politics." The corollary to that definition was the definition of politics as "present-day history."

Metadiscipline	Specialized Discipline
Trained in history	Trained in a subject area
Can deal with all areas	Deals only with own subject
May lack knowledge	May lack technique

You can see from this chart that there are problems with both approaches. In many cases, we now find people with areas of specialized knowledge who study history and use what they learn to work in their particular areas, merging the two oppositions, so to speak.

❖ IS HISTORY OBJECTIVE OR SUBJECTIVE OR A COMBINATION OF THE TWO?

Many people have the belief that history is objective, based only on facts. This perspective suggests that historians tell us what happened in the past and how things changed over time. It's as simple as that. A fact-based chronology.

Now it is true, no doubt, that historians base their writings on facts—or on what they think are facts. After all, historians are not supposed to be writing fiction. But even if all historians were to write their histories based only on factual material, it is obvious that they cannot deal with all the facts involved with what they are studying. They have to select those facts—those events—that they consider to be most significant and most revealing from all the material they have.

Thus, there is an element of interpretation involved in history based on the selection process. That explains why historians often differ with one another when they write about the same topic. Berkhofer (1969), in the passage quoted above, mentioned that over the years, as new concepts and theories are developed, historians change their interpretations.

But at any given moment in time, different kinds of historians, with different theories and methodologies and beliefs about what is important and what is unimportant, clash over how to write about a given subject. Marxist historians focus their attention on topics such as the economic system, the class system, imperialism, the control of the media by the ruling class, alienation, and other concepts derived from Marx and similarly inclined thinkers. Psychoanalytically inclined historians, who write psychohistories of important figures, are concerned with the families of their subjects, their personalities, and similar topics. Nixon, for example, was the subject of any number of psychohistories that attempted to explain Nixon's career in terms of his psychological makeup and problems.

Historians used to focus their attention mostly on important military and political figures and pay little attention to "ordinary people," to everyday life, to cultural matters and artistic works and other seemingly unimportant matters. Now, in recent years, with the development of the "Annales" school of history, championed by historians such as Ferdinand Braudel, many historians are also looking at things such as the growth of certain crops by farmers, the consumption of bread, and similar topics. These topics, which seem mundane and trivial, provide valuable information about the past and may explain more about what caused things to happen, such as great migrations of people, than events in the lives of kings and queens and the decisions made by parliaments.

❖ KINDS OF HISTORICAL RESEARCH

G. Phifer (1961), in his article "The Historical Approach" (in *An Introduction to Graduate Study in Speech and Theatre,* edited by C. W. Dow), suggests that there are seven types of historical studies. They are listed below, in slightly modified form:

1. *Biographical studies,* focusing on the lives of important persons

2. *Movement or idea studies,* tracing the development of political, social, or economic ideas and movements

3. *Regional studies,* focusing on particular cities, states, nations, and regions

4. *Institutional studies,* concentrating on specific organizations

5. *Case histories,* focusing on social settings of a single event

6. *Selected studies,* identifying and paying close attention to a special element in some complex process

7. *Editorial studies,* dealing with the translating or processing of documents

There are also different kinds of historians. Thus, intellectual historians are basically interested in how ideas have affected history and focus their attention on the concepts and theories of important thinkers, writers, artists, political figures, and the way the beliefs of these individuals have shaped the beliefs of ordinary people. Biographical historians focus on the lives of important figures. For example, many historians have written about Richard M. Nixon, an enigmatic and psychologically complicated figure. Quantitative historians, on the other hand, use statistics and other numerical data to make their arguments.

I could make an analogy with medicine. We find (especially as we grow older) many different kinds of medical specialists practicing, who sometimes disagree about what a symptom means and how best to treat a medical problem. It is often the case that the same kinds of specialists (for example, neurologists or urologists) disagree about how a specific medical problem should be dealt with. That is why in medicine, the rule is "get a second opinion." In history, if you don't like a particular interpretation, the rule is "get a second historian." I might add that researchers in all fields disagree about many things; as I've pointed out elsewhere, even economists with the same statistical data often disagree about how to interpret them.

❖ THE PROBLEM OF WRITING HISTORY

We find another complicating factor to the historical approach, and that is connected with the way historians write. Generally speaking, they take the material they have gathered—from primary sources, such as newspaper articles, records from diaries and journals, and data from governmental agencies, and from secondary sources, such as statements by individuals of consequence, material from scholarly books and scholarly articles, autobiographies and biographies, ideas from philosophers, artists, and others—and weave a narrative (that is, tell a story) out of this material.

Primary Sources	Secondary Sources
Newspaper articles	Articles by other historians
Records from diaries	Articles and books by scholars
Data from agencies	Ideas from philosophers
Speeches	Editorials
Interviews	Commentaries
Autobiographies	Biographies

Now, all of this material that historians use must be considered suspect—including data—because researchers often make mistakes in gathering it. People have biases or lie about things when answering questionnaires. Newspaper articles are sometimes full of errors, and so are books and articles from the scholarly and general press. People who write their autobiographies tend to focus on the positive aspects of their careers and downplay the negative ones. Wherever one looks, there are problems in finding and interpreting historical data.

The need historians have to tell stories, to write narratives, also poses problems, for the narrative form imposes some limits on writers. Historians want their books to be interesting, coherent, and stylishly written, as well as being factually correct. Historians also want to give their books an element of drama and suspense. So putting materials into a narrative may lead to simplifications or exaggerations or other deviations from the reality of situations being dealt with. Historians writing narratives do not recognize, I would suggest, the degree to which the requirements of historical writing shape their perceptions. If they are legitimate historians, who are trying to be fair and objective, they would not willingly distort things. Of course, some historians are so ideological that they twist things around to make history fit their ideological preconceptions.

Nor would they recognize that they often are reductionistic—taking complicated matters and simplifying them. It is the common tendency in research to use overly strict limitations on the kinds of concepts and variables to be considered as causes in explaining a broad range of behaviors or processes. Reductionism tends to suggest that certain elements used in the analysis may be more relevant than other elements, based on the researcher's preconceptions and scientific orientation.

❖ THE PROBLEM OF MEANING

Historians have to find patterns to make human behavior meaningful. A random collection of facts about some topic doesn't tell us anything. Neither does a simple chronology. The question that must be asked is whether historians impose a pattern on the material they are dealing with (because of their theories about how to interpret historical data and other material) or whether they elicit from this material or, to be more precise, discover in this material a pattern. Are historians ingenious thinkers who impose their conceptual theories on past events to explain what happened, or are they gifted analysts who find in past events the pattern that helps explain them? This question is analogous to the debate over structuralist critics who interpret literary works, films, television shows, videos, and other kinds of texts.

There are two views about what the structuralists do. One says it is all "hocus pocus," and the structuralist imposes on the text some ingenious structure that is in the mind of the structuralist critic. The other says it is "God's truth," and structuralist critics are astute at finding structures that are hidden in these works.

These differences are shown in the chart that follows, which is applied to history:

God's Truth	Hocus Pocus
Discover what's in text	Impose structures on texts
Elicit patterns from history	Impose patterns on history
Theory helps discover pattern	Theory creates pattern

One of the things that history does is help us find meaning in the events of the past, and to do this, historians have to find patterns to help organize the data they work with; whether the patterns historians write about are discovered or are imposed is always something we must keep in mind when we read works by historians.

Another way of stating the problem is to point out that facts don't speak for themselves. Someone has to interpret the facts and put them into perspective. This process of establishing perspective requires some theory that explains how society works.

❖ HISTORICAL PERIODS

Dividing the past into periods is another method historians use to make sense of things. Thus, history departments have courses on ancient history, medieval history, modern history, contemporary history, and so on. In addition to these very broad categories, historians often use much narrower ones, such as centuries or, in the case of United States history, decades. They make distinctions between American culture, political thought, and social practices in the many decades such as the "Gay Nineties" or "Roaring Nineties," and every decade since then, as the following chart shows:

Decade	Typical Characterization
1920s	Era of the Robber Barons
1930s	The Depression Years
1940s	World War II and Postwar Period
1950s	Eisenhower Stability
1960s	Post Vietnam: Flower Children & Hippies
1970s	The Quiet Decade
1980s	Reagan Years, Me-Decade
1990s	Generation Xers
2000s	Generation Z, Internet Generation
2010s	Aught Generation?

Each of these decades is, some historians argue, different from the others, and each can be characterized by particular kinds of ideas, social practices, economic conditions, art styles, fashions, and so on that were dominant.

These ideas have filtered into society, in general, and now newspapers often have articles about social trends, such as "Returning to the Fifties," or about the impact of "the Sixties" on contemporary American culture. Of course, historians often disagree about how to characterize the decades, but I've offered some generally held descriptions of each. It is also worth noting that these decades didn't necessarily all start on January first and end on December 31st of the decade; often, there was a considerable amount of overlap.

It is natural to use our knowledge of the past to try to understand the present because we believe the past has influenced the present. That is one of the things history teaches us. How the past has influenced the present and what impact the past may have on the future is a different matter. To the extent that future developments in social thought shape the consciousness of historians, we can also argue that the future influences the past as we learn to interpret and understand it.

Fredric Jameson, an important theorist of postmodernism.

❖ BAUDRILLARD AND JAMESON ON POSTMODERNISM

Postmodernism is based on the notion of periods as well—the term *postmodernism* suggests "after" **modernism** and "different from" modernism. This topic is discussed in the glossary, but it is useful to say something about postmodernism and media here. There are many different definitions and understandings of postmodernism, but most theorists of postmodernism suggest that it is connected to the rise of mass media and what Jean Baudrillard, a prominent French theorist of the subject, described as simulations and "hyperreality." For Baudrillard, media and simulated models have replaced manufacturing as the basic way of organizing societies.

As Steven Best and Douglas Kellner explain in *Postmodern Theory: Critical Interrogations* (1991),

> For Baudrillard the models of the United States in Disneyland are more real than their instantiations in the social world, as the USA becomes more and more like Disneyland. . . . The hyperreal for Baudrillard is a condition whereby models replace the real, as

exemplified in such phenomena as the ideal home in women's or lifestyle magazines, ideal sex as portrayed in sex manuals. (p. 119)

Another important theoretician of postmodernism, Frederic Jameson, deals with the impact of postmodernism on media and culture in *Postmodernism: or, The Cultural Logic of Late Capitalism* (1991). He discusses some characteristics of postmodern culture:

> this whole "degraded" landscape of schlock and kitsch, of TV series and *Reader's Digest* culture, of advertising and motels, of the late show and grade-B Hollywood film, of so-called paraliterature, with its airport paperback categories of the gothic and the romance, the popular biography, the murder mystery, and even the science fiction or fantasy novel. (pp. 2–3)

What is important to recognize about postmodernism, Jameson (1991) argues, is that it is just a name for a new form of capitalism and is connected, in direct ways, to the development of consumer cultures.

❖ THE HISTORICAL AND THE COMPARATIVE APPROACH

I'm making a somewhat simplified argument here to clarify the differences between historical and comparative research methods. In reality, the two are not necessarily antithetical. History, for our purposes, will deal with the past and with changes over time. Comparative analysis, on the other hand, deals with changes over space—with the difference, say, between the U.S. Constitution and the constitution of some other country, such as the Japanese constitution, or between the American Revolution and the French Revolution. A historical approach to Disneyland would deal with its evolution over the years, and a comparative approach would deal with Disneyland in the United States and in France or Japan (or both).

Let me suggest the differences between these two approaches in the following chart:

Historical Research	Comparative Research
Change over time	Differences over space
Before and after	Here and there
Early articles on Disneyland and later ones	Articles on Disneyland in the United States, France, and Japan

Because, as de Saussure argued, we make sense of concepts differentially, we can choose either the time axis or the space axis for our research. But there is nothing to prevent historians from doing both—looking at changes over time and differences in space—when they do their research. Fernand Braudel, the great French historian whom I quoted at the beginning of the chapter, uses both a historical and a comparative approach, which greatly enriches his book.

❖ HISTORY IS AN ART, NOT A SCIENCE

We must keep in mind that many scholars regard history as an art, not a science. At first, history was written by amateurs—that is, people who were not trained in universities to be historians but who were involved, in some cases, in events of consequence or interested in writing about these events. History is now much more professionalized, and most historians are based at universities where they do their research and teach history courses and, in some cases, historiography—the art of being a historian. Some historians now use quantitative methods and adapt various scientific approaches to their research; they see history as a social science, not as an area in the humanities, not as an art. There is, therefore, considerable disagreement among historians about how they should do historical research and write history.

❖ DOING HISTORICAL RESEARCH

So what does this mean for you? If you keep in mind the following questions, they will guide you as you proceed with your research.

Can you narrow your focus? Have you narrowed your topic of research so you can deal with it in the amount of time at your disposal and the length of paper that is required of you? That is, you can't do a history of news in 15 pages that is not superficial, but you can write about the history of a news program such as *60 Minutes* that need not be superficial.

Can you find primary and secondary sources? You may be interested in some very focused subject but may not be able to obtain information about it—even through the Internet. So you have to be careful that you choose a topic for your research that has primary sources (records, data, interviews, statistics) and secondary sources (articles and books by scholars and others) that you can obtain.

Are your sources reliable? All historians face the problem of how reliable their sources are. We know that people who are interviewed— primary sources—sometimes lie about their opinions (for a variety of reasons). In the same light, people who write articles about themselves and their activities may put a spin on what actually happened, or they may give a biased and only partially true account to newspaper reporters or others who interview them. You always have to consider the reliability of your sources. One way to get around this is to find a few other sources and see whether there's agreement about the topic you are investigating.

Are the authorities you are citing reliable? As I mentioned earlier, historians often disagree with one another. So if you are citing historians, can you be sure they are correct? And if you are citing written materials from primary sources—those involved in an event—can you be sure they are telling the truth? It is a good idea to find primary sources—that is, people who can give you detailed firsthand information (but remember to be suspicious) as well as secondary sources, such as writings by historians, which can give you perspective and background. Also, if you can find a few primary sources written about a given event, then you see whether they agree with one another. For example, consider the matter of Watergate. There's an almost endless number of books and articles by people who were in the White House with Nixon, by Nixon, by reporters, and by historians who have studied the matter. By balancing primary and secondary sources, you may find that a consistent story will emerge.

What concepts or theory of history are you using? You may not recognize that you are using concepts or a theory of history, but when you write history, you have to have an organizing principle that tells you what material is good and what isn't, what you should focus on and what you shouldn't. What concepts or theory of history do you hold?

History is the record of progress.

History is the study of class conflict.

History is bunk!

History is the story of great figures.

History is the study of everyday life.

What does anything mean? Let us suppose that you are researching the way the 1999 World Series was televised (to give ourselves a good media research topic) and have found material about the series in newspapers, sports magazines, scholarly journals, books by sociologists and psychologists, and statements from athletes who were involved in the series, television executives, media critics, and various other sources who were directly or indirectly involved in the games. You might also have video recordings of the series.

As a historian, your task is not only to describe the televised version of the 1999 World Series (and the various controversies about how it was televised) but to say something about how the series and the way it was televised reflect society and culture in the United States. You not only have to describe and interpret the televised version of the series, but you also have to speculate about the economic, social, and cultural significance of the series—that is, say what you think the event means. When speculating, however, be sure to use appropriate language to make clear that you are offering hypotheses or interpretations or opinions; do not offer your speculations as "facts." A good historian may offer an interpretation of what an event means, but she or he always makes clear the difference between facts and interpretation of facts.

What's the impact? In addition to speculating about the meaning of the event you are dealing with, and let's assume, once again, that you are writing about the televised version of the 1999 World Series, you should concern yourself with what impact the series might have had on baseball, on our attitudes toward professional athletes, on owners of teams, on television networks, on society and culture in the United States, and on people in other cultures—to name a few of the topics you might wish to consider. We do this because one of the tasks of the historian is to assess the impact that events might have on our lives and on the societies in which we live.

❖ HISTORICAL ANALYSIS: APPLICATIONS AND EXERCISES

1. Investigate reviews of the historian Arnold Toynbee. Compare reviews in newspapers and popular magazines with reviews in scholarly journals. What conclusions do you reach about any differences you might find in the two kinds of publications about Toynbee's status as a historian?

2. Do a research project on new trends in historical analysis. What new approaches have historians come up with in recent years? Why have they developed these approaches?

3. How has postmodernism affected historical research? Find scholarly articles and books on the subject and report on what you learned about this question. Attach copies of the first page of the articles that you found.

❖ CONCLUSIONS

Most of the research we read about has a historical dimension to it, as the researchers describe and explain what they did and what they found. In a sense, when we write about things in the past, whether we are writing about the remote past (kings and wars) or the recent past (experiments we conducted), there is no escaping history. We can learn from historians important things, such as being accurate, organized, logical, and honest. As Jacques Barzun and Henry F. Graff (1957) write in an old but excellent book, *The Modern Researcher*,

> It is from historical scholarship—originating with the antiquarian—that the world has taken the apparatus of footnotes, references, bibliography, and so on, which have become commonplace devices, not to say household words. It is from the historical study of texts by philologists and historians that writers at large have learned to sift evidence, balance testimony, and demand verified assertions. . . . Whatever its purpose, a report is invariably and necessarily historical. Insofar as it reports facts it gives an account of the past. (p. 5)

Historians have provided researchers with some fundamental ways of searching for facts and recording them. One other important thing we've learned from the really first-rate historians is to be mindful of style when writing up our findings. The new research methodologies we have created do not displace the historical perspective but build on it.

When we write up our reports, we are writing, if you think about it, what can be described as short-term microhistories of our activities and findings and using this material to speculate about the present or the future (or both). There is no escaping the historical dimension, whether it is establishing a sense of context to give your research a grounding or talking about other research similar to the research you will be conducting.

❖ FURTHER READING

Appleby, J. (with Jacob, M.). (1994). *Telling the truth about history.* New York: Norton.

Barzun, J., & Graff, H. F. (1957). *The modern researcher.* New York: Harcourt, Brace & Company.

Benjamin, J. R. (1998). *A student's guide to history* (7th ed.). Boston: Bedford.

Berkhofer, R. F., Jr. (1969). *A behavioral approach to historical analysis.* New York: Free Press.

Breisach, E. (1995). *Historiography: Ancient, medieval & modern* (2nd ed.). Chicago: University of Chicago Press.

Foucault, M. (1973). *Madness & civilization: A history of insanity in the age of reason* (R. Howard, Trans.). New York: Vintage.

Godfrey, D. G. (2005). *Methods of historical analysis in electronic media.* London: Routledge.

Howell, M. C., & Prevenier, W. (2001). *From reliable sources: An introduction to historical method.* Ithaca, NY: Cornell University Press.

Iggers, G. G. (1997). *Historiography in the twentieth century: From scientific objectivity to the postmodern challenge.* Middletown, CT: Wesleyan University Press.

Noble, D. (1965). *Historians against history.* Minneapolis: University of Minnesota Press.

Phifer, G. (1961). The historical approach. In C. W. Dow (Ed.), *An introduction to graduate study in speech and theatre.* East Lansing: Michigan State University Press.

Startt, D. (2003). *Historical methods in mass communication.* San Ramon, CA: Vision Press.

The Game of LOVE

PASS | You're Engaged Now | Buy Flowers | Oops. BABY | PASS | Go to a French Restaurant | Get a Divorce Now

BLIND DATE

NO SHOW

PASS

COOK a meal

ELOPE | No Alimony | PASS | DIAMOND RING | BLIND DATE | GO TO RENO | PASS

PASS

Oops. BABY!

Road Trip

TAKE A TRIP

The ethnomethodological emphasis on cultural studies . . . stresses that the researchers should not try to suggest interpretations of people's worlds of meaning, to try to move into their minds. The interpretation of meaning is regarded as an activity that is characteristic of everyday situations of interaction: we look at what other people do, and infer on that basis what they "mean" or "think," and then respond on the basis of the interpretation we have made. It is one of the key tenets of ethnomethodology that the researcher should not compete with laypeople over such interpretations of meaning; the researcher should not try to offer the ultimate interpretation of what things "really" mean. Rather, the ethnomethodologist is concerned to study the methods or the rules of interpretation that people follow in their everyday lives. Ethnomethodology, as the name implies, is concerned with studying the "ethno-methods" of popular interpretation. Its object of study consists of observable, concrete, incarnated social activities through which actors produce everyday situations and practices and are capable of acting in those situations.

—Pertti Alasuutari, *Researching Culture: Qualitative Method and Cultural Studies* (1995, p. 36)

9

Ethnomethodological Research

E thnomethodological research is one of the most fascinating and also one of the most troublesome kinds of research there is. One reason for this situation is that ethnomethodology tends to resist being easily defined. Nobody (somewhat of an overstatement) is really sure what ethnomethodology is. Another problem is that some scholars consider its findings interesting but not terribly significant because they seem to deal with trivial and unimportant matters.

❖ DEFINING ETHNOMETHODOLOGY

The term **ethnomethodology** was thought up by a distinguished sociologist, Harold Garfinkel. In an article titled "The Origins of the Term 'Ethnomethodology'" (based on a transcript of a symposium on the subject), Garfinkel explains how he thought up the name:

> "Ethno" seemed to refer, somehow or other, to the availability to a member of common-sense knowledge of his society as common-sense knowledge of the "whatever." If it were ethno-botany, then it had to do somehow or other with his knowledge of and his grasp of what

were for members adequate methods for dealing with botanical matters. Someone from another society, like an anthropologist in this case, would recognize the matters as botanical matters. The member would employ ethnobotany as adequate grounds of inference and action in the conduct of his own affairs in the company of others like him. It was that plain, and the notion of "ethnomethodology" or the term "ethnomethodology" was taken in this sense. (qtd. in Turner, 1974, pp. 16, 17)

Garfinkel makes a number of important points about ethnomethodology in this passage selected from his talk (and I will add others taken from his writings and those of other ethnomethodologists):

- The focus of ethnomethodology is on people's "commonsense" knowledge of society.

- There is an interest among ethnomethodologists in people's "adequate grounds of inference."

- There is a concern among ethnomethodologists for actions people undertake in the company of others like themselves.

- Ethnomethodologists are interested in studying everyday life, which is generally neglected by sociologists.

- The ethnomethodologist's concern with people's understanding of things suggests that ethnomethodologists do not offer their interpretations of the meanings of people's activities but search for the way *they* make sense of things and find meaning in things—especially conversations people have and things people do.

Thus, ethnomethodology is interested in how people think and act in everyday life situations, in contrast to, for example, laboratory experiments or focus groups or other situations in which people recognize that they are, one way or another, being studied. "Common sense" becomes a subject of inquiry, not just a "given" that is neglected for other concerns.

These interests of ethnomethodologists have implications for advertising, in that advertisers want to know how people make sense of the world and how they react to "commonsense" appeals. Advertisers want to be able to "reach" targeted segments of the population and to influence them, which means advertisers want to understand people's "grounds for inference." Thus, ethnomethodology has important applications when it comes to making commercials and print advertisements.

Ethnomethodologists assume that people have common understandings—which they don't always articulate—and this leads ethnomethodologists to examine how people reason and what's behind their everyday activities. It isn't easy to find these common understandings or to determine how people reason.

Garfinkel offers several other definitions of ethnomethodology in his book *Studies in Ethnomethodology,* a collection of his papers that was published in 1967. Let me offer a sampling.

> The following studies seek to treat practical activities, practical cir-cumstances, and practical sociological reasoning as topics of empiri-cal study, and by paying to the most commonplace activities of daily life the attention usually accorded extraordinary events to learn about them as phenomena in their own right. (p. 1)

I will shortly describe some of the research Garfinkel did, and you will see that his findings are quite fascinating.

In Chapter 2, his essay "Studies of the Routine Grounds of Everyday Activities" makes the same point in slightly different terms:

> Although sociologists take socially structured scenes of everyday life as a point of departure they rarely see, as a task of sociological inquiry in its own right, the general question of how any such com-mon sense world is possible. . . . As a topic and methodological ground for sociological inquiries, the definition of the common sense world of everyday life, though it is appropriately a project of sociological inquiry, has been neglected. My purposes in this paper are to demonstrate the essential relevance to sociological inquiries, of a concern for common sense activities as a topic of inquiry in its own right and, by reporting a series of studies, to urge its "redis-covery." (p. 36)

These quotations point, then, to the subject of ethnomethodological research—whose most important tasks are the following:

- To define the commonsense world of everyday life

- To show the relevance of everyday activities to sociological theory

- To rediscover the significance of the commonsense world of people

We must keep in mind that the researcher does not try to interpret the meaning of everyday activities but, rather, to find the rules or codes by which people interpret statements made to them by others, through which they make sense of the world.

A SHORT THEATRICAL PIECE ON ETHNOMETHODOLOGICAL ANALYSIS

Grand Inquisitor:	*29–35–25–29–2*
Arthur:	(Laughing) I never heard that joke before. It's very funny!
Grand Inquisitor:	*How about 29–35–18–19–1?*
Arthur:	(Laughing) I love that joke about the rabbi and the minister's wife.
Grand Inquisitor:	*Don't you think it is quite absurd to reduce jokes to formulas?*
Arthur:	Not at all. Let me tell you a joke. The comedians have a conference every year. Since they know all the jokes in the world, they've reduced them all to numbers to save time when they tell them. A comedian gets up in the hall where they are all meeting and yells "24–16–3–44." Nobody laughs. One comedian in the back of the hall leans over to his friend and says, "He never could tell a joke."
Grand Inquisitor:	*I give up.*

❖ GARFINKEL'S INGENIOUS AND MISCHIEVOUS RESEARCH

Garfinkel (1967) tells us in his chapter on the routine grounds of everyday activities that he likes to take familiar scenes in people's everyday lives and "ask what can be done to make trouble" (p. 37). He asks his students to do things in their everyday lives (talking with friends, having dinner at home) that "produce and sustain bewilderment, consternation, and confusion; to produce the social structured affects of anxiety, shame, guilt and indignation; and to produce disorganized interaction" (pp. 37, 38). How does he do this? Rather easily, it turns out. Why does he do this? Because his little "experiments" enable ethnomethodologists to discover important and interesting things about the way people relate to one another.

What these case studies show is that important segments of everyday life escape our attention and are really fertile ground for understanding how people live and make sense of things. Our common understandings and background expectancies are so routinized and strong that it doesn't take much, as the various experiments of Garfinkel's students showed, to cause all kinds of problems and difficulties when these expectancies are not met.

Let me offer some examples.

Clarifying Comments. In one experiment (a term that is, perhaps, somewhat loosely used here), he asked students to take everything anyone said to them literally and to ask them to clarify their remarks. Thus, when a person was telling one of his students that he had a flat tire, the student asked him what he meant by flat tire? That led to the friend's getting flustered. In another example from the same experiment, a friend of one of his students asked him how his girlfriend was feeling. The student asked whether his friend meant physically or mentally? The person asking the question looked peeved and went on to a different subject.

Acting Like Boarders While at Home. In this experiment, Garfinkel asked 49 of his students to spend between 15 minutes to an hour at home acting like boarders. That is, they were to be very circumspect and polite, were to avoid getting personal, were to use formal address, and were to speak only when spoken to.

In something like 80% of the cases, the families of the students were "stupefied" and "astonished" and tried to make sense of the strange actions of the students. Some thought the students had been working too hard, were ill, had broken up with boyfriends of girlfriends, and so on. A number of the members of the families got angry.

The reason for this behavior by the families was that the normal behavior of the students (and people, in general, in family situations)—taking snacks when they feel like it, grabbing food, taking larger portions for themselves than others take at the dinner table, interrupting others while they are speaking—this normal behavior was no longer going on, and the members of the students' families got confused.

What the experiment revealed is that we take certain kinds of actions for granted, and when someone acts out of character one way or another, we get disturbed. A member of a family acting like a boarder, even though other family members might not recognize the behavior for what it is, disturbs the equilibrium and violates everyone's expectations. We can describe this in terms of figure and ground: When the figure suddenly changes, it stands out against the ground of expectations and becomes problematic.

Describing a Household as If One Were a Boarder. In this experiment, students were asked to spend between 15 minutes to an hour in their household assuming that they were boarders (but not to act as if they were boarders). They were to describe what they saw as if they knew nothing of the people involved. They were only to describe what they observed, as objectively as possible, and not make any assumptions about the motives of those involved or the propriety of people's behavior.

What the students learned, to their surprise, was the degree to which members of the family's treatments of each other were so personal. Garfinkel (1967) writes,

> Displays of conduct and feeling occurred without apparent concern for the management of impressions. Table manners were bad, and family members showed each other little politeness. . . . Many [students] became uncomfortably aware of how habitual movements were being made; of *how* one was handling the silverware, or *how* one opened the door or greeted another member. Many reported that the attitude was difficult to sustain because with it quarreling, bickering, and hostile motivations became discomfitingly visible. (pp. 45, 46)

Many of the students argued that their descriptions of their families were not *true* ones and that their families really got along together well and were happy.

❖ USING ETHNOMETHODOLOGY IN MEDIA AND COMMUNICATION RESEARCH

The question arises now, How can we use ethnomethodology in our research in communication and media analysis? Let me suggest a few answers to this question. What ethnomethodology provides us, we must remember, is a way of studying the codes and unconscious belief systems that lie behind our utterances and everyday actions. We can adapt ethnomethodological approaches to the media by asking the same questions ethnomethodologists ask—not about conversations but about dialogue in films and television shows, lyrics in songs, and similar phenomena.

There are differences between the analysis of dialogue in media and the analyses that ethnomethodologists make of real-world conversations in that dialogue in mass-mediated texts is created by writers. In a sense, therefore, when we do research on dialogue in a film or other mass-mediated text, we are dealing with a writer's perception of the world, but because writers create texts for large numbers of people, who presumably share their perceptions, we can assume that analyzing dialogue in mediated texts is not that different from analyzing dialogue in everyday situations.

We can still look for the unconscious, nonarticulated background understandings that people share, except that they are reflected in dialogue expressed by actors and actresses and in their actions and typical behavior, which are written by writers or, in many cases, teams of writers. A situation comedy such as *Frasier* had a dozen writers thinking up the ideas for stories and writing the scripts, but we must assume that these writers shared a common perception of the world with the people who watched the show.

Let me suggest the difference between what might be described as pure ethnomethodological research, as practiced by sociologists (and other researchers, such as linguists and psychologists), which focuses on everyday life routines, and the adapted or applied form of this research, which uses films, television programs, songs, and other mediated texts.

Pure Research	Applied/Adapted Research
Everyday life	Mass-mediated texts
Ordinary people	Actors, actresses, singers, etc.
Routine interactions	Scripted interactions
Search for codes	Search for codes

Although there are differences, the goals of both are the same—discovering the background expectancies and codes that lie behind everyday behavior. Let's consider a topic of great importance to most people—love (as in romantic love).

❖ LOVE IS A GAME

Many years ago, in the 1940s and 1950s, before rock 'n' roll and before rap, many romantic ballads were popular. These ballads were sung by crooners and told stories, usually about romantic love. (Many radio stations play these "golden oldies" for people who grew up in those years, so these songs are still being listened to but not by young people, as a rule.) One song that I found particularly interesting is a ballad called "It's All in the Game," which states that love is a wonderful game. In my classes, I often ask my students what the metaphor "Love is a game" implies about love. They supply the following notions about what we might describe as logical imperatives or commonsense beliefs found in the metaphor "Love is a game."

1. *Someone wins and someone loses.* Games generally have winners and losers, and so we can expect winners and losers in the wonderful game called love. But what does it mean to "win" at love? Or to "lose" at love?

2. *Sometimes you are winning and other times you might be losing.* In other words, like most games, we're never sure whether we'll win or lose at the end. That helps make it exciting.

3. *Love is not serious.* Games aren't really serious, so if love is a game, it isn't serious either. We play games to amuse ourselves, but when we grow bored with these games, we stop playing. Or we find another way to amuse ourselves or another person with whom to play the game.

4. *There are rules to follow in games.* Games are rule bound, and you must follow them if the game is to be a game. You can't make up the rules to suit yourself as you proceed. Or you shouldn't, that is.

5. *You have to watch out for cheating.* Some people cheat at games and so you have to be careful that you are not victimized. Cheating in the game of love suggests things such as lying about how you really feel or, perhaps, having someone else you are playing the game of love with, also at the same time . . . that is, playing with more than one person at a time.

6. *Games end after a while.* Eventually someone wins a game or the players get bored and stop playing the game.

We can see, then, that describing love as a game means that we adopt a certain set of understandings about what love is and how to "play" the game of love. Certain logical implications and expectations are contained in the notion that love is a game that are not found in other notions about love. Metaphors (love is a game) and similes (love is like a game) play an important **role** in the way we think about things; they are not just literary devices used by poets and writers. I would suggest that recognizing that people see love as a game and tracing out the implications of this metaphor is a form of applied ethnomethodological research.

❖ HUMORISTS AS CODE VIOLATORS

We are ready to undertake another form of applied ethnomethodological research with our study of humor. Humor is a subject that has perplexed philosophers, psychologists, sociologists, linguists, communication theorists, and many other kinds of scholars and thinkers for thousands of years. Let me suggest that one way to look at humorists—which is relevant to our interest in applying ethnomethodological theory—is as code violators. If we are interested in codes, schemas, and scripts (whatever you want to call the background understandings we have that we learn from growing up in a given culture and subculture), then humor is useful if, in fact, as I have suggested, it is connected to code violations.

Consider **jokes,** which are generally defined as having the following characteristics:

- They are short narratives.
- They are meant to amuse people.
- They have punch lines.
- They generate mirthful laughter.

A joke can be diagrammed as follows:

A-> B-> C-» D-> E-> F-> G-> H (punch line)
↓
I (laughter)

The punch line represents an unexpected resolution of the narrative being told, one that surprises us and amuses us and, if the joke is good, causes laughter. We tend to use the term *joke* loosely for things such as riddles, which take the form of questions and answers, and witticisms and puns, which involve wordplay. But technically speaking, a joke is a funny story with a punch line. Let me offer an example. I will use a letter to characterize each part of the joke.

A. A minister comes home early and finds his wife lying in bed naked. There is a strong smell of cigar smoke in the apartment.

B. He looks out the window and sees a priest, smoking a big cigar, leaving the apartment house.

C. In a fit of rage, with superhuman strength, the minister lifts up the refrigerator in his apartment, and just as the priest crosses beneath the window, the minister drops the refrigerator on the priest, killing him.

D. Then, consumed by conscience, the minister jumps out the window.

E. A few seconds later, the priest, the minister, and a rabbi appear before St. Peter in heaven.

F. "How did you get here?" St. Peter asks the priest. "I don't know," replies the priest. "I had been visiting a parishioner who was ill, and a refrigerator dropped on me, killing me."

G. "And how did you get here?" St. Peter asks the minister. "I dropped the refrigerator on the priest," replies the minister. "And then, I felt so guilty about what I'd done, I jumped out the window and killed myself."

H. "And how did you get here?" St. Peter asks the rabbi. "I don't know," replies the rabbi. *I was minding my own business, sitting in a refrigerator and smoking a cigar . . ."* (punch line)

I. Laughter (response to punch line)

I have put the punch line in italics here. If this joke is told by a good joke teller, it generally elicits laughter. We have to learn how to tell jokes successfully and to listen to jokes correctly, which means we must respond, on cue, when told a joke. The cue is the punch line. We have to pay attention to the joke teller so we laugh at the correct time, not letting too much time between the punch line and our laughter.

We have several codes violated in this joke. First, we have the matter of logical thinking. Priests are celibate . . . or at least they are supposed to be celibate. The minister jumps to conclusions about the priest, because he is smoking a cigar. Second, the minister violates the code, "Thou shall not kill." Third, the minister drops a refrigerator on the priest, an act that is quite impossible. And fourth, the rabbi violates the code of common sense. One does not sit in refrigerators smoking cigars and one cannot sit in refrigerators. Of course, we know why the rabbi was sitting in the refrigerator "minding his own business."

It may be worth looking at jokes to see what kinds of codes of behavior are assumed and then violated by the punch lines. It also may be worth looking at the monologues of comedians to see how they deal with and, in many cases, violate our ideas of normalcy and common sense. Humor involves some kind of a play frame that states "this is not for real" or "I don't really mean this" and that helps makes jokes, many of which are insulting to women, ethnic groups, racial groups, professional groups, and others, take on a veneer of acceptability so that people are willing to tell these jokes to one another. As Freud pointed out, humor is connected to masked aggression, and one of the joys of listening to jokes is participating, in a guilt-free way, in aggression. We realize now that humor can have very negative psychological consequences, which is why the media try to censor humor that is too insulting to people.

Character	Code Violated
Priest	Celibacy (assumed violation)
Minister	Thou shall not kill
Minister	Physical capacity of human beings
Rabbi	Thou shall not commit adultery
Rabbi	Humans sitting in refrigerators

❖ ON THE TECHNIQUES OF HUMOR

As I mentioned earlier, I made a content analysis of humor (from jokes, plays, comic books, literature, etc.) and elicited from the material I examined 45 techniques that, in various permutations and combinations, can be used to generate humor. In an earlier chapter, I listed these techniques by their categories. In Table 9.1, I list these techniques alphabetically and number each technique. These techniques enable us to examine any example of humor and determine the techniques found in the work that generates laughter.

Table 9.1   Techniques of Humor in Alphabetical Order

1. Absurdity	16. Embarrassment	31. Parody
2. Accident	17. Exaggeration	32. Puns
3. Allusion	18. Exposure	33. Repartee
4. Analogy	19. Facetiousness	34. Repetition
5. Before/after	20. Grotesque	35. Reversal
6. Bombast	21. Ignorance	36. Ridicule
7. Burlesque	22. Imitation	37. Rigidity
8. Caricature	23. Impersonation	38. Sarcasm
9. Catalogue	24. Infantilism	39. Satire
10. Chase scene	25. Insults	40. Scale, size
11. Coincidence	26. Irony	41. Slapstick
12. Comparison	27. Literalness	42. Speed
13. Definition	28. Mimicry	43. Stereotypes
14. Disappointment	29. Mistakes	44. Theme and variation
15. Eccentricity	30. Misunderstanding	45. Unmasking

If we apply this chart to the joke about the priest, minister, and rabbi, we find the following techniques at work:

- *Mistakes (29):* The minister smells cigar smoke and thinks it comes from the priest's cigar.

- *Reversal (35):* The minister attempts to get revenge against the priest.

- *Exposure (18):* The rabbi reveals that he's the source of the cigar smoke.

- *Facetiousness (19):* The rabbi says he was innocently sitting in a refrigerator.

- *Absurdity (1):* The rabbi was smoking in a refrigerator.

This analysis suggests, then, that jokes can be extremely complex texts, with all kinds of different things going on (techniques operating) that generate humor and laughter. It is possible to use this typology of humor techniques to study jokes and other forms of humor to see whether certain techniques are being used or whether the humor is based on language, logic, identity, or visual phenomena and action.

❖ ETHNOMETHODOLOGY AND THE COMMUNICATION PROCESS

In addition to using ethnomethodology to analyze phenomena such as routine conversations, dialogue in narratives, song lyrics, and jokes, it has other uses, as well. For example, intercultural communication can be studied to look for the national codes used by members of each culture, to determine why there may be problems when people from different cultures and countries try to communicate.

The same process can be used to examine the communication practices of subcultures in a given culture and, in particular, of marginalized subcultures such as drug abusers, prostitutes, and different kinds of criminals. We can make ethnomethodological studies of the communication practices of certain movements, such as feminist and gay liberation movements. The communication practices of certain occupations and organizations also lend themselves to ethnomethodological research. How does an organization decide on recordkeeping? What codes tell people in organizations "record this" or "don't record that." In short, many areas of communication can be analyzed using ethnomethodological research techniques.

❖ ETHNOMETHODOLOGICAL RESEARCH: APPLICATIONS AND EXERCISES

1. Using Garfinkel's method, in which you pretend you are a boarder, write a detailed description of a meal with your family or with some friends. Describe what happened as carefully as you can, assuming you don't know the people and without making any assumptions about their motives.

2. Find a transcript for a situation comedy such as *Seinfeld* or *Frasier* and analyze the conversation from an ethnomethodological perspective. What assumptions do the characters have about others and about life? Are there any behavioral codes that inform the dialogue?

3. Make an ethnomethodological analysis of the lyrics of a song that has interesting metaphors or metonymies in it. Use the "love is a game" analysis as a model.

❖ CONCLUSIONS

We can take the concerns and methods of ethnomethodologists—for the codes that shape and inform our everyday behavior (what we say and do and think)—and apply them to everyday behavior found in mass-mediated texts. These mediated expressions are not "pure" like the ones found in everyday life, but they still must make sense to the millions of people who watch films and television programs, listen to the radio and to music, read books, and tell jokes to one another. Thus, these mediated expressions of everyday life, and other areas discussed above, offer us a fertile ground for ethnomethodological research.

❖ FURTHER READING

Button, G. (Ed.). (1991). *Ethnomethodology and the human sciences.* Cambridge, UK: Cambridge University Press.

Francis, D., & Hester. S. (2004). *An invitation to ethnomethodology: Language, society and interaction.* London: Sage.

Garfinkel, H. (1967). *Studies in ethnomethodology.* Englewood Cliffs, NJ: Prentice Hall.

Heritage, J. (1985). *Garfinkel and ethnomethodology.* Oxford, UK: Blackwell.

Kessler, S., & McKenna, W. (1985). *Gender: An ethnomethodological approach.* Cambridge, UK: Cambridge University Press.

Lynch, M. (1993). *Scientific practice and ordinary action: Ethnomethodology and social studies of science.* Cambridge, UK: Cambridge University Press.

Rawls, A. (Ed.). (2006). *Seeing sociologically: The routine grounds of social action.* Boulder, CO: Paradigm.

Turner, R. (Ed.). (1974). *Ethnomethodology: Selected readings.* Baltimore: Penguin.

There is a series of phenomena of great importance which cannot possibly be recorded by questioning or computing documents, but have to be observed in their full actuality. Let us call them the imponderabilia of actual life. Here belong such things as the routine of a man's working day, the details of his care of the body, of the manner of taking food and preparing it; the tone of conversational and social life around the village fires, the existence of strong friendships or hostilities, and of passing sympathies and dislikes between people; the subtle yet unmistakable manner in which personal vanities and ambitions are reflected in the behaviour of the individual and in the emotional reactions of those who surround him. All these facts can and ought to be scientifically formulated and recorded, but it is necessary that this be done, not by a superficial registration of details, as is usually done by untrained observers, but with an effort at penetrating the mental attitude expressed in them.

—Bronislaw Malinowski, *Argonauts of the Western Pacific* (1961, pp. 18, 19)

10

Participant Observation

W e learn a great deal about the world, and about aspects of the world we're interested in, from reading about people and events, from listening to the radio and watching television, from talking with people, and from observing them. Reading, listening to the radio, and watching television gives us information about people and events, but it is mediated—that is, it is filtered through someone else's consciousness and shaped by someone else's decision about what to point a camera at or what question to ask.

❖ DEFINING PARTICIPANT OBSERVATION

Much research provides knowledge about people, but this knowledge is often somewhat abstract and gained by studying people in experiments and other controlled situations. **Participant observation** is different; it is a **qualitative research** technique that provides the opportunity to study people in real-life situations. It is a form of "field research" in which observations are carried out in real settings and where there is a lack of the kind of control and structure you have in experiments, for example. In participant observation, as the name suggests, researchers become involved in some group or organization or entity that they are studying. The researchers have to balance two roles: that of being participants and that of being observers. Researchers also have to avoid "going native," which means becoming so identified with the group that they lose their objectivity.

There are, then, several decisions you must make about your participant observation research. First, you have to decide whether to conceal your observations from the group you are studying, which raises ethical questions. If you tell the group that you are studying them, it may affect their behavior. Second, you have to decide whether to just observe the group or to participate in the group's activities and, if you participate, to what degree—keeping in mind that you want to avoid "going native."

Participant observation is typically carried out by a researcher in one of the two following roles:

(a) *Participant as observer,* where the researcher participates with the group being observed and is a functioning part of the group. As such, the person is an "insider" enjoying a close understanding of the context and the process while performing the added role of an observer and recorder.

(b) *Observer as participant,* in which the observer is a neutral outsider who has been given the privilege of participating for the purpose of making observations and recording them.

Both methods are legitimate, and each has advantages and drawbacks. Basically, it is a trade-off between familiarity, on one hand, and neutrality, on the other.

There is a difference between everyday observation and participant observation. In our everyday lives, we are always observing people and events and trying to make sense of things. We are concerned about matters such as what people say to one another, relationships, or how people use body language. But our speculations are random and fugitive—that is, quickly moving on to other matters. Scientific observation is different. It is focused—on what the observer wants to find out—and it is objective and systematic.

Here are some of the things we hope to discover by doing participant observations of what people do and say to one another. This is an adaptation of the who, what, where, etc. questions I discussed earlier. I am taking liberties here with a song from my youth that had a line in it that went as follows: "How come you treat me the way you do?" Our focus here is on members of some group that is being observed:

Where do people do what they do?

What common ideas and background knowledge do people have?

What do people do?

Who does what to whom?

Who originates actions and who reacts and how do they react?

Why do they do what they do?

When (and how often) do they do what they do?

How do they do what they do?

How long do they do what they do?

You, as a researcher, must always keep in mind the following questions about your participant observation: What do you want to find out about the people involved in this group? Is there some question that you want to answer? Is there some problem you hope to solve? Why are you doing this particular participant observation and dealing with this specific group?

A SHORT THEATRICAL PIECE ON PARTICIPANT OBSERVATION

Grand Inquisitor: *Where are we?*

Arthur: In a gym where people are working out.

Grand Inquisitor: *The machines here sort of remind me of some of our torture devices.*

Arthur: There are certain similarities.

Grand Inquisitor: *I notice there are men and women here of all ages. Don't they work? How do they have time to come here? Why are they here?*

Arthur: You've asked some interesting questions.

Grand Inquisitor: *The outfits of the women are curious: Many of them wear spandex clothes that cover them completely but are very revealing. I don't think I should be here, though I'd like to try some of the torture machines.*

(Continued)

(Continued)

| **Arthur:** | Notice that people don't talk to one another very much … and that men often wear shirts that reveal their muscles and that the gym is full of mirrors so people can look at themselves—at their big arms or small butts. |
| **Grand Inquisitor:** | *I rather like the ambience of suffering and pain that I see all about me. But these people are torturing themselves—we never thought of that during the Inquisition.* |

❖ SIGNIFICANT CONSIDERATIONS TO DEAL WITH WHEN DOING PARTICIPANT OBSERVATION

Here are some important matters to focus attention on when doing a participant observation of your group.

1. *The setting.* Where are you doing your observation, and what impact does the setting have on the behavior of the people being observed? Does the setting facilitate certain kinds of behavior and retard other kinds of behavior? For example, at a bar, you'd expect some flirting might go on and wouldn't expect people to be praying.

2. *The participants.* Who are you observing? How many people are involved? How are they related to one another? What is their function in the group being studied? What is the nature of the group being studied? It is important to record pertinent demographic data, if you can obtain this information, about each of the participants:

   Age

   Socioeconomic class

   Gender

   Race or ethnic group

   Occupation

   Education

3. *The nature and purpose of the group.* You should describe the group and explain what kind of group it is. What is it that brings the people in the group together? Is the group tightly

organized, or can people enter and leave it in a casual manner? Is the group ongoing, or is it based on chance events and one that only occasionally comes together? Does the group have many rules that members observe, or are there few (or no) rules?

4. *The behavior of people in the group.* What do the members of the group do? How do they do it? Why do they do it? Who gives the group its direction? How do people in the group interact with one another? What do they say to each other? Who is involved with decision making in the group? Who says what to whom with what effects? We are basically interested in what people say to one another and what they do and the relationship that exists between what people say and do.

5. *The frequencies and durations of behavior.* As an observer, you want to record whether certain behaviors occur frequently or just take place occasionally and how long the people you are observing spend doing certain things. Are the behaviors you are studying typical or unique? When do they tend to take place? Is there something that tends to provoke or lead to certain behaviors?

6. *Record what you see.* It is important that you record what you see in as much detail as possible. If you have access to informants, you should tape-record your interviews with them (if you can do so) so you have an accurate record of what they said. You should keep written records that are as detailed and complete as possible and should concern yourself with what people actually say and do and not with your impressions of things. Now, with inexpensive video cameras and cell phones with video capabilities, it is possible to make videos of interesting events.

7. *Self photographs and videos by members of the group.* Have members of the group take photographs or make videos that are connected to the topic you are investigating and discuss what their photographs and videos reveal. These photographs and videos will reveal what those who make them consider to be important and provide additional insights into the group. You can also ask the people taking photos and making videos to keep journals to document their activities.

Some participant observers develop tally sheets that enable them to keep track of an aspect of behavior they are observing. For example, if you were doing a participant observation of young children playing in a sandbox, you might make a tally to record when and how often specific children talked to one another or took one another's toys. You might have to redesign your tally sheet a number of times as you do your participant observation, because you will discover certain behaviors that you hadn't planned on recording are important.

If you have detailed data on a tally sheet, you can develop tables and charts showing your findings, which means there can be a quantitative aspect to participant observation, although many participant observers are not concerned with quantitative matters.

What I've been discussing to this point is at a rather high level of abstraction. Let me move down the ladder of abstraction and deal with some of the problems participant observers face when they do their research in the field. We must keep in mind that participant observation is a kind of fieldwork; the methods used in participant observation derive, in part, from those of anthropologists who studied preliterate tribes and cultures.

❖ A CASE STUDY IN PARTICIPANT OBSERVATION: READERS OF ROMANCE NOVELS

Janice Radway's (1991) book, *Reading the Romance: Women, Patriarchy and Popular Literature,* is an exemplary case study in participant observation. Radway was interested in what the people who read romance novels are like and why they read these works. Originally, she wanted to find out the way romance readers interpreted the novels they read, but when she became involved with a group of readers (the Smithton, New York, romance readers) she discovered the more important question was the way they used the novels and integrated them into their lives. As she explains,

> What the book gradually became, then, was less an account of the way romances as texts were interpreted than of the way romance reading as a form of behavior operated as a complex intervention in the ongoing social lives of actual subjects, women who saw themselves first as wives and mothers. (p. 7)

Radway's notion that she would use these readers to see how they interpreted romance novels gave way to something more important—the way the Smithton romance readers used these novels in their everyday lives. Radway asked the women in the group to fill out questionnaires to help her understand them better and lived, for a short while, with the leader of the group. She also tape-recorded her sessions with the group.

Her conclusions about the importance of spending time with actual romance novel readers are important. She writes,

> The nature of the group's operation suggests that it is unsatisfactory for an analyst to select a sample of romances currently issued by American publishers, draw conclusions about the meaning of the form by analyzing the plots of the books in the sample, and then make general statements about the cultural significance of the "romance." (Radway, 1991, p. 49)

Her point is that even if we take a representative sample of romance novels and analyze their plots and other features, we cannot assume, from the texts alone, that we understand what they reflect about American culture or know how readers of these novels are affected by them. We learn from Radway's book that sometimes, while conducting a participating observation study, we have to switch our focus when we discover something more important than our original notion of what we wanted to investigate.

❖ PROBLEMS CONNECTED WITH PARTICIPANT OBSERVATION

In theory, participant observation is easy. You find a group that you are interested in studying, become connected with it (or find some way to participate in it), observe the group, record your observations as unobtrusively as possible, and write up what you've found. In practice, participant observation is much more complicated.

The Problem of Focus

When you do participant observation, you have to be looking for something. You don't just observe everything that everyone does in the group you are studying. Thus, if you are a student and are studying the behavior of your classmates in a class (and here, taking notes is not a problem), you have to find a focus or topic that is narrow enough to examine given the amount of time at your disposal. Are you interested in the relationships that exist between your professor and certain students or the relationships between some students?

Sometimes, you will find that you started looking for information on one topic but discovered something else that is more important, so you have to be ready to shift focus.

The Problem of Observers Affecting Behavior

This matter—of observers affecting (by their presence) what is going on in a group—is known as **reactivity.** Does your presence, as a participant observer, change the way people normally relate to one another?

If you are studying a very small, cohesive group, your presence—as a stranger—may have some impact on the way the group normally operates. Over time, this reactivity may subside, as people get to know you and accept your presence. In larger groups, or groups that are not tightly organized, this is not such a problem.

The Problem of Unrecognized Selectivity

There is a problem of maintaining your objectivity in choosing what to focus your attention on, what to record in your notes, and what to omit. At times, without recognizing what they are doing, participant observers neglect certain behavior that is very important because they think a different behavior, which is actually relatively trivial, is more interesting. It's quite difficult to maintain your objectivity while doing participant observation and develop the facility to determine what is important and what is of secondary interest.

The Problem of Mind Reading

Mind reading, as I use the term, involves observers going beyond recording *what* people do and assuming they can read people's minds and figure out *why* people are doing something. As researchers, we are always looking for meaning, but we must be careful that we don't assume that our interpretations of some person's behavior are what the person meant by that behavior.

One way to avoid mind reading is to ask people why they did something or said something and to observe whether there is a connection between what people say and what they do. Of course, we must remember what we learned in the interviewing chapter—people don't always know why they do things, and sometimes they don't tell interviewers the truth when answering their questions.

The Problem of Validity

Here you must consider how representative the activities you observed were and whether the "reactivity" effect might have shaped the behavior of the group in certain ways. Participant observation is a high-risk kind of research. It may yield important insights, but your findings can also be of questionable validity.

❖ BENEFITS OF PARTICIPANT OBSERVATION STUDIES

Let me suggest some benefits that come from doing participant observation research. First, it helps you understand what's going on in a setting that you are studying. If you spend time with a group of people, you start seeing things that were not apparent or evident when you first started studying them. Our minds search continually for meaning, and one way we find meaning is by finding relationships and patterns. Systematic observation of groups helps us discover these patterns and relationships.

Second, participant observation helps you determine which questions to ask informants. Participant observers frequently make themselves known to the members of the group they are studying and thus are free to ask people questions. It only makes sense to use these opportunities to ask your informants questions that will be useful to you and that will provide insights about the group and the people in it.

Third, participant observation is, relatively speaking, an unobtrusive way of getting information about groups and their behavior. A great deal depends on the skill of the researcher and the setting. In certain cases, it is possible to take notes and record interviews with informants; in other cases, researchers have to try to remember what they can and then record their notes later. But in optimal situations, the observer becomes "taken for granted," and members of the group behave the way they usually do.

❖ MAKING SENSE OF YOUR FINDINGS

Once you have done your observation and recorded what you saw, you have to make sense of your research. That is, you have to interpret it. As I mentioned earlier, facts don't mean anything by themselves; they have to be put into context and explained.

Dealing With Actions

By *actions* I mean what certain individuals in the group you were observing did and said. You have to consider such matters as the following:

Who originates actions?

Who responds to these actions?

How do they respond?

Participant observation, we must remember, focuses on what people do with one another, do to one another, and say to one another. We observe behavior; we cannot observe what people think, and it is dangerous to assume that we can know what they are thinking on the basis of their actions. We focus on process, then on the various events that go on in the group, on sequences of actions and behaviors that, we hope, will reveal information of value.

Dealing With What People Think

We cannot observe what people think, but we can ask individuals about their thoughts and, if possible, tape-record their answers. As I mentioned earlier, one of the things that participation observation does is help us determine what questions to ask informants.

Using Concepts to Interpret Your Findings

One thing we do when we look at the material we have gathered from our participant observations is to look for concepts that will help us understand the behavior we've observed. We make sense of the world by applying concepts that offer explanations of things we observe.

Let me offer an example. Suppose we observe someone who washes his hands 200 times a day. We have a concept that explains that behavior: We say that person is an obsessive-compulsive. And that concept is part of a broad field known as psychoanalytic theory. We can see the relationships in the following chart:

Theory   Psychoanalytic theory

Concept   Obsessive-compulsive behavior

Behavior   Washing hands 200 times a day

A person who never heard of the concept "obsessive-compulsive" would not be able to explain this behavior except in relatively vague and useless everyday terms—*freaky, weird, strange,* and so on—terms that could be applied to many different kinds of behavior.

Concepts function in between abstract theories and specific behavior. We use the concepts we know to interpret or explain behavior that we observe. Naturally, the more concepts we know, the more we can understand what we see. So, to a degree, your conceptual knowledge plays a very important role in enabling you to make sense of the behavior you observed and interviews you made from your participant observation. Our conceptual knowledge is used in all our research, of course; we need concepts to understand what we can learn about people from interviewing them and observing their behavior.

❖ AN ETHICAL DILEMMA

An ethical dilemma that participant observers face is whether to pretend to join the group you are observing because you want to associate with the people in it or whether you should tell people in the group that you are doing research on them. Personally speaking, I think it is the ethical thing to do to tell people that you are observing them and not to pretend that you aren't. If you don't tell people what you are doing, you are, in a sense, using them, and you are also lying to them about your interest in the group. In addition, you will make things more difficult for yourself because you won't be able to tape-record interviews or take notes as easily as you can if people know you are conducting research on them.

I don't believe that people will change their behavior that much—at least not over the long run—because they know they are being observed. A great deal depends on your ability to "fade into the woodwork," to keep to the background, to keep your presence muted.

❖ ETHICS AND RESEARCH INVOLVING HUMAN BEINGS

When doing research involving human beings, you have a responsibility to deal with those you are studying in an ethical manner. Let me suggest some ethical rules that I think we should keep in mind:

1. *You shouldn't deceive people.* This means, when conducting participant observation, you should tell the group you are studying what they are doing.

2. *You should not use people as a means toward other ends, even if you think those ends are positive in nature.* Ethicists often make this point—you shouldn't use people for your own purposes, even if you think your findings will be important.

3. *You should not do anything that will have negative effects on those you study.* As the result of a famous study by Stanley Milgram about obedience, in which those who participated in the study ended up with many psychological problems, research involving human beings in universities now has to be accepted by boards that deal with ethical considerations.

4. *You must be honest in designing your research and reporting your findings about those you study.* You have to avoid letting an outcome you may (perhaps unconsciously) desire shape your research and your findings.

❖ PARTICIPANT OBSERVATION: APPLICATIONS AND EXERCISES

1. Taking the role of a participant observer, observe the behavior of people at a restaurant or cafeteria. Answer questions listed in the book about things we hope to learn from making a participant observation and use the list of significant considerations to deal with, as well. What problems did you face in making your analysis? How did you solve these problems?

2. Make a series of photographs about your typical day, from the time you get up in the morning until you go to bed. When you look at these photographs, do you find anything about them that reveals some aspect of your life that you were unaware of? When you compare your photographs with those that your classmates have made of their typical days, do you discover anything interesting in common with the photos made by your classmates? Do you find any surprising differences in them?

3. Buy a DVD of some situation comedy and use techniques you've learned about participant observation to observe the behavior of the people in the situation comedy. Base your analysis upon at least 3 hours (six episodes) of viewing the shows.

❖ CONCLUSIONS

Participant observation is one of the more widely used forms of research and one of the most interesting. It is also one of the most difficult, because human beings are so difficult to fathom and because interpersonal and individual/group communication and relationships are so complicated. But participant observation is one of the few ways we can do research in natural (nonlaboratory) settings and obtain information about what people do in contrast to what they say they do.

It strikes me that we also can use the same methods that we use in participant observation in analyzing mass-mediated texts. If we have a television show that is serial in nature, such as a soap opera or a hospital show or a science fiction show, one way to interpret the show is to think of it as being similar to a group that one is observing and use some of the techniques of participant observation to analyze a selected set of episodes. This is an unconventional way of conducting participant observation, but it might yield rather interesting results.

❖ FURTHER READING

Burawoy, M. (1991). *Ethnography unbound: Resistance in the modern metropolis.* Berkeley: University of California Press.

DeWalt, K. M., & DeWalt, B. R. (2001). *Participant observation: A guide to fieldwork.* Lanham, MD: AltaMira Press.

Heron, J. (1996). *Co-operative inquiry: Research into the human condition.* Thousand Oaks, CA: Sage.

Hume, L., & Mulcock, J. (2005) *Anthropologists in the field: Cases in participant observation.* New York: Columbia University Press.

McIntyre, A. (2008). *Participatory Action research.* Thousands Oaks, CA: Sage.

Reason, P. (Ed.). (1994). *Participation in human inquiry.* Thousand Oaks, CA: Sage.

Smith, C. D., & Kornblum, W. (1996). *In the field.* New York: Praeger.

Spradley, J. (1997). *Participant observation.* New York: Holt, Rinehart & Winston.

Part IV

Quantitative Research Methods

As an experiment in content analysis, a year's publication of The Saturday Evening Post (SEP) *and of* Collier's *for the period from April 1940 to March 1941 was covered. It is regrettable that a complete investigation could not be made for the most recent material, but samples taken at random showed that no basic change in the selection or content structure has occurred since this country's entry into the war. . . . We put the subjects of the biographies into three groups: the spheres of political life, of business and the professions, and of entertainment (the latter in the broadest sense of the word). Looking at our table we find for the time before World War I very high interest in political figures and an almost equal distribution of business and professional men, on the one hand, and of entertainers on the other. The picture changes completely after the war. The figures from political life have been cut by 40 per cent; the business and professional men have lost 30 per cent of their personnel while the entertainers have gained 50 per cent. This numerical relation seems to be rather constant from 1922 up to the present day. . . . We called the heroes of the past "idols of production"; we feel entitled to call the present day magazine heroes "idols of consumption." Indeed, almost everyone of them is directly, or indirectly, related to the sphere of leisure time: either he does not belong to vocations which serve society's basic needs (e.g. the heroes of the world of entertainment and sport), or he amounts, more or less, to a caricature of a socially productive agent.*

—Leo Lowenthal, "Biographies in Popular Magazines" (1944, pp. 508, 510, 516)

11

Content Analysis

C ontent analysis is one of the most commonly used research
methodologies by scholars dealing with media and communication. This is because it can measure human behavior, assuming, that is, that verbal behavior is a form of human behavior. In
contrast to opinion polls, which measure what people say they did
(or will do) but do not show us what people have actually done, content
analysis deals with actual behavior—by people talking with one
another, by characters in films and television programs, or the way
"heroes" are written about in magazine biographies.

❖ DEFINING CONTENT ANALYSIS

The term *content analysis* tells us, broadly, what the methodology does:
It analyzes the content of something. But there's much more to content
analysis than that. Let me offer an excellent definition of the term
found in Charles R. Wright's (1986) *Mass Communication: A Sociological
Perspective:*

> Content analysis is a research technique for the systematic classifica-
> tion and description of communication content according to certain
> usually predetermined categories. It may involve quantitative or

qualitative analysis, or both. Technical objectivity requires that the categories of classification and analysis be clearly and operationally defined so that other researchers can follow them reliably. For example, analysis of the social class memberships of television characters requires clear specification of the criteria by which class is identified and classified, so that independent coders are likely to agree on how to classify a character. . . . It is important to remember, however, that content analysis itself provides no direct data about the nature of the communicator, audience, or effects. Therefore, great caution must be exercised whenever this technique is used for any purpose other than the classification, description and analysis of the manifest content of the communication. (pp. 125–126)

A number of concepts mentioned in this passage require definition and clarification—*operational definition, coding,* and *manifest content*—which I will explain in the following pages.

Let me offer a second definition that helps clarify what content analysis is. This comes from George V. Zito's (1975) *Methodology and Meanings: Varieties of Sociological Inquiry:*

Content analysis may be defined as a methodology by which the researcher seeks to determine the manifest content of written, spoken, or published communication by *systematic, objective,* and *quantitative* analysis. It is, then, a quantitative method applicable to what has traditionally been called qualitative material—written language. . . . Since any written communication (and this includes novels, letters, suicide notes, magazines, and newspaper accounts) is produced by a communicator, the *intention of the communicator* may be the object of our research. Or we may be interested in the audience or *receiver* of the communication, and may attempt to determine something about it. (p. 27)

Zito enlarges the sphere of content analysis to all forms of communication, from the personal to the mass mediated. Many scholars would add that content analysis cannot tell us the effects on audiences of the material being studied, I should add. Content analysis tells us what is in the material being studied, not how it affects people who are exposed to this material. On the other hand, if you find, for example, that children's television shows have a great deal of violence in them, whether it is comic or not, you cannot help but wonder about what impact this violence is having upon children. Fortunately, other research methods have explored this question in great detail.

Like many other research methodologies discussed in this book, most of us do a personalized form of content analysis all the time—of what people say to us, of what we read in the papers and magazines. We are always searching for meaning and trying to figure out why people do things and what their actions mean. But content analysis is different from our attempts to make sense of communication in that content analysis is much more systematic and objective. And it is quantitative; it measures and counts certain things.

❖ WHY WE MAKE CONTENT ANALYSES

We use content analysis as a research method for a number of reasons. First, we want to get information about a topic and believe that content analysis, rather than other research methods, will help us get the information we're seeking. Thus, we might want to know how much **violence** there is on American television and whether there's more violence now than there was in earlier years. Content analysis is the methodology that will help us obtain the answers to these questions. We may also be interested in whether the amount of violence on American television differs from the amount of violence on British or French television (or some other country of interest to us) and use content analysis to find out what the situation is.

A SHORT THEATRICAL PIECE ON CONTENT ANALYSIS

Grand Inquisitor:	*What is your name?*
Arthur:	Conrad. Actually it's my pseudonym.
Grand Inquisitor:	*Where are you from?*
Arthur:	Connecticut.
Grand Inquisitor:	*What do you do?*
Arthur:	I'm a con artist.
Grand Inquisitor:	*What's your favorite food?*
Arthur:	Consommé with confiture.
Grand Inquisitor:	*What's your biggest personal problem?*
Arthur:	Too controlling.
Grand Inquisitor:	*What's your best attribute?*

(Continued)

(Continued)	
Arthur:	Confidence!
Grand Inquisitor:	*Are you married?*
Arthur:	Yes. My wife's name is Constance.
Grand Inquisitor:	*What does she do?*
Arthur:	She's a concierge in the Continental Hotel.
Grand Inquisitor:	*Is there anything else that you want to tell me about yourself?*
Arthur:	You want me to continue? Don't you think I'm to be congratulated?
Grand Inquisitor:	*Au contraire!*

Also, we may have some **hypothesis** (essentially a guess) about some topic and want to see whether our hypothesis is correct. For example, we may offer a hypothesis that with the rise of feminism, the way women are portrayed in fashion ads has changed and there is less "sexploitation" of women's bodies now than in earlier years. Or we may hypothesize that with the rise of feminism, the portrayal of women in the media has changed: We see them more often, and their roles are different in that they are more often shown in professional roles. Frequently, researchers doing content analysis state the problem they want to investigate in the form of a hypothesis, to give their research more focus.

It's one thing to devise—based on existing theory or previous research—interesting topics to investigate or hypotheses to explore; it's another thing to actually *do* a content analysis. I will now discuss some methodological considerations that we must keep in mind when planning a content analysis.

❖ METHODOLOGICAL ASPECTS OF CONTENT ANALYSIS

Factual information—what we sometimes term *factoids*—by itself doesn't tell us very much. If one were to say, "In 1998, there were approximately 30 acts of violence per hour on American television," we wouldn't know very much, because we wouldn't know what this datum, the "factoid," means. What we need is some perspective, something with which to compare the 1998 factoid. Here are some ways to make this comparison.

Determine Your Research Question. Before you begin, you have to decide what you are going to measure and what you hope to find out. It is useful to conduct a library search on the subject of your proposed content research before beginning to see whether others have done work on the same topic, work that might be useful to you. Also, make sure that your research topic is one that you can do with the time you have to make the analysis. Generally speaking, the narrower the focus, the better—especially for student projects.

Use a Historical Approach When Making a Content Analysis. Only if we use a historical approach and can say (and I'm making all these figures up for illustrative purposes), "In 1978, there were approximately 10 acts of violence per hour on television" do we have information of value. For now we know that in 1998, there was three times as much violence, per hour, on American television as there was 20 years ago. The historical approach has given us some perspective.

Use a Comparative Approach When Making a Content Analysis. If we also do a comparative study of television violence and discover that in Sweden, for example, in 1998, there were three acts of violence per hour on television, we have information that helps us gain additional perspective on the matter of violence on American television. Assuming that the content analysis has been done correctly, we can say that American television is 10 times more violent than Swedish television.

My point, then, is that content analyses are most valuable when they have either a historical perspective or a comparative perspective—or both perspectives. And having numbers is important. If a researcher says, "There's a lot of violence on American television," we should want to know what that researcher means by "a lot." What is "a lot" to a professor of communication may be "a little" to the manager of a television station.

Be Careful About Defining Your Terms Operationally. There are several kinds of definitions. The definitions you find in dictionaries are known as *constitutive definitions*—they define words in terms of other words and concepts. They are quite general and abstract. The definitions used in content analyses are *operational definitions,* which use operations and indicators to define concepts.

An operational definition tells how you will measure something and forces you to explain how you understand or interpret a concept.

Thus, if you are dealing with media violence, you will have to describe what kind of actions or behaviors constitute violence. Is threatening talk violence? Is comedic violence (the kind found in children's television cartoons) violence? Is there an important difference between comedic and serious violence?

This matter of offering an operational definition of your term is very difficult and is the weak point in many content analyses. If others don't accept your definition of violence, they will reject your findings as being irrelevant or unsound.

Categories must be mutually exclusive. You must not define your concept in a way that it can be applied to more than one kind of behavior. If you define violence too broadly or too narrowly, there will be problems. If your definition is too broad, researchers will argue that your measurements aren't reliable or of any value, because you deal with too many things. If your definition is too narrow, researchers will say you neglected important matters.

For example, some scholars do not consider the smacking and banging about by characters in animated comics and cartoon strips to be examples of violence. They see violence as something serious. Others would disagree with this assessment.

In *Violence and Terror in the Mass Media: An Annotated Bibliography*, George Gerbner (1988) writes, "Reliable observation and systematic analysis usually require limited and objective definitions. Most research studies have defined media violence as the depiction of overt physical action that hurts or kills or threatens to do so" (p. xi). The book lists and briefly describes 673 articles on media violence by psychologists, sociologists, and other scholars. But one problem with all these articles is that there is no agreement among all of them on how to define violence in the media. The reason for this is that violence is such a complicated phenomenon. According to the definition above, it is questionable whether the mayhem in animated cartoons and comics is really violence, because the characters don't seem to be affected by what happens to them.

In the same light, your concept must deal with all the behaviors that can be studied. If your operational definition leaves out certain kinds of violence (perhaps because they are difficult to measure and quantify), your results will also be held to be unreliable. So it is very important that your operational definition be carefully worded and thought out.

Determine Measurable Scoring Units. What this means is you've got to figure out what your basic or standard unit of measurement will be. If you are doing a content analysis of the comics page of a newspaper, you could take the comic strip frame as your basic unit. If you are doing a content analysis of magazine articles, you could take number of words; if you are studying a newspaper article, you could take number of column inches as your basic unit. If you are doing television programs, you could take number of minutes as your basic unit. The important thing is that your basic unit has to stay the same in all the examples you study.

Determine How to Do Your Coding. Coding is a process by which we classify the data we have obtained from the material we have studied and give each item in a category a symbol or number. We do this coding so that we can carry out various forms of cross-tabulations that we may wish to do when interpreting our research.

In dealing with television violence, for example, we may classify the different kinds of violence we find on television into a number of different categories and give each category some number or symbol. In the case of violence, there are many different kinds of violence we might observe: men against women, women against men, adults against children, children against adults, and so on.

Because *violence* is so vague a term and because it is so hard to operationalize a definition of violence, it is difficult to deal with and to code in such a way that anyone replicating your study would code everything the same way. I will return to these considerations later.

Measure Only the Manifest Content. When making content analyses, we examine only the manifest content of texts—that is, what is explicitly stated—rather than the latent content, the "hidden" material that is behind or between the words. If a male character in a comic strip says "I love you" to a female character, you have to take that statement at face value and use it in your content analysis. You must not assume, because of his previous actions in the story, that he's lying or insincere and thus discount his statement.

❖ ASPECTS OF VIOLENCE

In the chart below, taken from my book *Essentials of Mass Communication Theory* (A. A. Berger, 1995), I offer a number of different understandings of the term *violence*—to show how difficult it is to deal with this concept.

Keeping in mind de Saussure's (1966) admonitions about concepts being defined negatively, consider the possibilities when it comes to aspects of violence. I will list 31 polar oppositions that reflect various kinds of violence and, by doing so, will show how complicated an issue violence is.

1. Mediated violence	Violence we see directly
2. Real mediated violence (wars)	Fictive mediated violence
3. Comic violence	Serious violence
4. Intended violence	Actualized violence
5. Violence to individuals	Violence to groups
6. Inferred violence	Documented violence
7. Police violence (just)	Criminal violence
8. Verbal violence	Physical violence
9. "Fake" violence (wrestling)	"True" violence (bar brawl)
10. Violence against heroes	Violence against villains
11. Violence against women	Violence against men
12. Violence in the past	Violence in the future
13. Violence by human agents	Violence by mechanical agents
14. Defensive violence	Offensive violence
15. Violence by children	Violence by adults
16. Weak violence (insults)	Strong violence (murder)
17. Accidental violence	Intentional violence
18. Visual images of violence	Prose descriptions of violence
19. Violence by the insane	Violence by the sane
20. Violence as means to end	Violence as end in itself
21. Causes of violence	Effects of violence
22. Violence as action	Violence as reaction
23. Many minor acts of violence	One major act of violence
24. Violence as emotional response	Violence as rational decision
25. Violence against others	Violence against self
26. Violence ordered by others	Violence decided by self
27. Sign of depravity	Cry for help
28. Violence caused by fear	Violence caused by hatred
29. Institutional violence	Individual violence
30. Violence as instinctive	Violence as cultural
31. Violence as integral (sports)	Violence as extraordinary (murder)

We can see, then, that violence is extremely complex and difficult to define—especially from an operational point of view. Because of the complexity of the concept, many content analyses of violence in the media have been challenged.

❖ ADVANTAGES OF CONTENT ANALYSIS AS A RESEARCH METHOD

There are a number of advantages to content analysis, which explains why it is such a popular form of research:

- It is unobtrusive.

- It is relatively inexpensive.

- It can deal with current events, topics of present-day interest.

- It uses material that is relatively easy to obtain and work with.

- It yields data that can be quantified.

One of the main advantages of content analysis is that it is unobtrusive. Unlike research methods such as interviewing and participant observation, the researcher does not "intrude" on what is being studied and thus does not affect the outcome of the research. In addition, unlike some other research methods, content analysis is a relatively inexpensive kind of research. It doesn't cost very much to obtain material to be studied—to duplicate printed matter or to make videos of television programs. Of course, the scope of the content analysis is a factor. If you're going to make a very large-scale analysis of television news programs, for example, and use hundreds of hours of program material, then coding this material can be very time-consuming and expensive. But for most content analyses, costs of obtaining the material to be analyzed are not great.

Content analyses can be made of topics of current interest. That is, you can deal with matters of concern of the moment—though, as I've suggested earlier, data by itself doesn't mean very much. You need to be able to put your data in perspective, which is provided, generally speaking, by making historical or comparative content analyses. Sometimes, however, just obtaining data on some topic of current interest is useful, such as political advertisements or political commercials in a campaign.

In addition, the material used to make content analyses is readily available. If you are doing a content analysis of printed material, you can often find it at a good library. And many television programs from the past can be obtained at certain research libraries. Contemporary television programs can be taped, of course. What is most important, however, as far as our interest in **quantitative research** methods is concerned, is that the data you collect from your content analysis can be expressed in numbers. These numbers provide detailed information that can be interpreted to gain insights into the mind-set of those who created the texts. Possibly—although this is debatable—they can be used to infer the way audiences of these texts might be affected by them.

❖ DIFFICULTIES TO CONTEND WITH IN MAKING CONTENT ANALYSES

Like any research method, researchers have to face certain problems when making content analyses. I dealt with some of these topics earlier in my overview of content analysis. Now I will add a few points to the previous discussion:

- Finding a representative sample

- Determining measurable units

- Obtaining reliability in coding

- Defining terms operationally

- Ensuring validity and utility in your findings

The first problem is determining what is a representative sampling of the textual material you are studying. If you are studying Saturday morning network children's television, you have to decide which programs are representative and how much of each program to analyze. If your sampling is not representative, your findings will not be convincing.

Sometimes this problem is dealt with by choosing a random sampling of whatever it is you are analyzing and assuming that a random sampling will provide you with a representative sampling or at least one for which that it cannot be argued that there was observer bias in the choice of texts to be analyzed.

You also have to determine what your measurable units are. With printed text, this is usually done in column inches or square inches or words in newspaper or magazine articles. You can also use television shows or magazine issues. However you do it, you must find a way to make sure your units are standard. If you are studying fashion advertisements in magazines, the individual advertisement would be the unit; it doesn't make much difference whether your ads are in a magazine the size of *Vogue* or in the Sunday magazine section of the *New York Times.* For such cases, the number of inches is not important. If you are dealing with comic strips, the frame would be the fundamental unit.

You do have to figure out how to code your material so that every coder will classify the elements in the texts being analyzed the same way. This matter of coder reliability is important because if different coders code a certain action in a text different ways, your results will not be useful.

To obtain coder reliability, you must make operational definitions of the various activities in the text that are to be coded. Thus, you must classify all of the actions you want coded (for example, different kinds of violence) and then offer operational definitions for each of them. I have discussed the difficulties of making operational definitions earlier.

The simplest (but also quite effective) way of testing reliability ("intercoding reliability" in content analysis jargon) is to have several coders analyze identical content and then compare the results. The researcher looks for percentage of agreement and, of course, the higher the agreement level, the greater the reliability. Typically, a reliability level of 90% or higher is considered acceptable.

You also must be sure that your findings are valid and useful—namely, that you actually measured what you planned to measure and that your results will be of some interest. This means you must pay a good deal of attention to formulating your research question, so you have a chance of finding interesting things and getting good results.

There is also the problem of the intensity of the violence to be considered. One television show may have many acts of relatively "weak" violence while another show, of the same length, may only have one act of violence, but it is so powerful that its impact on viewers is strong and long lasting.

❖ DOING A CONTENT ANALYSIS: A LIST OF STEPS TO TAKE

I've discussed the methodological problems connected with doing content analyses, some of the difficulties involved in doing this kind of research, and some of the benefits gained. What follows is a list that takes you step by step through the process.

1. Decide what you want to find out and offer a hypothesis—that is, an educated guess—about what you expect to find. (For example, it is reasonable to hypothesize that as a result of the growth of feminism and the increased power of women in the government and other aspects of society, the number of words spoken by women in comic strips will increase as we move from 1960 to 2000. Whether that hypothesis is correct or not has to be tested by making a content analysis.)

2. Explain what you'll be investigating and tell why this research is worth doing.

3. Offer an operational definition of the topic you'll be studying. If you're studying violence, tell how you define it.

4. Explain your basis for selecting the sample you'll be analyzing. How did you determine which examples to investigate?

5. Explain what your unit of analysis is.

6. Describe your classification system or system of categories for coding your material. Remember that the categories must be mutually exclusive and that you must cover every example of what you're analyzing.

7. Determine your coding system.

8. Test for intercoding reliability and make any necessary adjustments, such as increased training and practice for the coders or an adjustment of the operational definition and code guides.

9. Using your coding system, analyze the sample you have selected.

10. Present your findings using quantified data that you've obtained from your content analysis.

11. Interpret your results using your numerical data and other material that may be relevant to your research.

This list describes the steps researchers commonly use in doing content analyses. Of course, there's a big difference between having a list of steps to follow and actually doing the analysis and wrestling with problems such as how to select a sample and how to classify and code the material in the sample. And there is also the matter of interpreting your findings, for interpretations invariably "go beyond" the data and thus are open to criticism.

SAMPLE CODING SHEET FOR COMPARATIVE NEWSPAPER COMIC STRIP PAGE ANALYSIS

1. Name of newspaper		
2. Dates of publication: month, day	2000	2010
3. Page numbers for each day	2000 page(s)	2010 page(s)
4. List of names of all comic strips on each page(s) for each date	2000	2010
	_____	_____
	_____	_____
	_____	_____
	_____	_____
	_____	_____
5. Number of male and female figures on each page for each date	2000	2010
6. Number of words spoken by all male characters on each page for each date	2000	2010
7. Number of words spoken by all female characters on each page for each date	2000	2010

NOTE: This content analysis deals only with the number of words spoken by male and female characters on the comic strip pages of a newspaper in 2000 and 2010 (or any dates chosen by your instructor). It does not deal with age, gender, race, or other topics that might be investigated.

❖ CONTENT ANALYSIS: APPLICATIONS AND EXERCISES

1. Using the list of oppositions in kinds of violence, make a content analysis of the kinds of violence found in an episode of some crime television show. Prepare a coding sheet for the analysis. Did you find anything surprising in your analysis? If you can find an episode of the show done a number of years earlier, you can see whether there have been any interesting changes in the way violence is used.

2. Make a content analysis of the words spoken by males and females in a day's comic strip page in some newspaper from the week of May 15 in 1990 and 2010 (or some other day, as long as they were both weekdays). Base your analysis on the list of steps to take in making a content analysis, found in this chapter, and the coding sheet shown above. What problems did you face in making your content analysis? What were your findings? Did they surprise you in any way? You can also study other topics in the comics, such as the kinds of violence found in them, the number of male and female figures found in them, and so on.

3. Find some idols of production and idols of consumption in magazines. Duplicate the first pages of the articles (find three of each) and bring them to class. What problems did you face in finding your "idols"? What interesting things did you find in the articles? Where did you go looking for idols of production?

❖ CONCLUSIONS

Like other research methods, there's a big difference between knowing something about the methodology of content analysis and actually doing the research. But there's no such thing as a perfect methodology—one that does not have weaknesses and limitations. Do not be surprised if you run into difficulties in doing a content analysis (or any other kind of research, for that matter), and don't be too hard on yourself, either.

It takes a good deal of practice and experience to learn how to manage the difficulties that researchers face. The important thing is to think clearly and work carefully, and if you have the opportunity, share what you've learned. Leo Lowenthal's (1944) content analysis of *The Saturday Evening Post* and *Collier's*, which I quoted at the beginning of this chapter, led to important insights about the way what he termed "idols of production" had been eclipsed by "idols of consumption." They still dominate many of our magazines and have played a major role, over the years, in shaping America's consumer society.

❖ FURTHER READING

Adams, W., & Adams, F. S. (1978). *Television network news: Issues in content research.* Washington DC: George Washington University.

Gottschalk, L. A. (1995). *Content analysis of verbal behavior: New findings and clinical applications.* Mahwah, NJ: Lawrence Erlbaum.

Krippendorf, K. (2004). *Content analysis: An introduction to its methodology* (2nd ed.). Thousand Oaks, CA: Sage.

Neuendorf, K. A. (2001). *The content analysis guidebook.* Thousand Oaks, CA: Sage.

Riffe, D., Lacy, S., & Fico, G. (2005). *Analyzing media messages: Using quantitative content analysis in research.* Mahwah, NJ: Lawrence Erlbaum.

Roberts, C. W. (Ed.). (1997). *Text analysis for the social sciences: Methods of drawing statistical inferences from texts and transcripts.* Mahwah, NJ: Lawrence Erlbaum.

Weber, R. P. (1990). *Basic content analysis.* Newbury Park, CA: Sage.

There is no perfect data collection method. However, self-administered questionnaires are preferable to personal interviews when three conditions are met: (a) You are dealing with literate respondents; (b) you are confident of getting a high response rate (which I put at 70%, minimum); and (c) the nature of the questions you want to ask does not require a face-to-face interview and the use of visual aids such as cue cards, charts, and the like.

Under these circumstances, you get much more information for your time and money than from the other methods of questionnaire administration. If you are working in a highly industrialized country, and if a very high proportion (at least 80%) of the population you are studying has its own telephone, then consider doing a phone survey whenever a self-administered questionnaire would otherwise not be appropriate.

—H. Russell Bernard, *Research Methods in Anthropology:
Qualitative and Quantitative Approaches* (1994, p. 264)

12

Surveys

Surveying is a research method that we use to get information about certain groups of people who are representative of some larger group of people of interest to us. For example, manufacturers of products want to know how people feel about their products (and those of their competitors) and use **surveys** to find out. We use surveys to determine the following:

- What do people know?
- What do people think?
- What do people own?
- What do people do?
- What have people done?
- What are people planning to do?
- What are people's attitudes?
- What are people's tastes?
- What are people's prejudices?
- What are people's beliefs?
- What are people's values?

Politicians frequently use surveys to find out what issues are of importance to people and, during election periods, who they intend to vote for. Most surveying is done by interviewers, but one particular kind of survey—the questionnaire—does not use interviewers but is sent through the mail or distributed in publications (or through other means, such as on the Internet). Both terms—*surveys* and *questionnaires*—are often used loosely.

❖ DEFINING SURVEYS

In their book *Field Projects for Sociology Students,* Jacqueline P. Wiseman and Marcia S. Aron (1970) offer an excellent definition of surveys:

> Survey research is a method for collecting and analyzing social data via highly structured and often very detailed interviews or question-naires in order to obtain information from large numbers of respondents presumed to be representative of a specific population. (p. 37)

This description calls our attention to four key points about surveying:

1. It is done to collect and analyze social, economic, psychological, technical, cultural, and other types of data.

2. It is based on interviewing people (respondents) and asking them for information.

3. It is done with representative **samples** of a population being studied.

4. It is assumed that information obtained from the sample is valid for the general population.

❖ KINDS OF SURVEYS: DESCRIPTIVE AND ANALYTIC

There are two basic kinds of surveys: *descriptive* surveys and *analytic* (or explanatory) surveys. I will deal with each kind of survey briefly. The *descriptive survey,* as the name suggests, describes the population being studied. These surveys seek to obtain information about demographic factors such as age, gender, marital status, occupation, race or ethnicity, income, and religion and to relate this information to opinions, beliefs, values, and behaviors of some group of people. For

ex Stats Canada

example, broadcasters use surveys to find out how **popular** their programs are, and manufacturers use surveys to determine who uses their products. The focus of descriptive surveys is on present-day behavior.

The second kind of survey, the *analytical survey*, seeks to find out why people behave the way they do. Researchers often use data from descriptive surveys to develop hypotheses and use analytical surveys to test their hypotheses about what causes certain kinds of behavior. Analytical surveys attempt to determine whether there are causal relationships between certain kinds of behavior and various social and demographic characteristics of people.

As you might imagine, it's much easier to obtain descriptions of people's behavior than it is to find out why people behave the way they do. There are so many different variables behind people's choices that it is hard to know why people act the way they do. People are affected by so many different factors that it's difficult to determine what, if anything, is of primary importance. You have to consider biological, psychological, social, economic, and political factors (among other things) in dealing with human behavior, and it is difficult to determine how each or any of these factors is involved in human behavior.

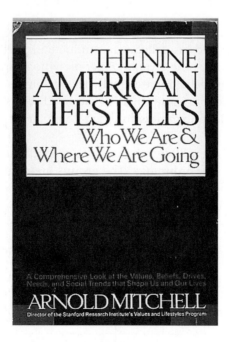

This book, by Arnold Mitchell, explains the thinking behind the VALS typology.

❖ THE VALS TYPOLOGY SURVEY

In 1983, Arnold Mitchell, director of the Stanford Research Institute's **Values and Lifestyles (VALS)** program, published *The Nine American Lifestyles: Who We Are & Where We Are Going.* In his preface, he makes some interesting points. He writes,

> People's values and lifestyles say a good deal about where we are going, and they help explain such practical, diverse questions as: why we support some issues and oppose others; why some people are strong leaders and others weak; why some people are economically brilliant and others gifted artistically—and a few are both; why we trust some people and are suspicious of others; why some products attract us and others don't; why revolutions occur.
>
> By the term "values" we mean the entire constellation of a person's attitudes, beliefs, opinions, hopes, fears, prejudices, needs, desires, and aspirations that, taken together, govern how one behaves. . . . We now have powerful evidence that the classification of an individual on the basis of a few dozen attitudes and demographics tells us a good deal about what to expect of that person in hundreds of other domains. Further, the approach often enables us to identify the decisive quality-of-life factor or factors in a person's life. (p. vii)

Mitchell developed what is known as the VALS typology based on a large survey he and his colleagues conducted in 1980. The typology argues that there are nine groups of people who share similar values, which shapes their behavior, especially as consumers. The advertising industry was extremely interested in the VALS typology because the advertising people thought it would help them target certain groups of interest to them.

The first VALS typology (there was a second one that was developed later) had eight groupings. The groups are names and classified according to whether they are need driven, outer directed, inner directed, or both outer and inner directed:

Name	Group Classification
Survivors	Need driven
Sustainers	Need driven
Belongers	Outer directed
Emulators	Outer directed
Achievers	Outer directed

I-Am-Me's	Inner directed
Experientials	Inner directed
Societally conscious	Inner directed
Integrated	Outer and inner directed

This typology grew out of a huge survey that Stanford Research (not connected with the university) conducted, which describes the role of the survey in developing the typology as follows:

> The Values and lifestyle (VALS) typology . . . rests upon data obtained in a major mail survey conducted by VALS in 1980. . . . The survey asked over 800 specific questions on a great range of topics. Sample size exceeded 1600. Respondents constituted a national probability sample of Americans aged eighteen or over living in the forty-eight contiguous states. Statistical analysis of survey results quantified and enriched the basic concepts of the VALS typology and enabled us to provide detailed quantitative and human portraits of the VALS types, together with their activities and consumption patterns. (Mitchell, 1983, pp. 3, 4)

This survey was very large with a significantly sized sample, suggesting a high degree of reliability. What is interesting, for our purposes, is that VALS developed a short form of the survey for the convenience of the Stanford Research Institute's clients and discovered that it achieved an overall level of agreement of 86%.

We learn two things from this study. First, it is possible—if done correctly—to obtain useful results from a relatively small survey. The short form of the VALS survey was almost as accurate as the long form. Second, after one obtains results from a survey, it is necessary to interpret the results, and usually this takes the form of creating a typology—of aggregating or classifying the people who completed the survey into various kinds of groups. The fact that Stanford Research came up with a second VALS typology that is quite different from the first typology suggests that this aspect of survey research analysis is based on interpreting the data and finding ways to classify it, and some interpretations and classifications of data are better than others.

❖ METHODS OF DATA COLLECTION

Conventionally, surveys collect data through two methods:

1. Interviews (individual or group interviews; in-person or telephone interviews)

    2. Self-administered questionnaires—supervised administration (one-to-one or group administrations) or unsupervised administration, when the questionnaire is mailed (or e-mailed) to people or freely distributed via magazines, the Internet, and so on

Survey interviews are quite different from depth interviews, described earlier in the book. Survey interviews have lists of questions that people are asked to answer and are not structured so that interviewers can explore subjects that come up, by chance, as in less structured depth interviews. Survey interviews are shorter than depth interviews and more structured so information can be obtained to make valid generalizations about the population being studied.

Questionnaires are conventionally understood to be lists of questions given or sent to people who are asked to answer the questions and return the questionnaires to the senders. That is, they are self-administered surveys. Questionnaires should always be accompanied by cover letters explaining the purpose of the questionnaire and pointing out how it is in the interest of the respondent to answer the questionnaire. They should also be attractively designed and easy to fill out and return. It's a good idea to provide a stamped, self-addressed envelope to respondents. The easier you make things for your respondents, the better chance you have of getting the questionnaire returned.

The advantages and disadvantages of these two methods of surveying are noted briefly in the following chart:

Personal Interviews[1]

Advantages	Disadvantages
Interviewer can explain questions in detail	Can be intrusive (too personal)
Interviewer can use a variety of data collection methods	Time-consuming and expensive
Interviewer can spend a lot of time with respondents	Hard to find people in sample at times
You know who is answering questions	People are reluctant to answer some questions

[1]Telephone interview is comparatively shorter, is cheaper, and can be less intimidating, but because not everyone has phones, the sample may be biased or unrepresentative.

| A higher likelihood of achieving a desired response rate | Needs well-trained interviewers |
| Not intimidating | Interviewer and respondent may have a language barrier |

Self-Administered Questionnaires

Advantages	Disadvantages
Inexpensive	People may misinterpret questions
No interviewer bias to worry about	Low response rates the norm
You can ask about very personal matters	You don't know who actually filled out the questionnaire
You can ask complex, detailed questions	Sampling errors frequent

You can see from this chart that there are advantages and disadvantages to each of the three ways of collecting information. The choice you make should be based on what you want to find out, how much time you have, and how much money you have.

❖ ADVANTAGES OF SURVEY RESEARCH

There are a number of advantages to conducting surveys, which explains why they are so widely used. They are also widely reported on in newspapers and magazines, in part because people are interested in what the surveys reveal . . . even though individuals are often reluctant to participate in them.

- Surveys are inexpensive.
- Surveys can obtain current information.
- Surveys enable you to obtain a great deal of information at one time.
- Surveys provide quantitative or numeric data.
- Surveys are very common, and some of the information you seek may have already been discovered in a survey.

Surveys are, relatively speaking, inexpensive, especially when you consider the amount of information surveys are able to obtain. And the information you obtain is very current. Surveys enable researchers (who work for manufacturers, marketers, political parties) to find out, for example, what products people own, what products they intend to purchase, what issues are important to them in elections, who they might vote for in elections, and all kinds of other information of interest to the people making the survey.

What is particularly important is that surveys obtain information that can be quantified and analyzed statistically and thus can reach a higher degree of precision about the group being studied that other forms of research cannot duplicate. These data can be summarized in such a way that readers are able to see, rather quickly, what the data reveal about the population being studied.

I use the phrase "population being studied" because many surveys are interested only in one segment of the population—for example, people planning to buy cars, voters in a given state, housewives, or audiences of television shows. Survey information is so important in the television industry that programs live or die based on their popularity—which is determined by data about viewers obtained from surveys.

One thing you should keep in mind is that so many surveys are conducted that the information you are interested in obtaining may have already been found in another survey. So you should make sure that you aren't expending a great deal of time and energy to find information that is already available. The other side of this coin is that people have developed resistance to being surveyed and may not cooperate with you. The following note comes from an online media report, *Media Professional,* for October 1997, citing findings from a September 1997 issue of *Business Marketing:*

Business Researchers Struggle to Get Valid Response Levels

Business researchers are finding it harder and harder to get 50% response rates to the surveys. As the number of surveys has increased, buyers have become less likely to respond to an individual survey. In addition, companies are beginning to discourage employees from spending their time responding. 50% response is the generally accepted threshold for accuracy.

❖ PROBLEMS WITH USING SURVEYS

There are a number of general problems connected with using surveys and questionnaires (and interviewing of all kinds) that you, as a researcher, should keep in mind:

- People often don't tell the truth, especially about personal matters.

- People make mistakes about what they've done, even if they are trying to tell the truth.

- Obtaining representative samples is frequently quite difficult.

- People often refuse to participate in surveys.

- Relatively small percentages of people answer and return questionnaires.

- Writing good survey questions is difficult to do.

Sometimes people won't tell the truth. They may be afraid, for example, that if they tell you what programs they typically watch you'll think they are stupid, or maybe they are afraid that you'll think they watch too much television.

People also make mistakes about their behavior. They may, for example, understate the amount of television they watch in a given day. In other cases, people give incorrect answers because the questions are unclear or ambiguous or, somehow, threatening. Frequently, people intend to answer questionnaires but mislay them or forget about them. That's why it is often necessary to send follow-up letters to remind people to fill out their questionnaires and mail them back to you. It is crucial that you get questionnaires back from people in your sample; otherwise, the sample will not be representative.

Many people refuse to participate in surveys. Personally speaking, I know that I get irritated when I'm called around dinnertime and asked whether I'll answer some questions for some marketing survey. Like many people, I dislike giving certain kinds of information about myself to others, especially if I believe they'll be profiting from the information I provide.

❖ A NOTE ON MEDIA USAGE SURVEYS: SHARES AND RATINGS

When doing surveys dealing with what television programs people are watching, researchers distinguish between audience **ratings** and audience **shares.** Barry L. Sherman (1995) explains in *Telecommunications Management: Broadcasting/Cable and the New Technologies,*

> *Rating* refers to the percentage of people or households in an area tuned to a specific station, program, or network. For example, if, in a Nielsen sample of 1000 homes, 250 households were tuned to the

ABC network, the rating for ABC during that time period would be (250 div 1000), or 25%. For ease of reporting, the percentage sign is dropped in the ratings book. *Share* refers to the number of people or households tuned to a particular station program or network correlated with sets in use. Continuing the above example, if only 750 of the sampled households were actually watching television in the time period covered, ABC's share would be (250 div 750) = 33%. Since there are always more sets in a market than there are sets in use, the share figure is always higher than the rating. (p. 389)

Because radio stations, television stations, and networks make money by delivering audiences to advertisers, the size (and nature) of the audiences of these stations and shows is of crucial importance. The larger the audience (as long as the **demographics** are acceptable), the more a station or network can charge for running commercials.

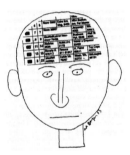

As you might imagine, the share is of particular interest because it tells station owners how well their station is doing compared with other stations with the actual listening audience. And like much information gathered in research, relationships—generally stated in percentages—are crucial.

❖ OPEN-ENDED AND CLOSED-ENDED SURVEY QUESTIONS

One can use two kinds of survey questions: open-ended and closed-ended questions (or, in other terminology, constructed response questions and selected response questions). An open-ended question asks for an answer that the respondent should construct by himself or herself, writing down in the space provided for this. Closed-ended questions ask respondents to select from lists of answers provided by the survey designer—lists such as multiple-choice questions or Likert scales. Examples of the two follow.

Multiple-Choice Question. The two major criteria for generating good questions are (a) that they are mutually exclusive (the respondent should be able to select one response only, unless multiple responses are requested) and (b) that the questions are exhaustive (all possible choices should be mentioned, which is typically achieved by adding "other" as a choice). An example follows:

Which one of the following network television stations do you most regularly watch for national news?

a. NBC

b. CBS

c. ABC

d. FOX

e. Other

Likert Scale Questions. In *Research Methods in Anthropology,* H. Russell Bernard (1994) discusses **Likert scales:**

> Perhaps the most commonly used form of scaling is attributed to Renis Likert (1932). Likert introduced the ever-popular 5-point scale. . . . The 5-point scale might become 3 points or 7 points, and the agree-disagree scale might become approve-disapprove, favor-oppose, or excellent-bad, but the principle is the same. These are all Likert scales. . . . Likert's method was to take a long list of possible scaling items for a concept and find the subset that measured the various dimensions. If the concept were unidimensional, then one subset would do. If it were multi-dimensional, then several subsets would be needed. (pp. 297, 298)

In the following Likert scale, a question is offered, and people are asked to choose from among five positions: strongly agree, agree, neutral, disagree, and strongly disagree. This example of a Likert scale is applied to a question about news programs:

The most important aspect of local news is accuracy.

1. Strongly agree

2. Agree

3. Neutral

4. Disagree

5. Strongly disagree

You can see that a Likert scale enables you to quantify opinions and beliefs and thus obtain more precise indications of beliefs and opinions than you can with many other methodologies.

❖ WRITING SURVEY QUESTIONS

Writing good survey questions is an art. After you have decided what information you want, you have to write your survey questions. Good survey questions have the following characteristics:

- They are clear and not ambiguous.
- They are short.
- They use simple, easily understood language.
- They ask for only one piece of information per question.
- They avoid showing bias.
- They aren't "leading" or "loaded" questions.
- They don't embarrass respondents.
- They ask questions that the respondents can answer.
- The questions are logically grouped with questions related to one another being near one another.
- The scales for measurement of opinion are clear. (The Likert scale is highly recommended because it provides considerable detail . . . much more than "Like/Dislike" or "Good/Neutral/Bad.")
- The order of the questions is worked out logically.

Expressing yourself clearly, so that people understand exactly what you want to know, is quite difficult. It's surprising how people can misunderstand, misinterpret, and become confused about questions you thought were simple to answer. You've got to be very careful about your choice of words and the structure of your sentences.

One way to achieve clarity is to write sentences that are short and to the point. The shorter your sentences are, the less chance they will be misunderstood. Another matter to keep in mind is to ask for only one item or piece of information in a question and not write double-barreled questions. The following question is double-barreled and is an example of the type of question to be avoided. These questions usually have an "and" in them:

Do you think this product tastes good and is nutritious?

This question should be separated into two questions: one about the taste and the other about the nutritional value.

In writing your questions, you must avoid showing bias slanting your questions in certain ways that reveal your beliefs and opinions. A similar problem involves writing leading questions, in which you ask your respondents, more or less, to agree with you about something or hint that they should answer a question in a certain way. Biased questions and leading questions both impose your ideas and perspectives on your respondents and defeat the purpose of surveys, which is to obtain information about how your respondents feel.

A SHORT THEATRICAL PIECE ON SURVEYS

Grand Inquisitor: *During the Inquisition, we made a survey of our heretics.*

Arthur: That's quite a surprise. What did you find?

Grand Inquisitor: *We gave them one multiple-choice question:*

Which would you prefer:

A.   To be boiled in oil

B.   To be stretched on the rack

C.   To be quartered by four horses after your joints were cut

D.   To be forced to die of old age

Arthur: What did you find?

Grand Inquisitor: *It was quite a surprise. It seems that 100% of those who answered their multiple-choice question checked "D." They said they wanted to be forced to die of old age.*

(Continued)

> *(Continued)*
>
> **Arthur:**   Did your findings have any effect on the Inquisition?
>
> **Grand Inquisitor:**   *No. Because 100% of the inquisitors answered the multiple-choice question they were asked the same way, they wanted to save the heretics "the hard way"—namely, A, B, or C. I suspect that people often use surveys to suit their own purposes and do whatever they want, regardless of survey results.*

Of course, interest groups sometimes want to obtain certain results, so they word their questions to more or less guarantee that they'll get the answers they want. Consider the following yes or no questions on the same subject:

1. "Do you think innocent babies should be murdered before they are born?"

2. "Do you believe women have the right to reproductive freedom and control over their own bodies?"

Obviously, Question 1, which is full of trigger words meant to evoke emotional responses, is not impartial and "leads" respondents to answer in certain ways. What really causes problems for researchers is when respondents answer both questions "yes." This is a problem because the respondent has agreed with two contradictory positions.

❖ MAKING PILOT STUDIES TO PRETEST SURVEYS

Because people have a genius for misinterpreting and misunderstanding questions—even ones that you think are simple and straightforward—you should make pilot studies. That is, you should test your surveys and questionnaires (the technical term for them, used by social scientists, is *instruments*) on a small group of people to see what problems arise. You should consider the following questions when assessing your **pilot study:**

- Can people easily understand all your questions?

- Do your questions enable you to obtain the information you want to obtain?

- Are there questions you didn't ask that you should ask?

- Are there questions you asked that you shouldn't ask?

- Does your pilot suggest you should try a different method of data collection?

The advantage of doing a pilot study is that it frequently helps you discover problems in your questionnaire that you couldn't have anticipated, which you then can solve before you undertake a larger study.

❖ CONDUCTING ONLINE SURVEYS

The Web is a convenient and inexpensive source for conducting surveys. Students can take advantage of sites such as SurveyMonkey to conduct relatively simple surveys free of charge. In an article in *The Chronicle of Philanthropy*, Marilyn Dickey (2006) discusses some things to keep in mind when selecting a site to make a Web survey. I offer an abbreviated version of the points she makes.

- Is the site easy to use? Are the instructions clear?

- Does the site offer the question formats most suitable for your needs?

- Can the survey be conducted on the Web, or do people taking it have to print out questionnaires, etc.?

- Is there a limit on how many questions you can ask?

- Can the data you collected be downloaded to Excel or a statistical program?

- Can you make good visual presentations (charts, graphs) with the program?

- Can the results be viewed on Windows and Macintosh computers?

Since you are students, you don't have to worry about many of these matters. If your instructor asks you to use SurveyMonkey or some other program, it will provide you with any number of different kinds of questions you can ask and other help.

Whatever kind of survey you conduct, whether on the Web or with selected samples of people, you must still keep in mind the rules for asking survey questions and other factors connected with any kind of surveys.

- What do you want to find out?
- What questions should you ask to find out?
- How do you avoid ambiguous or unclear questions?
- What kinds or types of questions will you use in the survey?
- What kind of answers are you looking for?
- Who will you ask?

We make surveys to get answers to questions that are of interest and importance to us. Surveys can provide us with a great deal of information, but we must always keep in mind that when people answer survey questions, they don't always understand them and they don't always tell the truth.

❖ ON THE MATTER OF SAMPLES

The logic behind sampling is relatively simple. If you have a homogeneous population—that is, everyone is the same—a relatively small sample of this population will provide reliable information about the larger population. (We use the term *population* to cover all the members of a group.)

A reliable sample must be (a) representative and (b) adequate in size. I will demonstrate graphically how random selection works. Let us suppose we have a country with 1 million people in it and they all have the same genetic makeup, which can be symbolized as X'. Everyone in the population can be represented as X', with 1 X' representing 50,000 people.

General Population

X' X' X' X' X'	X' X' X' X' X'
X' X' X' X' X'	X' X' X' X' X'

Sample Needed

X' (small fraction of)

Obviously, if you take even a very small sample of this particular population, you will obtain accurate information about their X' genetic makeup because everyone is the same. (Notice that in this case, it doesn't matter how you chose the sample.) Researchers can make a *simple random sample* and obtain reliable information. (Simple random samples can be made by numbering everyone in a population and using a table of random numbers to select certain members of the population to study. In the example above, any sample that is chosen will work.)

But suppose the population is heterogeneous or mixed, as shown below:

General Population

X A B A B X A X B B X X

A X B B A A B B X X A A

Sample Needed

X A B

In the sample of this mixed or heterogeneous population, you would have to make sure you had Xs, As, and Bs in the same proportion that they are found in the population to survey. For these kinds of populations, it is often useful to make *stratified random samples.* To make a stratified random sample, you have to find representative groups and survey them randomly, so you can have some confidence that you will get all groups.

You use stratified random samples when you wish to get some information about a characteristic in the population. Researchers select variables they are interested in and find respondents who have these characteristics.

There is a third method of sampling, using *cluster samples,* to survey groups of people of interest to the researcher, such as newspaper-reading habits of people in a given city or area. This is based on the fact that people belong to various groups in their daily lives. It is difficult to determine who to choose from the clusters who will be representative. The sampling unit is not individuals but naturally occurring groups of people—that is, already formed groups. These three kinds of samples will be explained in more detail now.

❖ OBTAINING RANDOM SAMPLES

The next topic I wish to cover is the matter of obtaining samples. I will deal with the three kinds of **random samples** discussed above:

1. Simple random samples

2. Stratified random samples

3. Clustered samples

There are many ways of obtaining accurate samples, but for all practical purposes, for students and others without great financial resources, random sampling is the most convenient method to use in obtaining a representative sample of the population being studied.

Simple Random Samples

A simple random sample is a sample in which each member of a population being studied has an equal chance of being selected. The term *simple* is used because this kind of sampling involves only one step using a table of random numbers (provided in Table 12.1) to obtain a random sample.

Table 12.1   A Table of Random Numbers

3941	1132	2271	6394	2438	1718	9548	5896	8618	0050
8915	2115	3784	4481	2866	1355	5590	6508	2495	5138
3962	6179	1507	3479	1272	7027	6268	8060	2718	1907
5449	4219	6262	2850	3516	6536	8036	8426	2901	4058
1342	2102	0902	5347	6769	3745	4938	0033	0902	7502
3594	1295	7766	0363	4732	6404	7003	4242	0000	5088
8876	7784	6445	0692	8029	5724	3604	6483	4323	1212
6445	0933	0887	9527	2189	8361	5930	4306	2759	9745
2167	3139	0986	2788	1920	5657	2932	5317	5960	8905
4581	7409	1191	1600	7184	6254	1835	4708	8613	6355
1849	3920	9947	3851	5875	6967	0823	0488	4030	0148
2408	6779	0796	7244	1625	8894	6075	8806	0273	1308
5688	4251	2068	2522	5905	8829	2734	0393	7240	4636
4518	4551	0008	9625	5584	1192	7829	7179	2902	1097
2590	6006	9961	1445	7221	3680	2901	6035	4834	1864
6752	1976	8687	5756	1527	0836	9931	2886	9392	0119

7967	7274	8498	0571	2632	3852	2433	3065	9471	5105
3511	9317	2022	6734	2506	2144	3194	4113	9709	7590
6637	9376	6538	5231	7599	6353	8136	0551	5810	5646
4815	7212	2329	8475	7429	2425	0271	8565	7581	9879
2253	4501	1808	3738	4078	3186	6108	9174	0207	6776
9288	8788	4298	4206	6595	1772	2838	0897	0881	0977
4954	4053	3599	8702	5157	1085	6589	0702	3249	8629
4096	6024	7876	9322	1771	2559	1251	1008	7846	9745
0903	1025	7333	9908	9048	3399	3003	9799	5244	1133

a. Generated by using PERL.

You obtain a random sample by assigning sequential numbers to everyone in the population being studied and then use the table of random numbers to select your sample. Let's suppose you wish to choose a random sample of 10 students from a class of 100 students. You list all students in alphabetical order and you assign a number, starting at one and going to 100, to each member of the class. Then you consult your table of random numbers and select your sample based on the random numbers. Computers can also generate such tables.

You then choose the first random number; if it is 13, you take student number 13 from your list of 100 students as the first person in your sample. If the next number is 26, you take student number 26 as the second person in your sample. And you continue doing this using the first 10 numbers in your list of random numbers to obtain your simple random sample. For students doing research projects and for others doing relatively uninvolved research, the simple random sample is probably the best choice.

Individuals who are used in simple random samples cannot be used again; they are removed from later selections of random samples that might be needed to obtain other information. This is known as random sampling *without replacement*. (In more complicated kinds of sampling, they are replaced, but this is not the norm for inexpensive surveys.)

Stratified Random Samples

This technique enables us to obtain greater precision in our sampling by using other information we have about the population being studied to obtain representative samples. In doing stratified random sampling, you take your population and divide it into subcategories that are relevant to the subject under investigation. These subcategories, technically known as *strata* (the plural of the term *stratum*), should be mutually exclusive; that is, nobody can be a member of more than one stratum.

In making a stratified random sampling, you select some characteristic of the population being studied that you consider to be important and select your random sample from this group. For example, suppose you wish to study television news reporters in your city. You could study matters such as their gender, their race, their age, the amount of experience they have, or their college major. If you decide to study their college major or race, you then make your random sample based on these factors. You do simple random sampling within each stratum.

Clustered Samples

To make random samples, you need a list of all members of the population being studied—which, in many cases, is impractical. To get around this problem, researchers do clustered sampling, which involves sampling members of groups or categories. You divide your population into naturally occurring groups of people, such as people in particular ZIP codes or areas of a city or state, and sample from within each group. It is not as accurate as random sampling, but it saves a great deal of time and money.

❖ EVALUATING THE ACCURACY OF SURVEYS

There are three considerations involved in evaluating surveys:

1. Sample size

2. Margin of error

3. Confidence level

The error of measurement strongly depends on the sample size.[2] The margin of error decreases as your sample gets larger but in smaller increments, as can be seen in Figure 12.1.

---

[2]Technically speaking, the error of your measurement decreases with the square root of your sample size, which explains why larger samples don't provide the equivalent amount of accuracy. The law of diminishing returns is at work. A survey of 1,500 people gives you almost as much accuracy as a survey of 2,000 people.

Figure 12.1 Sample Size and Standard Error Relationship

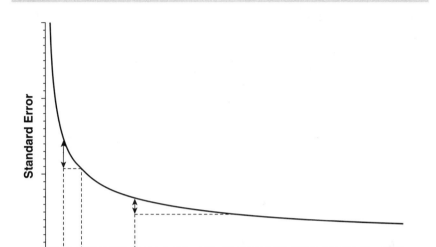

Generally speaking, the larger the sample, the more confidence you can have that your findings will be accurate, but this works only up to a point. The most famous example of a sampling error occurred in the 1936 presidential campaign between the Democratic candidate, Franklin Delano Roosevelt, and the Republican candidate, Alf Landon. A magazine, *The Literary Digest,* surveyed some 2,300,000 people. This sample was based on responses to questionnaires sent to readers of the magazine and to some 10 million people who had telephones. This sample, however, was not a representative sample of the entire voting population; it was composed, to a large degree, of the wealthier elements in American society, essentially wealthy Republicans, so the results were all wrong. *The Literary Digest* had, unknowingly, asked an essentially Republican (and very unrepresentative) sample of American society which candidate it would vote for and got a highly inaccurate picture of the American voting public.

So the size of the sample doesn't necessarily tell you very much. Of course, you could ask everyone in the population you wish to study and avoid sampling—this is called a *census.* But that is not practical. So you have to find a representative sample of the population you are studying. And the figure for the sampling error will provide you with an indication of the degree of accuracy of your research.

The confidence level indicates, as its name suggests, how confident you can be that a particular result obtained in the sample of your survey reflects the corresponding parameter of the population. The confidence level is closely connected with the interval estimation when the result is reported not as a single number (point estimation) but as a band (range) where the parameter is assumed to belong with a certain level of confidence. The interval estimation is centered to the point estimation, and its width is proportional to its standard error (SE) and the level of confidence we would like to have. The more confident we want to be, the broader should be the interval of estimation. The most often used level of confidence is 95%, which corresponds to the interval with a lower limit of 2 standard errors to the left of the sample statistic and an upper limit of 2 standard errors to the right of the sample statistic. For example, if we found after a survey that 54% of the clients prefer Product A and that the standard error of this estimation is 3%, then we can conclude with 95% confidence that between 48% and 60% (54% – 6%; 54% + 6%) of the clients in the target population will prefer Product A. This means that if we repeat this survey 100 times, keeping the same sample size, in 95 cases, the preferences for Product A will be somewhere between 48% and 60%.

If we want a higher level of confidence—let's say 99%—then the corresponding interval will be broader approximately 3 standard errors to the left and to the right of the sample statistic; for the example above, it would mean preferences for Product A will be between 45% and 63%. In case of lower confidence—for example, 68%—the confidence interval will be smaller (1 SE), and the preferences for Product A will be between 51% and 57%.

A general rule of thumb is that the point estimation for a proportion in surveys of 1,500 people (assuming that the surveys are carried out correctly) has a standard error of estimation of plus or minus 3%, and surveys of 350 people have a sampling error of plus or minus 5%. Many national political polls use samples of 1,000 to 1,200 people and obtain results that are accurate to plus or minus 3%. If the election is close and Candidate A is leading Candidate B by 51% to 49%, it means that either of the candidates can win, because the error is bigger than the difference between the two candidates, and it is possible for Candidate B to get 51% of the votes and for Candidate A to get only 49%. It could also be that Candidate A has 54% of the vote and Candidate B only 46%. All things being equal, Candidate A has a much better chance of winning than Candidate B.

❖ SURVEYS: APPLICATIONS AND EXERCISES

1. Using your classmates as your universe, prepare a question-naire about the amount of television, radio, video games, and other media they use in a typical day. Also find out about their cell phones, MP3 players, and other possessions involved with their media use during a typical day. Use the discussion of writing survey questions to make your survey. What are the most important things you want to find out? How can you avoid confusing questions, showing bias, obtaining incorrect information, or embarrassing those answering the questionnaire? Later, in class, compare the questionnaires in terms of the first five questions asked in each questionnaire.

2. Find a scholarly article that uses surveys and analyze the questions it asks. Do you find any problems with the questions? If so, explain. Could you have asked better questions? If so, write them down for classroom discussion. What problems did the writers of the survey face when designing it? How did they overcome them?

3. Using a Web survey program such as SurveyMonkey, conduct a survey about a topic that your instructor will give you or a topic of interest to you. Pay attention to the way you frame your questions to ensure you will obtain information of value to you.

❖ CONCLUSIONS

As you can see, using surveys and questionnaires is a rather complicated matter. These instruments are used because they are relatively inexpensive and enable researchers to obtain a great deal of information. But great care must be taken in designing surveys and questionnaires and in obtaining sample populations to survey.

It's not a bad idea to think of surveys and questionnaires in terms of a puzzle metaphor: How can I solve this puzzle—that is, obtain reliable information about the population I wish to study given the difficulties involved in dealing with people and designing good instruments? You must consider what questions you ask to which members of your population or group being studied and how reliable the information you obtain will be. Despite the problems involved with this research method, surveys and questionnaires remain two of the most widely used means of obtaining reliable quantifiable data by researchers.

❖ FURTHER READING

Alreck, P. L., & Settle, R. B. (1994). *The survey research handbook.* New York: Irwin Professional Publications.

Babbie, E. R. (1990). *Survey research methods* (2nd ed.). Belmont, CA: Wadsworth.

Fink, A. (2009). *How to conduct surveys: A step-by-step guide* (4th ed.). Thousand Oaks, CA: Sage.

Fowler, F. J., Jr. (1995). *Improving survey questions.* Thousand Oaks, CA: Sage.

Fowler, F. J., Jr. (2009). *Survey research methods* (4th ed.). Thousand Oaks, CA: Sage.

Rea, L. M., & Parker, R. A. (1997). *Designing and conducting survey research: A comprehensive guide.* San Francisco: Jossey-Bass.

Rubinstein, S. M. (1994). *Surveying public opinion.* Belmont, CA: Wadsworth.

Sapsford, R. (1999). *Survey research.* Thousand Oaks, CA: Sage.

Smith, J., & Christian, L. M. (2008). *Internet, mail, and mixed-mode surveys: The tailored design method.* Hoboken, NJ: John Wiley.

Weisberg, H. F., Krosnick, J. A., & Bowen, B. (1996). *An introduction to survey research, polling and data analysis.* Thousand Oaks, CA: Sage.

Experimentation

Experimentation, more than other styles of research, promises clear causal inferences. Its strategy is to manipulate exposure to an hypothesized cause, while controlling for the contaminating influence of other possible causes by the use of control groups and by the random assignment of subjects to control and experimental situations. These arrangements are intended to maximize "internal validity," which means confidence that the independent variable did in fact "make some significant difference in this specific instance" . . . and that the observed effects are not really the result of some uncontrolled and perhaps unknown variable that is the true cause. However, to gain causal clarity, experiments must frequently sacrifice realism and generalizability to nonexperimental populations and situations (or "external validity"). Furthermore, although it is possible to design experimental controls for many types of testing and measurement effects, the risk of such effects is high.

—John Brewer and Albert Hunter,
Multimethod Research: A Synthesis of Styles (1989, pp. 46–47)

13

Experiments

Although we tend to think of the term *experiment* in connection with scientific work or with the research of social scientists, most of us in our daily lives frequently do what might be described as unscientific experimentation.

❖ EVERYDAY EXPERIMENTATION

Suppose, for example, that you have a bad cold. You might try one remedy, and if it doesn't work, try another; and if that isn't effective, you try something else—until you've found something that will help you (with symptomatic relief, if nothing else).

What is important here is that you try one thing at a time. If you take aspirin and a cold remedy and have some hot chicken soup and your cold gets better, you don't know whether it was the aspirin or the cold remedy or the chicken soup or some combination of the three that was the important factor in helping you feel better. So the principle is, try one thing (or variable) at a time and see what happens. We do the same thing when we try different foods or kinds of dishwashing detergent. We give these things a try, and if we like the results, we keep purchasing them. If the "trial" (read "experiment") is unsuccessful, we try something else.

Experimentation, like the other methodologies discussed in this book, can be very complicated, and it is impossible to deal with all the different kinds of experiments and aspects of experimentation in detail in this book. But I can offer a generalized overview of the nature of experimentation that will give you insights into what is involved in the process of experimentation.

A SHORT THEATRICAL PIECE ON EXPERIMENTS

Grand Inquisitor:	*Tell me about your next experiment.*
Arthur:	I want to find out whether a person on a cruise ship who eats X amount eight times a day gains more weight than a person who eats 2X amount four times a day. You can eat eight meals a day on cruise ships.
Grand Inquisitor:	*So?*
Arthur:	I am applying for a $500,000 grant to cover the expenses I will incur in this research.
Grand Inquisitor:	*Will I be involved in this experiment?*
Arthur:	Yes. You have your choice. You can either be the person who eats X amount eight times a day or 2X amount four times a day.
Grand Inquisitor:	*I'll choose the eight times a day regime. We developed big appetites in the Middle Ages. But why can't we just eat in restaurants? Why do we have to take cruises?*
Arthur:	The ocean is an important variable in this experiment. And I like cruises. But you make a good point. After the experiment on cruise ships, I'll replicate it at three-star restaurants in France.

❖ DEFINING EXPERIMENTS

For our purposes, we will understand an experiment to be a procedure or kind of test that

1. demonstrates that something is true,

2. examines the validity of an hypothesis or theory, or

3. attempts to discover new information.

In the first case, we try to show that what is held to be true about something is actually true. This might involve, for example, replicating an experiment to see whether the findings in the first experiment are correct. In the second case, we test a hypothesis or theory to determine whether it is valid. We might think that there is a relationship between heavy television viewing and violent behavior in young people (having, of course, operationally defined *heavy* and *violent*). In the third case, we want to discover something we did not already know. We might try to find out how MTV affects the attitudes of male viewers of a particular age range about certain subjects, such as how to relate to women or what's stylish and so on.

❖ THE STRUCTURE OF AN EXPERIMENT

Let me offer an overview of the steps taken when conducting experiments—or what might be described as the "structure" of a typical experiment.

*   Your experiment will involve two groups of people: the *experimental group* (also known as the *treatment group, intervention group,* or *stimulus group*) and the **control group.** Something will be done to the *experimental group,* but it will not be done to the *control group.*

*   Individuals must be randomly assigned to either the *experimental group* or the *control group.* How to do this is discussed in Chapter 12, on surveys and questionnaires, and involves the use of tables of random numbers (see Table 12.1).

*   A *pretest* is done. You measure the groups in terms of a *dependent* variable. There are two kinds of variables—*independent* and *dependent.* (Independent variables are ones that are varied by researchers, whereas dependent variables are ones presumed to be affected by independent variables.)

*   You perform the experiment and introduce one independent variable to the *experimental group.* Nothing is done with the control group.

• You conduct a posttest to see if there's a significant difference between the *experimental group* and the *control group* relative to the variable introduced.

An example of an experiment might be to take 100 sophomore males and divide them randomly into two groups of 50 students. You then test the students on something specific, such as their attitudes toward women. Then you show the *experimental group* a certain amount of violent MTV videos but don't have the control group see anything. Then, after showing the *experimental group* the MTV videos, you test the two groups again to see whether the exposure of the *experimental group* to the MTV videos has led to any changes in that group's attitudes toward women. (Note: This example describes one of several possible experimental designs—the classical pretest and posttest design. There are, of course, other designs or ways of structuring experiments.)

The logic of experiments is quite simple. We have two groups that are basically alike, and we expose one of the groups to X and don't expose the other group to X; then we see what affect X might have had on the group exposed to it. We can tell what the effect was by comparing the group exposed to X with the other group that wasn't exposed to X. It is assumed that the two groups are very similar to one another initially—a condition created through random assignment of subjects to groups (experimental or control). The underlying principle is that if the posttest shows differences between the two groups, the researcher would be able to conclude that the experimental treatment had an effect, because the treatment was the *only* variable distinguishing between the two groups.

In the hypothetical experiment described above, we are, in effect, comparing the *experimental group* before and after the exposure to the MTV videos and contrasting them with the *control group*. This experiment is diagrammed in the chart below.

Control Group	Experimental Group
1. 50 male sophomores	1. 50 male sophomores
2. Randomly selected	2. Randomly selected
3. Pretested	3. Pretested
4. *Not exposed to MTV*	4. *Exposed to MTV*
5. Postested	5. Postested

The two groups are treated the same until Step 4, when the *independent variable* (in this case, exposure to a certain amount of MTV) is examined to see whether it had an effect on the *experimental group.*

This offers us a sense of the logic of experiments. We must be careful to introduce only one independent variable; if we introduce two or more variables, we cannot know which, if any, of the variables affected the experimental group. The technical term for introducing more than one independent variable is *confound. Confounds* prevent researchers from determining what caused what in experiments.

Some experiments depart slightly from the classical form of experiments in that they don't use the control–experimental group model I've just described. In these experiments, the control group may be asked to perform certain tasks similar in nature, but different, from the experimental group. For example, an experiment conducted by Baba Shiv of Stanford University divided a group of students into two groups. He asked the first group to remember a two-digit number and the second group to remember a seven-digit number. The groups were told to walk down the hall of a building, where they had a choice of snacks: a bowl of fruit salad or some chocolate cake.

Shiv found that the students who were asked to remember seven digits asked for the chocolate cake twice as much as those who had to remember two digits. Shiv concluded that the cognitive load of remembering seven numbers overtaxed the prefrontal cortexes of those students, which is involved with willpower. Thus, the overtaxed prefrontal cortexes of the students who had to remember seven numbers made them less able to resist the chocolate cake. This experiment helps explain why we tend to indulge in foods we know we shouldn't eat when we are tired.

❖ ADVANTAGES OF EXPERIMENTS

Experiments, if carried out carefully and correctly, provide very strong evidence that a given independent variable (such as the exposure of the experimental group to mediated violence in the form of MTV videos) actually has any effect that might have been discovered. Also, experiments give strong evidence that this effect that was discovered was not the result of some unrecognized phenomenon.

We can, then, discover all kinds of new knowledge by conducting experiments. And the fact that experiments can be replicated makes it possible for other researchers to conduct the same experiment to confirm the validity of the experiment.

❖ DISADVANTAGES OF EXPERIMENTS

Probably the biggest problem with experiments is that they are artificial, conducted—generally speaking—in laboratories or in "nonnatural" situations. When people know that they are involved in an experiment, this information often affects their behavior.

There is also reason to believe that the design of experiments tends to overemphasize cause-and-effect relationships between matters being studied. It may be, for example, that many other factors are involved in the attitudes that male college sophomores have toward women.

In addition, there are often ethical problems involved in scientific experimentation. We see this in the case of medicines, in which the *experimental group* is given some new drug and the control group is denied the drug. Is it ethical to deny people a drug that may affect their health—or even save their lives in some cases? Of course, dealing with the media doesn't involve life-and-death matters, but it is possible that certain experiments might disturb people psychologically. For example, many of the people who were involved in the Milgram experiment (discussed later in this chapter) suffered from psychological problems caused by their participation in it and needed extensive counseling and therapy.

That is why universities all have research boards that review potential experiments to make sure that the people being experimented on are not disturbed or harmed in any way.

❖ A CHECKLIST ON EXPERIMENTAL DESIGN

This checklist is adapted from the list found in John W. Creswell's (1994) *Research Design: Qualitative and Quantitative Approaches* (p. 127). He describes this list as offering "key decisions" that experimental researchers have to make when designing their research. I have made some adaptations because I've not covered certain topics and kinds of experiments he deals with.

1. Who are the subjects (what population are they from) in your experiment?

2. How were the subjects selected? Was it randomly done?

3. Will the subjects be randomly assigned into groups?

4. How many subjects will be in the experimental group and the control group?

5. What is the dependent variable in the study? How will it be measured? How many times will it be measured?

6. What instrument(s) will be used to measure the outcome in the experiment? Why was it chosen? Is it reliable?

7. What are the steps you'll be taking in this experiment?

   a. A random assignment of your subjects

   b. Collection of demographic information

   c. Administration of a pretest

   d. The experiment itself (introduction of independent variable, also known as treatment or factor)

   e. Administration of a posttest

8. What threats are there to the internal and external validity of your experiment? How have you dealt with them?

9. Are you going to do a pilot test of your experiment?

10. What statistics will be used to analyze your data?

11. Are there any ethical questions that you must consider when designing your experiment?

This list offers a useful guide for those planning and conducting experiments, in that it provides an overview of the process of experimentation. Of course, there is a big difference between knowing the "theory" of experimentation and implementing that theory—that is, actually conducting an experiment.

❖ WHAT'S AN EXPERIMENT AND WHAT ISN'T?

In experiments involving human beings, it's difficult, in some cases, to determine what is an experiment and what isn't. In this respect, let us consider some research that Stanley Milgram, a social psychologist, conducted. Strictly speaking, one could argue that Milgram's research was not an experiment because he didn't have a control group. But is it that simple?

Milgram (1965) described his study as follows:

Two persons arrive at a campus laboratory to take part in a study of memory and learning. (One of them is a confederate of the experimenter.) Each subject is paid $4.50 upon arrival and is told that payment is not affected in any way by performance. The experimenter provides an introductory talk on memory and learning processes and then informs the subjects that in the experiment one of them will serve as teacher and the other as learner. A rigged drawing is held so that the naive subject is always assigned the role of teacher and the accomplice becomes the learner. The learner is taken to an adjacent room and is strapped into an electric chair.

The naive subject is told that it is his task to teach the learner a list of paired associates, to test him on the list, and to administer punishment whenever the learner errs in the test. Punishment takes the form of electric shock, delivered to the learner by means of a shock generator controlled by the naive subject. The teacher is instructed to increase the intensity of the electric shock one step on the generator for each error. The generator contains 30 voltage levels ranging from 15 to 450 volts, and verbal designations ranging from "Slight Shock" to "Danger: Severe Shock." The learner, according to plan, provides many wrong answers, so that before long the naive subject must give him the strongest shock of the generator. Increases in shock levels are met by increasingly insistent demands from the learner that the experiment be stopped because of growing discomfort to him. However, the experimenter instructs the teacher to continue with the procedure and disregard the learner's protests. (p. 128)

After the research, Milgram gave lectures on his controversial research, in which he displayed photographs of the naive subjects in his research. These photographs showed the incredible amount of strain on their faces, as many of them proceeded (so they thought) to shock the person strapped in the electric chair. He was investigating obedience and wanted to find out the degree to which people would be obedient in a difficult situation.

Milgram, who was a personal friend of mine, told me that he had asked many deans of schools of social and behavioral science how far they thought naive subjects would go up the electronic console, and most of the deans said they doubted that people would go beyond the third level. To Milgram's surprise, a considerable number of people went all the way to the most severe shock level on their shock-generating consoles.

This research, sometimes known as the "Eichmann" experiment, because it suggested that under the right conditions, people will do almost anything, was very controversial—as might be expected. It led to the decision to have all research involving human beings examined by university panels dedicated to preventing abuses in experimentation.

Let me suggest that there are other ways of looking at experimentation that would suggest that Milgram did, in fact, conduct an experiment. I know he certainly thought he did.

Here is a slightly different definition of experimentation, from James A. Schellenberg (1974), in *An Introduction to Social Psychology:*

> **Experimentation**—the observation of phenomena under controlled conditions. In *laboratory experiments* the investigator himself creates the setting for his observations, where *in field experiments* he manipulates only some of the variables in an established social setting. A third category of *natural experiments* is sometimes used to refer to cases where the investigator actually controls nothing, but where events happen to occur in a way similar to that which an investigator might wish to create through controlled conditions. (p. 348)

Schellenberg's list of kinds of experiments suggests that Milgram's research was a laboratory experiment but one that did not have a control group. The control group, in a sense, was the population not involved in the experiment.

❖ EXPERIMENTS: APPLICATIONS AND EXERCISES

1. Critique an article in a scholarly journal on media and communication that describes an experiment. Make a copy of the first page of the article to turn in with your analysis and critique of the experiment. Use the "Checklist on Experimental Design" in making your discussion of the article.

2. Design a simple experiment involving media effects that you can make with your classmates, with half of them as the control group and the other half as the group being involved in the experiment. What do you want to find out? How will you discover what you want to find out? What problems do you face in conducting this experiment? Compare the experiments that your classmates created to see if there are any commonalities in them. Did anyone have an ingenious experiment idea?

❖ CONCLUSIONS

We can see that defining experiments is difficult (because there are a number of different kinds) and conducting them is even more difficult (because people are so complicated and hard to figure out). Nevertheless, there have been and will be in the future a large number of experiments dealing with the media and related matters conducted by researchers from a variety of different fields such as psychology, **sociology,** and communication. This research, reported in a variety of journals, is the subject of great interest to commercial media organizations, the government, and the scholarly community.

This chapter provides an overview of experimentation that enables readers to analyze the methods used in experiments and to determine how well the experiments are carried out. It also provides a means for students to devise their own experiments. These experiments will be simpler than the ones carried out by well-funded researchers, but nothing prevents students with imagination and initiative from doing some experimentation on their own.

❖ FURTHER READING

Boruch, R. F. (1996). *Randomized experiments for planning and evaluation.* Thousand Oaks: Sage.

Campbell, D. T., & Russo, M. J. (1998). *Social experimentation.* Thousand Oaks, CA: Sage.

Christensen, L. B. (1997). *Experimental methodology* (7th ed.). Boston: Allyn & Bacon.

Keppel, G. (1991). *Design and analysis: A researcher's handbook* (3rd ed.). Englewood Cliffs, NJ: Prentice Hall.

Montgomery, D. C. (1997). *Design and analysis of experiments* (4th ed.). New York: John Wiley.

Rosenthal, R., & Rosnow, R. L. (1991). *Essentials of behavioral research: Methods and data analysis* (2nd ed.). New York: McGraw-Hill.

Ryan, T. P. (2007). *Modern experimental design.* Hoboken, NJ: John Wiley.

What gave Comte and his followers so much confidence was the discovery that statistics, invented much earlier but new in use, disclosed interesting regularities. It appeared, for instance, that suicides did not occur haphazardly but kept to certain numerical proportions depending on sex, age, occupation, and the like. Similarly, it was discovered after the establishment of the modern postal service that the number of letters mailed without stamp or address did not vary at random but in relation to the time of day, the total number of letters sent, and so on. This made it seem likely that the notion of accident in individual or social behavior was simply a cloak for our ignorance of the hidden "laws."

Between Comte's beginnings and Marx's later works, the march of the Industrial Revolution had brought forth a greatly increased supply of statistics. Marx fashioned his elaborate attack on the capitalist system out of the famous "blue books" published by the British government on every phase of life, from the sanitation of factories and the accidents in coal mines to the incidence of alcoholism and infant diseases. A new image of society began to emerge from these serried ranks of figures . . . the older conception of the social order as a group of individuals endowed with free will and moved by ideas, customs, and creeds, appeared less and less believable.

—Jacques Barzun and Henry F. Graff,
The Modern Researcher (1957, pp. 204, 205)

14

A Primer on
Descriptive Statistics

with Felianka Kaftandjieva

S tatisticians use mathematical methods to analyze, summarize, and interpret numerical data that have been collected. The research methods discussed in this book—content analysis, surveys, questionnaires, and experiments—yield these kinds of data. But numerical data do not mean very much until they have been analyzed and interpreted, using statistical methods.

The choice of the statistical method of analysis (choosing between the variety of methods available) depends on the data that have to be analyzed. Statisticians differentiate four different kinds of data, depending on so-called levels of measurement.

❖ LEVELS OF MEASUREMENT

Nominal Level. Typical examples of data on this level are demographic matters such as sex, nationality, and marital status. For each analyzed object, the only thing we are able to determine is to which one of a few categories it belongs. We can code these categories with numbers, but they would be used only as signs without any mathematical meaning.

For example, we can code sex as 0 for females and 1 for males, but nothing will be changed if we use 0 for males and 1 for female. We cannot use these numbers for any mathematical operation. We could equally well use such symbols as ►)- for males and *§& for females. From the point of view of statistics, nominal data are the simplest kind of data because of the limited number of operations that can be applied to them.

Ordinal Level. Data belong to this level when they can be ordered according to some criterion. Examples of such data are educational level or rank in the army. On the basis of these data, you can compare objects and say who has a higher education or a higher position in the army, but you cannot determine how big the difference is between them. In other words, the only possible operation with data on the ordinal level is comparison (although any data transformation that maintains the order of the data can be applied).

Interval Level. Temperature is a typical example of an interval level of measurement. Not only can we compare two days (or two bodies), finding which one is warmer, but we also can determine the magnitude of the difference. The interval scales, however, have no naturally defined zero point. The zero points for Fahrenheit or Celsius scales are subjectively determined, and they can be changed if a new temperature scale is invented. Because of the lack of an intrinsic defined zero point with interval data, it is meaningless to make statements such as, "Today is twice as warm as yesterday."

Ratio Level. Salaries, height, weight, and number of children (or wives) are data that belong to the ratio level of measurement, and all mathematical operations valid for real numbers can be applied to such data.

❖ DESCRIPTIVE STATISTICS

There are two kinds of statistics—descriptive and inferential. This primer deals with descriptive statistics. Descriptive statistics refers to methods that we use to obtain, from raw data, information that characterizes or summarizes the whole set of data. That is, descriptive statistics allow us to make sense of the data more easily. (Inferential statistics allow us to generalize from the data collected to the general populations they were taken from.) I will briefly discuss some of the most popular concepts from descriptive statistics.

Frequency Distribution

Statisticians are strange people. They tend to count everything—births and birds, deaths and debts, and so on. If we look at the beginning sentence of this primer from the point of view of a statistician, it would not look like a set of words but like a set of numbers such as the following:

4	4	5	3	3	9	2	4
10	3	3	9	4	10	8	4
7	3	3	2	3	9	11	12

In fact, this numerical set represents the length of the words (as a number of letters), used in the following sentence: "What gave Comte and his followers so much confidence was the discovery that statistics, invented much earlier but new in use, disclosed interesting regularities."

We are lucky that the sentence was not too long, and fortunately, we did not decide to count the length of the words in the whole paragraph. But even in this case, when we have only 24 words,[1] the numbers cannot reveal too much, because they are not organized. The organization of the data in a form that is comprehensive, as well as easier for analysis and interpretation, is usually called *data tabulation*, and it is presented either as a frequency table or in a chart form. The frequency table for the length of the words in the first sentence is presented in Table 14.1.

In the first column of this table, all observed different values are given, ordered in ascending order. The numbers in the second column show how many times this value was observed in the analyzed sample. This is called a *frequency distribution*, and we can conclude, based on it, that most of the words in this sentence are short (3–4 letters). Taking into consideration that the length of the words is closely connected with the readability of the text, we also can assume (even without reading the sentence!) that it is an easily understandable sentence.

---

[1]In statistical language, it can be written as $N = 24$, and statisticians would say that "the size of our sample is (equal to) 24."

Table 14.1   Frequency Distribution of Length of Words in Example Sentence

Length of Words (in letters)	Frequency (f)
2	2
3	7
4	5
5	1
6	0
7	1
8	1
9	3
10	2
11	1
12	1
Total	24

It is also obvious that the words used differ very much in their length. There are 2-letter words as well as 12-letter words. The frequencies also vary; as can be seen, there are no 6-letter words in the sentence, whereas there are seven 3-letter words.

The presentation of the information in Table 14.1 can also be presented in a graphical form, as shown in Figure 14.1. From this chart, it is even easier than from a frequency table to see that most of the words are located in the left part of the distribution.

For small samples, as in this case, it is quite possible to have no examples for some of the categories (for example, 6-letter words). The more different values there are in the data set, the bigger is the probability of empty cells (with $f = 0$) in the frequency table. In such cases, it is better to group data in broader intervals with equal size. Combining data, however, leads to losing information on one hand, and, depending on the number of intervals used and their width, the same information can be interpreted in different ways on the other hand.

It can be easily demonstrated with the distributions, shown in Figures 14.2a and 14.2b. Both charts present a frequency distribution of

Figure 14.1   Frequency Distribution—Length of Words

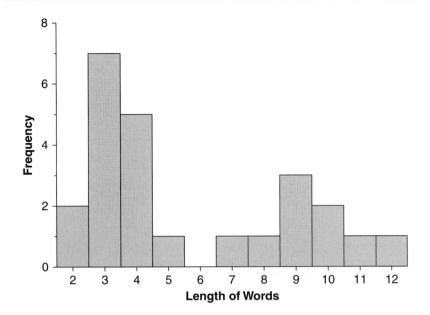

the length of the words in the same sentence, but they look different. The first distribution has two peaks, whereas the second has only one—on the left side. The reason for these differences is that the distributions are based on a different number of grouping intervals—in the first case, there are 6 intervals with a length of 2, while in the second case, the intervals are fewer (4) but broader (with a length of 3).

That is why it is preferable, first, to prepare a frequency table (or a chart of frequency distribution) for raw (nongrouped) data and then, after its analysis, if there is a need, to proceed to grouping data into intervals.

There are three main descriptive characteristics for each distribution:

1. *Location:* Where on the axis is the distribution positioned?

2. *Dispersion:* How broad is the distribution?

3. *Shape:* What is the form (appearance, pattern) of the distribution?

Different statistical measures for each one of these three characteristics of the distribution exist, and each one has its own advantages and disadvantages. The main reason for choosing a statistical measure, here, is the kind of data we have to analyze.

Figure 14.2   Frequency Distribution of the Length of the Words in the Same Sentence

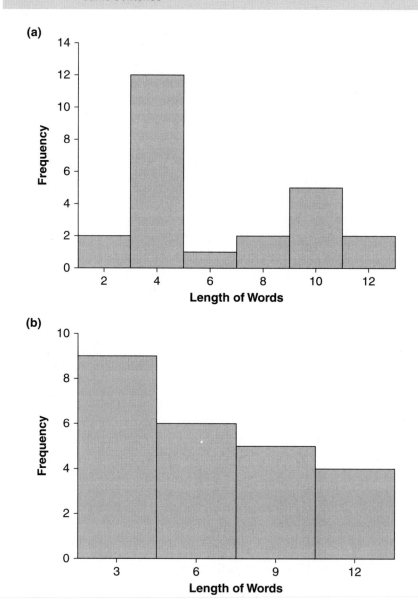

❖ MEASURES OF CENTRAL TENDENCY

The statistics describing the location of the distribution are usually called measures of central tendency because they indicate where on the scale is the central point of the distribution. There are three more commonly used statistics: mean, median, and mode.

The Mean

The mean (the arithmetic average) is the sum of all observed data values, divided by the sample size. In the example with our sentence, all we have to do to get the mean is add all observed values and to divide the sum by 24 as shown below:

$$\frac{4+4+5+3+3+9+2+4+10+3+3+9+4+10+8+\\4+7+3+3+2+3+9+11+12}{24}$$

The result of these calculations is 5.625. In other words, the average length of the words in the analyzed sentence is between 5 and 6 letters. Of course, statisticians like symbols and formulas, so in their language it would look like the following:

$$\overline{X} = \frac{\sum\limits_{i=1}^{N} X_i}{N},$$

where

$\overline{X}$ is the symbol for the mean;

X is the symbol for each one of the observed values, and that is why i can vary between 1 and N;

N is the size of the sample, 2; and

Σ is a symbol for the sum (Greek letter Sigma).

One of the main disadvantages of the mean is that it is most profoundly affected by extreme scores.

For example, let's imagine the following situation: A very bad surgeon had to do five surgeries in one day. Unfortunately, all the patients except one died, either during surgery or a few hours later. The lucky (or the most stubborn) patient not only survived but lived 45 years after the operation. So if we present the life of the all patients as the number of years they live after the operation, we would have this: 0, 0, 0, 0, 45 or, on average, $(0 + 0 + 0 + 0 + 45) / 5 = 9$ years, which is quite a good average result for any surgeon. The question, however, is, Would that surgeon be your first choice, if you need an operation? My answer would be definite: No!

This disadvantage of the mean usually takes place when the sample size is comparatively small ($N < 30$), but the mean sometimes leads to wrong conclusions even with bigger samples. Did you hear about the statistician who drowned in a lake averaging only 2 inches in depth? The main reason for this is that the mean takes into account all observed values, and they affect the final result in one and the same degree. The last warning concerning the mean is that it is a valid measure for the central tendency only for interval and ratio data.

The Median

The median (Me) is the point in the distribution that divides it into two halves. The median can be used as a measure for the central tendency for all kinds of data, except nominal. The easiest way to find the median for raw data is to order them from the lowest to the highest. If we do this for the words in our sentence, the result will be as follows:

0 0 2 2 3 3 3 3 3 3 3 4 4 4 | 4 4 5 7 8 9 9 9 10 10 11 12

Because of the even number of words in the analyzed sentence, the midpoint is between two values, and then the median will be equal to the average of these two nearest values:

$$(Me = \frac{4 + 4}{2} = 4).$$

In case of odd number of values, the median will be equal to the value in the middle point of the ordered data.

Let's, for example, edit the analyzed sentence, skipping the second word *much* (perhaps it is a bit too much to use *much* twice in one and the same sentence!). The modified sentence will be, *"What gave Comte and his followers so much confidence was the discovery that statistics, invented much earlier but new in use, disclosed interesting regularities."*

The change in the sentence will lead to the change in the observed values—they will be with one less ($N_1 = 23$), and the number of four-letter words will also be with one less. The ordered values will be as follows:

0 2 2 3 3 3 3 3 3 3 4 4 4 4 5 7 8 9 9 9 10 10 11 12

The middle point in this case is on the 12th observed value, and it is again 4 ($Me = 4$). In other words, the two versions of the sentence (with two or with one *much*) have equal medians.

The median does not depend on the extreme values, because it does not take them into account. For example the median for the length of the life of the patients of the inept surgeon will be equal to zero (0, 0, 0, 0, 45), and it is a much better indicator for the central tendency than the mean, equal to 9 years. That is why, especially for small samples, it is a better measure for the central tendency than for the mean.

The Mode

The mode (*Mo*) is the third measure of the central tendency, and it can be applied to all kinds of data. The mode is the most frequently observed value in the frequency distribution. In the case with the length of the words in the beginning sentence, the mode will be 3, because most words in the sentence (7) consist of three letters. In statistical language, it would appear in this way: $Mo = 3$.

Each frequency distribution has only one mean and median, but for some of the distributions, more than one mode can exist. The mode does not take into account the whole information about the distribution, and it is not a very stable estimator of the central tendency. That is why it is comparatively rarely used as a measure of central tendency—mainly in cases when the other measures cannot be applied (nominal data). If we compare the three measures of the central tendency for our case, we will notice that they differ rather considerably:

$$X = 5.625; Me = 4; Mo = 3.$$

Someone can reasonably ask, "Then, what is the REAL central tendency?"

The answer to this question is that all the three are real, but they mean different things. Which of them to use depends on the following:

- The level of measurement
- The sample size

In our case, the best estimator of the central tendency (the data are intervals, but the sample size is small) is the median. Moreover, its meaning is very clear—half of the words are below, and the other half is above (50/50). In any case, when any measure of the central tendency is reported, we have to be aware of its meaning before making any interpretations and conclusions.

Let me offer an example, taken from Brant Houston's (1996) *Computer Assisted Reporting*, which discusses the salaries of baseball players:

> Neill Borowski, head of computer-assisted reporting at *The Philadelphia Inquirer* . . . said that baseball fans were outraged by player's salaries because they always heard the average salary was $1.2 million. But the median salary was $500,000 and the mode, or the most frequent salary, was $109,000. These numbers indicate that there are a few players making really, really big money. The middle value, the salary amount that half the salaries exceed and half the salaries fall below, was $500,000. If you asked all baseball players for a count of hands for each salary, the largest number (the mode, not a majority) of the hands would go up for $109,000. (Okay, it's still a lot, but not as much as you thought. And it's being made by people who have to make all their money in 10 years or less.) (p. 75)

These figures are probably low because the salaries of baseball players have skyrocketed in recent years, but his point is well made. Most baseball players don't make the gigantic salaries that a relatively small and select group of ballplayers make.

❖ MEASURES OF DISPERSION

The statistics describing how broad the interval is on the measurement scale covered by the frequency distribution are usually called measures of dispersion. There are many such measures, but we will describe here only two of them—the easiest one and the most frequently used one.

Range

The range (R), as a statistical concept, can be used for all kinds of data except nominal data. It is equal to the difference between the maximum and the minimum observed values. That is why it cannot be applied to the nominal data: They cannot be ordered, and consequently, the minimum and maximum values do not exist.

In the case with the length of the words in the beginning sentence, the minimum value is 2 and the maximum value is 12, so the range is equal to 10 ($R = 12 - 2 = 10$). This statistic can be easily calculated, and its meaning is very clear—the range is the distance between the two end points of the frequency distribution. The range, however, depends very much on the extreme values, and this is the main reason that the range is not used often as a measure of the dispersion.

❖ STANDARD DEVIATION

The standard deviation (*SD* or *s*) is a measure of variability indicating the degree to which all observed values deviate from the mean. The mathematical formula used for calculation of the standard deviation is given below:

$$SD = \sqrt{\sum_{i=1}^{N} \frac{(X_i - \overline{X})^2}{N-1}}$$

where

SD is the symbol for the standard deviation;
$\overline{X}$ is the symbol for the mean;
X is the symbol for each one of the observed values, and that is why i can vary between 1 and N;
N is the size of the sample; and
Σ is a symbol for the sum (Greek letter Sigma).

It is obvious that the calculation of the standard deviation is much more complicated than the calculation of the range. Moreover, the standard deviation can be used only for interval and ratio data.

Despite these disadvantages, the standard deviation is the most frequently used statistic as a measure of the dispersion, because it takes into account all observed values and because the dispersion is expressed in the same units as the observed values.

❖ THE NORMAL OR BELL-SHAPED CURVE

In most of the cases, when the sample size is big enough ($N > 100$), the three measures of the central tendency are the same and are exactly in the middle of the frequency distribution. This kind of distribution is so often met that it is called "normal." Its graphical presentation looks like a bell (see Figure 14.3), and it is called the "normal curve" or "bell-shaped curve." It can be seen from this graph that if the distribution is normal, most of the cases are concentrated around the center of the distribution, and only a small number of cases are distributed at the ends.

Figure 14.3   Normal Distribution or "Bell-Shaped Curve"

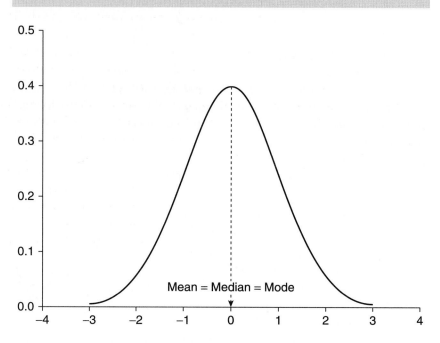

The normal distribution is also symmetrical. If we draw a vertical line through the middle point (mean-median-mode), the distribution will be split into two identical parts. Most of the characteristics (physical, chemical, biological, psychological, sociological) of the subjects or objects in a sample are approximately normally distributed. For example, beauty, intelligence, money, children, and lovers have normal distribution, and most of us are somewhere in the middle:

- Not too beautiful, but neither very ugly
- Not a genius, but not a fool either
- Not very rich, but at least not starving

At the same time, only a small percentage of people (and usually their names are well known) are really beautiful or geniuses or billionaires. Fortunately, people at the opposite end of the scales of beauty, intelligence, or money are also few in number; most people are in the middle. In other words, the chance of ending up in the middle (in everything) is greater than the chance of being on the top.

You might conclude that it isn't fair. And you will be correct. It is not fair; but it is "normal!"

For example, let's have a look at the results of the 1991 U.S. General Social Survey about educational levels shown in Figure 14.4. In this graphical presentation, raw data are grouped into 2-year intervals, and as can be seen, the shape of the distribution is close to the bell shape, but it is slightly asymmetrical, and its peak is a little bit higher than the top of the theoretical normal distribution. The two measures of the central tendency are identical (the mode and the median), equal to 12 years of education, and the mean is a little bit higher—12.88 years. Statisticians might be a bit disappointed with the fact that the distribution is not ideally bell shaped, but if we were educators, we would be happy with this asymmetry, because it shows that there are more people with a higher educational level than people with only a primary education. It is not "normal," but it is a hopeful sign.

The normal distribution is well studied from the theoretical point of view, and all its characteristics are well known. For example, if the frequency distribution is approximately normal, we can conclude immediately that about 68% of the observed values fall into the interval $X - 1\ SD$; $X + 1\ SD$, and 95% of the observed values fall into the interval $X - 2\ SD$; $X + 2\ SD$, as shown in Figure 14.5.

Figure 14.4   Frequency Distribution for U.S. Educational Levels

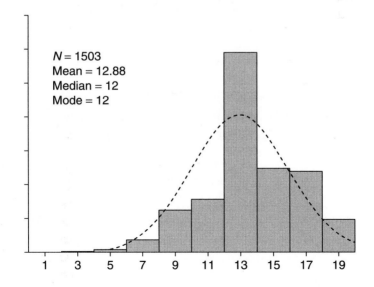

$N = 1503$
Mean = 12.88
Median = 12
Mode = 12

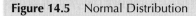

Figure 14.5   Normal Distribution

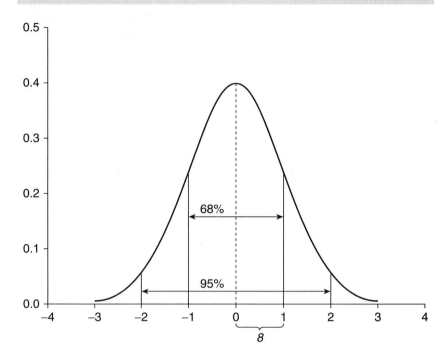

A lot of statistical tests and inferential statistics are based on the assumption of normally distributed data, but they may be applied only if the data gathered meet this assumption. That is why before applying any statistical method (valid only for normally distributed data), we have to test the hypothesis that our data are normally distributed. Otherwise, the results of the analysis will be meaningless.

A SHORT THEATRICAL PIECE ON STATISTICS

Arthur:	Statistics are very important. Perhaps you've heard the expression, "There are lies, damned lies, and statistics."
Grand Inquisitor:	*I've always felt that statistics can be used any way you want to use them.*
Arthur:	There's another saying, "Figures don't lie, but liars figure."
Grand Inquisitor:	*Why do people love statistics so much?*

Arthur:	There's comfort in numbers. You get a sense of certainty and seriousness from numbers that you don't get from words of logical arguments.
Grand Inquisitor:	*I read recently that half of the marriages end in divorce now. Why don't people choose, when* they *get married, to be in the other 50% that doesn't get divorced?*
Arthur:	Everyone who gets married thinks that they are in the other 50%. Remember, this is a country where we all think we're above average. When people get married, they should also get divorced at the same time, but not put in the date on the divorce papers. That would make things a lot easier.

❖ THE PROBLEMS WITH RATINGS

It is worthwhile to offer a cautionary note. People can use statistics selectively to prove all kinds of things. As the folk saying goes, "Figures don't lie, but liars figure." For example, you might want to look carefully at the statistics used by radio and television stations, networks, and other media organizations, because their data might be accurate as far as they go but neglect to deal with certain important matters (such as the demographic makeup and buying power of a show's audience), or they might put a positive spin on figures about audiences and the popularity of programs that is unwarranted. And there is reason to believe that the figures the Nielsen Ratings Company and other ratings companies use may not be accurate due to the methods of data collection used (see the quotation from Barry Sherman, 1995, in Chapter 12).

Joseph R. Dominick (1993) lists a number of reasons to question the accuracy of ratings in *The Dynamics of Mass Communication:*

> First, it is possible that the type of person who agrees to participate may have viewing habits different from those of the viewer who declines to participate. Second, in the case of both Arbitron and Nielsen reports (based on about 55 percent of the diaries sent out) it is possible that "returners" behave differently from "non-returners." Third, people who know that their viewing is being measured may change their behavior. A family might watch more news and public affairs programs than usual in order to appear sophisticated in the eyes of the rating company. Fourth, both ratings companies admit that they have a problem measuring the viewing of certain groups. Minorities, particularly blacks and Hispanics, may be

underrepresented in the ratings companies' samples. Lastly, the stations that are being measured can distort the measurement process by engaging in contests and special promotions or by running unusual or sensational programs in an attempt to "hype" the ratings.

Despite these problems, the ratings are useful and necessary—because the prices stations can charge for commercials are, in large measure, determined by the ratings their programs get.

❖ A CAUTIONARY NOTE ON STATISTICS

Actually, it's a good idea to be skeptical whenever statistics (and any research data) are given. You might ask yourself questions such as these:

- Who collected the data?

- How accurate are the data?

- How timely are the data?

- How complete are the data? (Did the researchers fail, for one reason or another, to obtain important data?)

- Are there other data that raise questions about the accuracy of (or that contradict) the data being dealt with?

- Are useful comparisons of data made?

- Are the methods used in the analysis appropriate for this kind of data?

- How have the data been interpreted?

❖ STATISTICS AND COMPARISONS

Let me say something about the use of comparisons and statistics. Often, data are presented using comparisons. Comparisons may be odious, but they are often very useful. Generally two kinds of comparisons are made:

Historical (before and after)

Spatial (here and there)

But there are other kinds as well. Let me quote some fascinating historical statistics from the *Harper's Index* found in the February 1987 issue of *Harper's* magazine:

- Number of shelters for battered women: in 1970—0; in 1986—1,100

- Percentage of the racial incidents reported in Los Angeles County whose targets were Asians: in 1985—15; in 1986—45

- Price of a unit of whole blood in New York City: in 1976—$29; today—$70.75

In some cases, a statistic by itself is interesting in that it gives an idea of the size or scope of some activity. Here are some more examples from the same issue of the *Harper's Index* that are not comparative but are fascinating:

- Number of roof thatchers in Britain: 900

- Average amount of gas a cow belches each day (in cubic feet): 35

- Number of condoms used every second in the United States: 7

The figure for condom usage is interesting, but it doesn't tell us a great deal. It would be much more useful to know what percentage of the American population uses condoms, which would enable us to determine how many people who use condoms are having intercourse in America every second. (How sociologists get these figures is another matter; our knowledge of statistics and problems with sampling might make us a bit skeptical about the accuracy of some research, although there are some methods that are very reliable if applied in the proper way.)

❖ DATA ON MEDIA USE IN AMERICA

Now I'd like to offer some statistics about the growth in ownership of media technology in American culture. These figures offer information that has important implications for anyone interested in the role of media in societies and deal with the percentages of households that have telephones, television sets, radios, wired cable, alternative delivery systems, and computers for 1997 and 2007. By offering two sets of figures, we can get some insights into trends in ownership of these items. They were obtained from www.census.gov (Table 1090: Utilization of Selected Media) and other sources.

Item	1997 (%)	2007 (%)
Telephone service	96	94.6
Radios	98	99.0
Television	95	98.2
Computers	40	78
Cell phones	34	82.4

According to a Gallup poll in 2005, Americans have the following devices in their homes:

Object	Percentage
VCRs	88
DVD players	83
Cell phone	78
Desktop computer	65
Digital camera	50

Statistics on media players and other products found in typical American families shows we have the following:

5   Radios

3.6 CDs or tape players

3.5 Television sets

2.9 VCRs/DVD players

2.1 Video game consoles

1.5 Computers

We can see, then, that we spend a considerable amount of money on purchasing devices that allow us to play and record media and communicate with one another on cell phones. The

Kaiser Family Foundation estimates that children between ages 8 and 18 spend 44.5 hours a week—that makes 6.5 hours a day—looking at computer screens, television monitors, or game player screens, to which we must also add cell phone screens, bringing the total to more than 8 hours a day we spend looking at screens, according to some estimates.

The U.S. Census has estimates for the amount of media typical Americans will consume in 2010. The Census estimates Americans will spend 3,500 hours a year with different kinds of media, which amounts to 9.8 hours a day with media. This 3,500-hour figure breaks down as follows (I've not included some relatively minor time expenditures):

Medium	Number of Hours Per Year	Number of Hours Per Day
TV	1,607	4.40
Cable	958	2.62
Recorded music	184	0.50
Newspapers	155	0.42
Video games	125	0.34
Reading books	108	0.29
Reading educational books	8	0.02

Obviously, we live in a media-saturated society that dominates our leisure times and has a profound impact on our society and culture as well as our individual lives. Now that some computers that cost around $250, around 62% of American households are connected to the Internet, and some families have more than one computer in their homes. Smart phones, which are actually powerful computers, are now becoming dominant. And now Apple's iPad and other brands of tablet computers have the power to make major changes in the way people use computers and consume media.

❖ ON THE PROBLEM OF INTERPRETATION

When dealing with statistical data, there is the matter of interpretation. The data we get from research always have to be interpreted. Figures don't mean anything in and of themselves, and that's where problems often arise. If we don't find problems in the research methodology or means of data collection in research projects (or in both), we often find different points of view (and sometimes mistakes) in the interpretation of the data that have been collected. So media stations and networks battle with one another, using statistics selectively, and we must be on guard and notice the qualifications they use and the way they "read" the data they have collected to suit their own purposes.

Statistics pose a dilemma. They must be interpreted, but the interpretations some people make are often highly speculative and based, in certain cases, on selecting only those statistics that suit the purposes of the person(s) using the data and neglecting other data. Researchers should be honest and tell not only the truth but also the whole truth, to the extent we can do so. One problem is that we tend to see what we would like to see, and very often we unconsciously neglect some facts.

❖ STATISTICS: APPLICATIONS AND EXERCISES

1. Using the latest *Statistical Abstract of the United States,* find data on some aspect of media use in America that you find interesting. Print out the page with the data and turn it in with your discussion of what was interesting about the data. Then find data on media use in France, Japan, and Argentina to compare with the data about American media usage. What do these comparative data reveal about media usage in the countries involved? Did you learn anything interesting from making this comparative analysis?

2. Find statistical data on the amount of television young children (ages 3–10) watch daily in America, France, Japan, and Argentina and the amount of advertising to which they are exposed. Does using a comparative approach offer important insights about children and the media in America?

3. What do you make of the following statistics about televised football? In a typical 3-hour game there are

11 minutes of action. A typical play takes 4 seconds.

17 minutes of replays

3 seconds devoted to cheerleaders

67 minutes of players standing around, getting back to the huddle, lining up, etc.

60 minutes of commercials

Given these statistics, why do you think televised football is so popular?

❖ CONCLUSIONS

In this primer on descriptive statistics, I've dealt with some of the more commonly used concepts, to help you interpret data better and make sense of some of the articles you might be reading about media usage and related concerns. There are many books on statistics that can further your knowledge of this useful and interesting subject. Two of the most widely used software programs are SPSS (formerly, Statistical Software for the Social Sciences; now, Statistical Product and Service Solutions) and SAS (Statistical Analysis System). These programs greatly facilitate making statistical analyses—and making bigger mistakes (than we made before we had them) if not properly used.

❖ FURTHER READING

Burdess, N. (2011). *Starting statistics: A simple guide*. Thousand Oaks, CA: Sage.

Freedman, D., Pisani, R., & Purves, R. (1997). *Statistics* (3rd ed.). New York: Norton.

Gonick, L., & Smith, W. (1993). *The cartoon guide to statistics*. New York: HarperCollins.

Kanji, G. K. (1999). *100 statistical tests*. Thousand Oaks, CA: Sage.

Moore, D. S. (1997). *The active practice of statistics: A text for multimedia learning*. New York: Freeman.

Salkind, N. J. (2008). *Statistics for people who (think they) hate statistics* (3rd ed.). Thousand Oaks, CA: Sage.

Sirkin, R. M. (1999). *Statistics for the social sciences* (2nd ed.). Thousand Oaks, CA: Sage.

Vogt, W. P. (1998). *Dictionary of statistics and methodology* (2nd ed.). Thousand Oaks, CA: Sage.

Wright, D. B., & London, K. (2009). *First (and second) steps in statistics* (2nd ed.). Thousand Oaks, CA: Sage.

Part V

Putting It All Together

[The doorbell rings.]

Mr. Smith: Goodness, someone is ringing.

Mrs. Smith: There must be someone there. I'll go and see.

[She goes to see, she opens the door and closes it and comes back.]

Nobody. [She sits down again.]

Mr. Martin: I'm going to give you another example . . .

[Doorbell rings again.]

Mr. Smith: Goodness, someone is ringing.

Mrs. Smith: There must be somebody there. I'll go and see.

[She goes to see, opens the door, and comes back.]

No one. [She sits down again.]

Mr. Martin: [who has forgotten where he was]: Uh . . .

Mrs. Martin: You were saying that you were going to give us another example.

Mr. Martin: Oh, yes . . .

[Doorbell rings again.]

Mr. Smith: Goodness, someone is ringing.

Mrs. Smith: I'm not going to open the door again.

Mr. Smith: Yes, but there must be someone there!

Mrs. Smith: The first time there was no one. The second time there was no one. Why do you think that there is someone there now?

—Eugene Ionesco, *The Bald Soprano* (1958, p. 22)

15

Nineteen Common
Thinking Errors to Avoid

❖ ❖ ❖

In this chapter, I will list and briefly explain some of the more common errors we make in our thinking processes—including errors known, in philosophical parlance, as *fallacies.* There is a strong relationship between logical and correct thinking and designing research projects. So it is important that we examine our thinking for mistakes that we inadvertently might be making. I assume, of course, that all of the thinking errors I am discussing are made by accident and are due to carelessness or not recognizing that some kind of thinking error has been made.

Researchers must be honest and report the results of their research; that is part of the ethics of research. But occasionally, researchers inadvertently make mistakes of one sort or another. That's to be expected. All anyone can ask when you do research is that you do the best job you can in designing your research and carrying it out and that you report your results—even if your findings surprise you or are, for some reason, distasteful to you.

A SHORT THEATRICAL PIECE ON CORRECT THINKING

Grand Inquisitor: *Are people bald because they have no hair, or is it that they have no hair because they are bald?*

Arthur: Isthay estionqway isway absurdway. Pons asinorum, post hoc ergo propter hoc, petitio principi, ad populam. Quid nunc.

Grand Inquisitor: *Why is it that newspapers give the age of people when they die but not when they are born?*

Arthur: I don't know. That's a very profound question. Probably because there is a bias in this country against babies. The elderly have great political power, but who cares about babies, since they don't vote.

Grand Inquisitor: *What's the difference between an alligator?*

Arthur: I give up!

Grand Inquisitor: *An alligator can swim in the ocean but not on the land.*

Arthur: Did you ever study critical thinking?

Grand Inquisitor: *I'm naturally very critical—especially of others. I prefer not to think, except when it is absolutely necessary. With all the great computer programs now, one needn't do so.*

❖ COMMON FALLACIES

1. *Appealing to False Authority.* We often use authorities when supporting our arguments—people who have expertise in certain areas—but we must be certain that the authorities we cite can speak with legitimacy on the subject we are dealing with.

An authority on medicine is not an authority on education, for example. Some commercials for health products have actually used actors who play doctors in television programs as "authorities" when really what they are is actors or, perhaps, "celebrities."

2. *Stacking the Deck (selected instances).* When we make arguments, we must be careful that we do not neglect information that negates our position and cite only information, data, and statistics that support our position. We must be scrupulously honest when doing research and deal with all data. The other side of this fallacy is to use examples that are not generalizable. For example, I once mentioned in a class that smoking is bad for people, and one of my students told us about his uncle who is 92 and smokes two packs a day. His uncle is obviously not a representative figure.

3. *Overgeneralizing (allness).* This error involves assuming that what is true of some X is true of all X. The term *generalization* comes from the Latin *genus* (kind, class, genre) and refers to a statement that is true for every member of the group or **class.** If there is one contrary instance, it negates the generalization. Therefore, it is generally a good idea to qualify generalizations so that one contrary instance will not invalidate them. Not everyone in England speaks the kind of English the queen does or that certain members of the upper classes do (what is known as "the received pronunciation"). Actually, a relatively small proportion of the people in England do. So we have to be careful and avoid making generalizations about how "the English" speak. We cannot assume that what is true of some is true of all. (This is the kind of thinking that is behind stereotyping.)

4. *Imperfect Analogies and Comparisons.* When we make an analogy, we compare two things and allege that they are similar in some important way or ways. In ancient days, supporters of royalty asserted that a country was like a body and needed a head (the monarch) to rule; otherwise, there would be chaos. This notion is silly, because a country is not like a body, which may explain why there are so few kings and queens nowadays. And when there were kings, there also was a great deal of chaos and confusion.

There are two kinds of analogies: *metaphors,* which state equivalence (My love is a red rose) and *similes,* which use *like* or *as* and state similarity (My love is *like* a red rose). When you make analogies, you must be certain that the analogy is correct and fitting.

5. *Misrepresenting Ideas of Other People.* We often inadvertently misrepresent the ideas people have because we are in a hurry or careless. We must be careful, for example, when we quote people that we do so accurately. Leaving off a word can alter the meaning of the material quoted to a considerable extent. And the same applies to leaving out sentences that qualify previously discussed material. Misrepresenting the ideas of people is also known as creating "straw men" that are easy to knock down.

6. *Pushing Arguments to Absurd Extremes.* We do this when we take a reasonable statement by someone and greatly exaggerate it so that it loses any semblance of credibility. When we do this, we fail to notice any qualifications that might have been made or any limitations made by the person whose ideas we are distorting. This kind of thinking—pushing arguments to absurd extremes—is quite common and is done because we do not like an idea, have an emotional reaction to a statement, or want to generate an emotional reaction to an idea. Thus, for example, advocates for the National Rifle Association often argue that any attempt to limit the sales of guns means the government (or whoever) will "end up taking everyone's guns away."

7. *Before, Therefore Because Of* (post hoc ergo propter hoc). This argument reasons that if X occurs before Y, X causes Y. Just because something takes place before something else does not mean it caused it. Determining what causes anything is very difficult. For example, suppose a person goes to a restaurant for lunch. Later that night, he has an upset stomach. It is possible, but not necessarily the case, that the lunch led to the upset stomach. It might have been dinner or a snack or might not be caused by anything eaten but by a flu bug or something else. So we have to be very careful about assigning causes to phenomena.

8. *Misleading Percentages.* Sometimes percentages can be misleading. You must give an absolute number so the percentages can be interpreted correctly. In some cases, a 50% increase in the sale of books, in a given period (from 100 to 150 copies sold), looks impressive when you see the percentage but turns out to be trivial when you see the raw data. You must always mention the raw numbers on which the percentages are calculated.

9. *Using Seemingly Impressive Numbers.* Quoting numbers without giving the reader a sense of what percentage of the base the numbers represent is also a means of misleading people.

Suppose one were to say that a survey shows that 500 economists believe that inflation is a danger. That figure means a lot
if there are 1,000 economists in the country but not very much
if there are 20,000 economists in the country. This mistake is the
reverse of the one discussed above, using percentages without
giving absolute numbers. You should always know the percentages that lead to the use of numbers.

10. *Misleading Use of the Term Average.* We saw, in the chapter on
statistics, that there are three ways of figuring out averages:
the mean, the median, and the mode. The mean is defined as
the total divided by the number. Suppose we are dealing with
salaries in the United States. You get a considerably different
figure if you use the median—the figure halfway between the
lowest and the highest salary—rather than the mean. That's
because very high salaries will skew the final figure considerably. If there are a lot of millionaires and billionaires in a given
population, the median salary will be skewed upward and
will not give us a true picture of people's salaries.

11. *Incorrect Assumptions.* You have to make sure that what you assume
to be the case in some situation is correct. If you begin your
research with incorrect assumptions, your research—which builds
on these assumptions—will be deeply flawed. It's a wise policy to
always check on your assumptions, because they may be incorrect.
For example, many people assume that murderous violence in
high schools is an urban phenomenon. What we've seen in the
United States, however, is that many killings and massacres that
have taken place in our high schools have been in the suburbs.

12. *False Conclusions.* Let us suppose that a survey is taken of a
class of 200 students, and 8 people in the class complained that
they did not like it. That does not allow you to argue that 192
people "liked" the class; all you know is that they did not com-
plain. Many students in the class might not have liked it but
did not indicate their feelings, for one reason or another.

13. *Mistaking Correlation and Causation.* Just because there is a correlation between X and Y does not mean that X causes Y. For
example, there may be a correlation between amount of higher
education and small families, but it does not mean that the
amount of education causes small families. There may be other
factors involved, such as the age at which people with higher
education get married. We have to distinguish between some

factor *causing* something to happen and that factor *contributing to* something's happening.

14. *Diversion of Attention by Using Emotional Language.* There is a wonderful joke about what a minister scribbled in the margin of one of his sermons. "Argument weak—yell like crazy." The point is that people who feel very strongly about some issue may become very emotional about it, and their use of emotion often blinds them and those listening to them or reading what they have written to the weakness in their argument. Sometimes people use "red herrings" (any means of distracting people from the issue at hand) to evade dealing with a question.

Father: Why did you come home after midnight when I told you to be back by 11:00 p.m.?

Son: You're always picking on me.

The question was why the son came home late, but the son has tried to divert to it to why the father is always picking on his son.

Let me offer another example of this, taken from a famous Jewish joke, which is another red herring—but in this case, more literally, a pink salmon.

> A beggar named Cohen meets a wealthy person and pleads for some money for his starving family. The wealthy person gives Cohen some money. A short while later the wealthy man goes to a restaurant and sees Cohen eating a very expensive dish there—salmon and mayonnaise. When the man asks Cohen about it, he says, "When I don't have money, I can't eat salmon and mayonnaise. When I do have money, I shouldn't eat salmon and mayonnaise. So when can I eat salmon and mayonnaise?"

Cohen has shifted the argument from why he isn't spending money to feed his hungry family to when can he eat salmon and mayonnaise.

15. *Begging the Question (petitio principii).* If we look at the Latin, *petitio* means request or petition, and *principii* means beginning or at the start. So *petitio principii* is an argument that assumes its conclusion. That is, we accept as true what we are supposed to prove. When we argue correctly, the premises and conclusions must be separate. We beg the question by assuming that the answer to the question we are asking is obvious, because it is in the conclusion; thus, by using different words, we "answer" the question. For example, the statement "Smoking

marijuana is good for you because it is healthful" really begs the question. Saying it is "healthful"—the conclusion—is used to support the argument that "smoking marijuana is good for you."

16. *Oversimplification.* When dealing with complicated issues, to make ourselves clear or do the best we can with a weak position, we sometimes oversimplify things. Often, elements of the reasoning error discussed earlier, misrepresentation, are at work here. When we have oversimplified arguments that have been made by others and weakened them by doing so, it generally is much easier to claim support for our own position.

17. *Ad Hominem Arguments.* The term *ad hominem* is Latin for attacking the person—literally "to the man." We don't focus our attention on the argument being made but on the person who has made the argument. And by insulting or casting doubt on the "good name" of that person, we indirectly attack his or her ideas. We focus on "who" is making the argument and not on "what" argument is being made.

18. *Ad Populum Arguments.* In Latin, *ad populum* means appealing to the populace. These arguments usually take the form "everyone knows . . ." or "everyone believes. . . ." This kind of argument is really an appeal to be guided by so-called public opinion, but the appeal is spurious. When you say "everyone knows," you cannot possibly know what everyone knows. What you are probably doing is taking your assumptions and generalizing from them—assuming that everyone agrees with you. These "everyone knows" arguments imply that they are based on common sense, but as "everyone knows," common sense tells us that the world is flat.

19. *"Pooh-Poohing Arguments."* Pooh-poohing involves ridiculing other people and failing to take their ideas seriously. It is a means of avoiding logical argument and often uses the "everyone knows" argument to suggest that an idea is so absurd it shouldn't be even considered. "Pooh-poohing" is a common evasive technique.

❖ CONCLUSIONS

It's very easy to make some of the mistakes discussed above. In part, this is because we often drop our guard when we become involved in a research project and don't examine our thinking processes as carefully as we should. There is no "perfect" research project; every kind of research has strong points and weak points, and there are almost always methodological problems that affect what we do and what we find. And then there is the matter of interpreting what we've found; different people may "read" the same data differently. Economists, for example, are notorious for taking the same data about the economy and interpreting them in wildly different ways.

That's why it is always a good idea to have other people look at your research design to see what suggestions they have to make. They may help you avoid making some of the thinking errors that I've discussed in this chapter or other kinds of mistakes I've discussed in the previous chapters. Although you might be able to discover thinking errors in the work of others, it is generally very difficult to see these errors in your own work. We all suffer from this problem—because we are so intimately involved in our research that we don't, or can't, see it objectively. It's a good idea to put your work aside for a short period of time so you can look at it more objectively. You wouldn't want to have your research attacked for appealing to false authorities, overgeneralizing, stacking the deck, making imperfect analogies, arguing on the basis of incorrect assumptions, or any of the other errors I've mentioned.

❖ FURTHER READING

Clayton, C. (2007). *The re-discovery of common sense: A guide to the lost art of critical thinking.* Lincoln, NE: iUniverse.

Conway, D. A., & Munson, R. (1990). *Elements of reasoning.* Belmont, CA: Wadsworth.

Corbett, E. P. J. (1991). *The elements of reasoning.* New York: Macmillan.

Cottrell, S. (2005). *Critical thinking skills.* New York: Palgrave.

Darner, T. E. (1995). *Attacking faulty reasoning: A practical guide to fallacy-free arguments* (3rd ed.). Belmont, CA: Wadsworth.

Dowden, B. H. (1993). *Logical reasoning.* Belmont, CA: Wadsworth.

Kelley, D. (1994). *The art of reasoning* (2nd expanded ed.). New York: Norton.

Kirby, G., & Goodpaster, J. R. (1995). *Thinking.* Englewood Cliffs, NJ: Prentice Hall.

Paul, R., & Elder, L. (2002). *Critical thinking: Tools for: Taking charge of your life.* Upper Saddle River: NJ: Financial Times/Prentice Hall.

Russow, L.-M., & Curd, M. (1989). *Principles of reasoning.* New York: St. Martin's.

Wilson, D. C. (1999). *A guide to good reasoning.* New York: McGraw-Hill.

Icon.

Rules of Good Riting

1. Each pronoun agrees with their antecedent.

2. Just between you and I, case is important.

3. Verbs has to agree with their subject.

4. Watch out for irregular verbs which has cropped up into our language.

5. Don't use no double negatives.

6. A writer mustn't shift your point of view.

7. When dangling, don't use participles.

8. Join clauses good like a conjunction should.

9. And don't use conjunctions to start sentences.

10. Don't write a run-on sentence it is difficult when you got to punctuate it so it makes sense when the reader reads what you wrote.

11. About sentence fragments.

12. In letters themes reports articles and stuff like that we use commas to keep strings apart.

13. Don't use commas, which aren't necessary.

14. Its' important to use apostrophe's right.

15. Don't abbrev.

16. Check to see if you any words out.

17. In my opinion I think that the author when he is writing should not get into the habit of making use of too many unnecessary words which he does not really need.

18. Then, of course, there's that old one: Never use a preposition to end a sentence with.

19. As far as incomplete constructions, they are wrong.

20. Check for speling. (Spell checkers aren't always write.)

21. Last but not least, avoid cliches like the plague.

—From the Canadian Society for Biomechanics Website
(http://www.health.uottawa.ca/biomech/csb/laws/writing.htm)

16

Writing Research Reports

❖   ❖   ❖

After you've done your research, whether it was qualitative or quantitative (or both), you have to write a report on your findings. That is, you have to communicate what you discovered to others. The quality of your writing will play an important role in the way people who read your report respond to your research. It is important that your report be well organized, grammatically correct, and well argued. Writing academic papers can be characterized as writing, in university settings, that observes basic scholarly conventions involving what is appropriate for the content and style of what is written. These matters are discussed below.

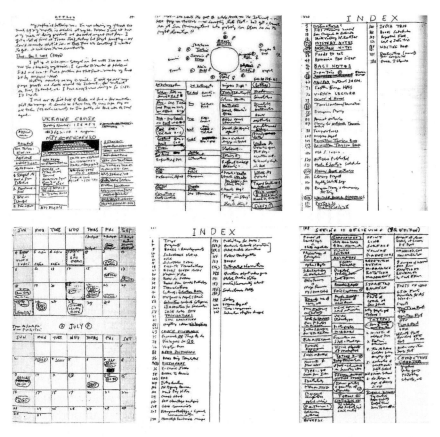

Pages from my journals which I use to plan my books and conduct research.

❖ KEEPING A JOURNAL

In 1956, one of my professors suggested I keep a journal. At the time, the idea struck me as silly. "I don't have anything to write about," I thought. But later that year, for one reason or another, I bought a bound book and started keeping a journal. I use Canson basic sketch books, which cost around six dollars. You can get them at most art supply stores or on the Internet. Since then I have written 88 journals, and this book, like all my other books, actually originated and took shape in my journals. For researchers and writers, journals are invaluable. They are also therapeutic. One reason **personal journals** are useful is that when you are writing in your journals, ideas pop into your head that would disappear if you didn't write them down, and the very act of writing in a journal tends to generate new ideas. On the basis of more than

50 years of keeping a journal, let me offer some suggestions that will help you make them more useful to you.

- The journal must be a bound volume.
- Number all the pages.
- Make the last page an index of the journal.
- Use the first four pages for drawing in monthly calendars.
- Write in dark ink.
- Write the date down for each day's entries.
- Reserve some pages for brainstorming on topics you are working on.
- You can use the bottom of your pages to put down e-mail and URL addresses.

I often draw four lines down a page to use it for brainstorming on some topic. By indicating in the index the page numbers of the topics you deal with on a given page, you can access them more easily. I also like to make little drawings in my journals, every once in a while, to give them more visual interest. You can write about ideas, hopes, thoughts, things that happened to you, and all kinds of other things. In a sense, you are creating a documentary about your life and ideas that you can access in later years. I sometimes use material and ideas in journals I wrote a number of years ago in my writings. You never can tell when an idea will come in handy.

A SHORT THEATRICAL PIECE ON WRITING REPORTS

Grand Inquisitor: *Why force poor, overworked students to write reports on their research? Why not let them dictate their reports on tape cassettes? They could have music in the background, do some rapping . . . it would be cool.*

Arthur: Because the written word lives! You can read over something that's been written and see how good the research is. There's also the matter of the quality of the writing. We live in an increasingly electronic age, but it's still important to be able to write.

(Continued)

(Continued)	
Grand Inquisitor:	*I'm developing a software program. You just tell it what your subject is and it writes the paper. It also takes tests for you.*
Arthur:	We now have programs that automatically grade papers on the quality of the writing and the research.
Grand Inquisitor:	*Are professors really necessary nowadays?*
Arthur:	We're going to be replaced by holograms, Internet courses, and paper-grading machines.
Grand Inquisitor:	*Why not give students degrees when they enter? It would save them a lot of stress.*
Arthur:	Are you, by chance, a university president?

❖ A TRICK FOR ORGANIZING REPORTS

Let me offer an anecdote that has an important moral. A number of years ago, I attended a conference at Stanford University. There were three speakers and a fourth person, a "respondent," who was there to offer his assessment of the research reports that were given. This is a common practice at conferences; the respondent assesses the reports, gives context, offers critiques, and so on.

Before the session started, I noticed him doing what seemed rather strange. He took four sheets of 8.5 × 11-inch paper and folded them in half and tore them so he had eight half sheets of paper. Then he took those sheets and folded them in half and tore them. He did this a few times and ended up with a stack of small slips of paper. One sheet of 8.5 × 11 paper yields 16 slips, so he ended up with 64 little pieces of paper approximately 2 inches × 3 inches in size.

Then, as the various speakers gave their reports, he'd write something down on a slip of paper. I noticed that he used one slip of paper for each idea. After the third speaker had given his report, there was a short break. The respondent spent the time assembling his small slips of paper and then gave a remarkable (since he had so little time to organize his talk) logically structured analysis discussion of the reports he had heard, with comments, criticisms, and suggestions.

The Secret: One Idea Per Slip of Paper

I would suggest that it is a very good idea for writers to use this methodology of one idea per piece of paper for organizing their reports. If you have one idea on a piece of paper, it is easy to take that idea from one location and put it in a different location when you start making your outline for your report. If you have two ideas on a slip of paper, you can't move your ideas around easily.

This notion of one idea on a slip of paper is at the heart of some computer programs designed to help writers organize their ideas. It's much easier to manipulate slips of paper (that is, single ideas) as you plan your report than it is to rewrite a report that is poorly organized. I have used this method of organizing material in many of my books, I might add. After I've got my stack of pieces of paper, I sit down at a table and put them on the table. Then I start trying out different ways of organizing them until I've got what seems to me to be the best way of structuring things.

Of course, as you write, ideas suddenly arise in your head—probably from the unconscious—that have some impact on what you are writing, that help you flesh out ideas or explain them in interesting ways. In *Writing the Australian Crawl,* the poet William Stafford (1978) says that "a writer is not so much someone who has something to say as he is someone who has found a process that will bring about new things he would not have thought of if he had not started to say them" (p. 17). There's no reason why reports of research can't be written in an interesting manner, even if there are some rather formal rules for the way these papers should be organized.

❖ OUTLINES, FIRST DRAFTS, AND REVISIONS

I've already suggested that you use little pieces of papers to organize your thoughts. You can arrange them and rearrange them until you have a logically coherent outline for your paper. Remember that when making an outline, if you have subtopics, you must have at least two of them. That is, if you have an A, you have to have a B. The next important thing to do is write a first draft as quickly as you can and print it out. Then you can start going over it and revising it, because all writing is rewriting. Very few writers get things right the first time, which is why rewriting plays such an important role in writing.

Your revisions should be done on hard copy—that is, print-outs of your first draft. For some reason, it is much better to make revisions on print-outs of written material than on monitor screens. Then, after you've made your revisions to your print-out, you enter your revisions into your draft on the computer and print it out again. You can then revise the second draft print-out and put your new revisions into your article in the computer. As a rule, you should plan on making three revisions of your written work to get it in an acceptable condition. Hemingway is rumored to have rewritten the closing sentence of one of his novels 30 times. You don't have to do that many revisions, but you do need to make at least three revisions.

❖ WRITING RESEARCH REPORTS

When you write your research reports, they conventionally have the following stylistic attributes:

Formal Style. Reports do not use colloquial language and usually generate an air of seriousness about themselves.

Third Person. Reports are written in the third person (one) rather than the first person singular (*I*), although some journals are much more casual about things nowadays.

Gender-Neutral Language. Reports use gender-neutral language. This is most easily accomplished by avoiding *he* and *she* and using the plural.

Awkward: Each respondent took his or her questionnaire . . .

Better: The respondents took their questionnaires . . .

Transitions to Guide Readers. Transitions are important guides to readers in that they cue them in to what is coming. The chart below lists some of the more important kinds of transitions:

Causes	Effects	Sequences	Meaning
Because	Therefore	First	We understand
This leads to	As a result	Next	This suggests
Since	Accordingly	Finally	This implies
Examples	**Contrasts**	**Conclusions**	**Time Relations**
For example	But	Therefore	Before
For instance	Nevertheless	Thus	After
To show this	In contrast	We find, then	At the same time

Active Voice. Some writers use the passive voice to give their research an air of authority, but I think the passive voice, which uses some form of the verb "to be," tends to deaden the prose rather than enliven it.

Active voice: We *found* in our research . . .

Passive voice: It *was discovered* by us in our research . . .

What gives research authority is the quality of the thinking and of the research, not using the passive voice.

Verb Usage. In writing your reports, it is important that you follow the conventions that exist about which verb tense should be used in each part of the report. Let me suggest you do the following:

Part of Report	Verb Tense to Use
Review of literature in introduction	Past
Discussion of procedures followed	Past
Discussion of meaning of research	Present
Discussion of future research	Future

These rules about verb tense usage are conventions that most researchers follow when describing their research in a report.

Jargon. Do not use jargon (that is, highly specialized terms) to the extent that this is possible. A good way to do this is to write for an imaginary audience of readers who are intelligent but who do not have any expertise or knowledge about the subject you are writing on. Define all terms that might be difficult for your readers and avoid abbreviations and acronyms (words formed from the initial letters of a name, such as NATO).

Undeveloped Writing. Undeveloped writing lacks detail and color. It tends to be vague and overly general, written at a very high level of abstraction. You can avoid this style by doing things such as offering examples, by defining terms you are using, by dealing with causes and effects of the phenomena you discuss, and by contrasting and comparing things.

❖ THE IMRD STRUCTURE OF QUANTITATIVE RESEARCH REPORTS

Conventionally, quantitative research reports are divided into four sections: an introduction, a description of the methodology that was employed, a report on the findings, and a discussion section. I will explain what we find in each section. Qualitative research reports can employ this design as well.

Introduction. In this section, we offer our readers a discussion of the background of the study, deal with why we made the study or conducted the research and why it is relevant, and generally, offer a brief review of relevant literature on the subject. (See Chapter 2 on library searches to get details on this topic.) It is customary to offer a statement of your hypothesis in this section and to deal with theories and research that have led you to make your hypothesis. The introduction, then, supplies a sense of context for readers and locates the research in a general area of knowledge. It also provides readers with information that will help them understand the report.

Method. This section deals with the design of the research or with the methodology employed in the research. It is detailed and very specific for two reasons: first, so your readers will see exactly what you did and, second, so your research can be replicated. It is important that research methods be described so other researchers can replicate your research should they wish to do so—perhaps because your findings are remarkable or they conflict with previous research on the same subject. In other words, in the method section, you deal with the operationalization (the activities carried out) in your research. You delineate the methods you are using to prove (or disprove) your hypothesis or discover answers to questions you have raised. You have to define all your terms carefully and describe how you went about collecting your data and answering the research question you posed for yourself in the introduction.

What follows is a list of things you might be doing that require an explanation and elaboration in your methodology section:

- Are you testing a theory?

- Are you testing competing theories?

- Are you testing a methodology?

- Are you replicating a study to test its findings?

- Are you trying to correct earlier research you did that had problems such as inconsistent results?

- Are you trying to find the answer to some question of interest?

- Are you trying to solve some social or political problem?

This section is often long and very detailed and usually draws the careful scrutiny of readers, because your methodology is of crucial importance. If people can find flaws in your methodology, your findings will be considered useless. Many battles between different kinds or schools of scholars involve conflicting ideas about methodological matters.

Results. The findings are reported in the results section. If you have numerical data, it is a good idea to present them in the form of charts and graphs in which results and relationships are easy to see. Usually, the results section is fairly brief because it doesn't take as much space to report what you found as it does to describe how you found what you found.

In this section, you offer your data and your analysis of these data. In addition, you discuss your results and their relation to your data.

Discussion. In this section, you discuss what you found, talk about any problems you faced in doing the research, describe any unexpected things that happened, deal with the relation between your findings and research by other scholars, offer suggestions for those doing research in the same area, and mention plans you might have for future research.

Here are some questions to consider for your discussion:

- Was your hypothesis supported by your research?

- Can you generalize from your findings?

- Were the questions you asked yourself at the beginning of your research answered?

- Did your findings lead you to ask other questions that might require new research?

- Were there ethical problems that presented themselves in your research? Or did your findings lead to ethical problems?

You may think of other questions to consider in addition to those listed above.

For good examples of the IMRD structure, see these articles: "Playing Violent Video and Computer Games and the Adolescent Self-Concept" (Funk & Buchman, 1996) and "Sexual Humor on Freud as Expressed in Limericks" (Kantha, 1999).

❖ WRITING CORRECTLY: AVOIDING SOME COMMON PROBLEMS

Your report may be well organized, but it is also crucial that your writing be grammatically correct. If you write a report full of spelling errors, punctuation errors, and unclear and awkward passages, your credibility as a researcher will be very suspect. Here are some of the most common errors people make when they write.

Awkwardness. Awkward passages are ungainly and stiff and are not well formed. For example, "The humanity of the death penalty is a problem that has long been a debate in many societies." Writing that uses the same sentence structure over and over again is also considered awkward.

Coherence Problems. Your sentences should flow together, using transitions to guide your readers. Short sentences that follow one after another, without transitions—that is, choppy writing—is sometimes called "Primer Style" writing. An example follows.

> My research involved making a content analysis. I selected some comic books to study. I decided to look for how much violence was in the comics I chose. I had trouble defining violence.

You can see that the writer offers a string of short, simple sentences with no transitions between them.

Dashes and Hyphens. Many writers mistake dashes for hyphens.

Dash:—

Hyphen: -

A dash (—) is made of two hyphens. Hyphens are used to link compound words (son-in-law) and cannot be used as dashes. Dashes are used to suggest a pause in a sentence that is longer than a comma or to set off an important phrase.

Comma Faults. Commas cannot be used to set off two independent clauses (that is, two complete ideas). You must use a semicolon or make some other kind of a change, such as inserting a transition. For example:

Comma fault: John loved research, he really enjoyed interviews.

Correct: John loved research; he really enjoyed interviews.

Correct: John loved research because he really enjoyed interviews.

Fragments. In writing reports, you must make sure that you use complete sentences and do not have sentence fragments—incomplete thoughts that you think are sentences. In other kinds of writing, such as personal essays, you can use fragments to emphasize things as long as you know what you are doing and use fragments rarely.

Fragment: You've learned about research. *But wait!*

Padding or Wordiness. This is writing that is too wordy, that uses many words in some passages where just a few words would do the same thing.

Wordy: I am of the opinion that . . .

Correct: I think . . . or I believe . . .

Spelling Errors. If you are not certain about the way a word is spelled, you should check its spelling in the dictionary. Spell checkers in computer programs are useful, but sometimes they make mistakes in that they don't recognize that a word that is spelled correctly doesn't fit in the sentence in which it is found.

Following is a table of some of the most common errors writers make.

Word	Function	Example
To	Connective	I'm going to Paris . . .
Too	Excess	Too many errors . . .
Two	Number	You made two errors . . .

(Continued)

(Continued)

Their	Possession	They took their books . . .
There	Place	Are you going there?
They're	They + are	They're too snobbish . . .
Who's	Who + is	Who's coming to the party?
Whose	Possession	Whose radio is that?
Its	Possession	The car lost its power . . .
It's	It + is	It's too late for tears . . .

Its causes many problems because it doesn't follow the rule usually found for possession in which possession is indicated by *'s*. *Its* is an anomaly, an exception. I should also point out that none of the possessive pronouns (his, her, mine, theirs, ours, yours, its) uses an apostrophe.

Clarity Problems. Passages that readers find hard to understand, for one reason or another, are described as unclear. They are usually ambiguous and sometimes unintelligible. Frequently, these passages are also awkward and full of grammatical mistakes. One reason people write unclearly is that they know in their minds what they mean, but they don't express what they know in their writing. Another reason people write unclearly is that their thinking is unclear. It's an excellent idea to read your paper aloud (or have someone else read it to you). This will help you catch awkward and unclear passages and recognize ideas that need development or clarification (or both).

Pronoun Reference Problems. A pronoun is a word used in place of a noun or another pronoun that precedes it. The first rule about pronouns is that there must be agreement between pronouns and their antecedents in number. For example, the term *everyone* is singular and takes a *his* or a *her* and not a *their* in the sentences in which *everyone* is used. The second rule about pronouns is that they refer to the noun or pronoun that immediately precedes them. If this rule is not followed, bizarre things can happen. For example, the following sentence involves incorrect pronoun reference:

Clutching his fried chicken, Bill got in his car, and proceeded to eat it.

As written, the *it* here refers to the car, not the chicken. The sentence would have to be reconstructed for it to make sense. A suitable revision of the sentence would be this:

Bill got in his car clutching his fried chicken and started eating it.

Repetitiveness. Some writers seem to know only one construction for a sentence, and when you read their reports, almost every sentence has the same basic structure. You must vary the structure of your sentences so you don't bore your readers. Also, you should vary their length. If all of your sentences have the same structure and are all the same length, people will find what you have written to be tedious and monotonous. You've got to consider the rhythm of your writing.

Verb Agreement Problems. Verbs have to agree with their subjects. A singular subject takes a singular form of a verb. A plural subject takes a plural verb.

I love Mary.	We love Mary.
You love Mary.	You love Mary.
He/she loves Mary.	They love Mary.

❖ MORE ON ACADEMIC WRITING STYLES

Because of scholarly journal requirements, many scholars incorporate their literature reviews into their articles, using parentheses and the names of authors and dates of their publications, as the following example show. This passage is taken from an article "Living on the Edge" by Robert McKercher and Candace Fu. It appeared in a 2006 issue of the *Annals of Tourism Research,* one of the most important journals in the field of tourism studies:

> Much of the published material on tourism and the periphery has focused on Fringe destinations such as Pacific Islands, arctic regions, or rural communities (Brown and Hall 2000; Gets and Nilsoon 2003; Hall 1994; Pearce 2002; Prideaux 2002; Wanhill 1995; Weaver 1998). Only a few studies have examined the periphery of existing destinations. These have explored such themes as attributes-based approaches toward periphality (Pearce 2002), residents' perceptions of the rural urban fringe (Weaver and Lawton 2001) and the periphery as a possible urban ecotourism venue (Dwyer and Edwards).

This style of using parentheses to cite relevant articles turns these scholarly articles, in a sense, into annotated bibliographies and makes the articles difficult to read. But these citations demonstrate that an author is up-to-date on the relevant literature and provide a service to readers by offering citations on articles of importance. Papers by students do not need to adopt this style of writing.

❖ A CHECKLIST FOR PLANNING RESEARCH AND WRITING REPORTS ON YOUR RESEARCH

This checklist draws on one found in a guidebook for student anthropologists edited by Conrad Kottak (1982, p. 33), *Researching American Culture*, and other works:

- Choosing your topic for research
    - —Find a subject that you are interested in and that can be researched in the time period available to you.
    - —Narrow your topic as much as you can. The narrower your focus, the better chance you have of being able to do your research.
- Designing your research project
    - —Determine what topic you'll be investigating or what group of people you'll be studying.
    - —Figure out how to obtain a representative sampling of textual material (for content analyses, for example) or a representative group of people (for surveys) or a place to be observed (for participant observations).
- Determining the appropriate method for doing your project
    - —For textual analysis, consider semiotic analysis, ideological analysis, rhetorical analysis, content analysis, or some combination of these methods.
    - —For subcultural group analysis, consider participation observation.
    - —For opinion and attitude research, consider interviewing, questionnaires, and surveys and focus groups.
    - —For field studies, consider ethnomethodology, participant observation, and interviewing.
    - —For events in the past, consider historical analysis and content analysis.
    - —For studying human behavior, consider experimentation and literature searches of the topic you are investigating.
- Organizing your data for presentation
    - —Put quantitative data into charts and tables.

—Use qualitative data to support or reject an argument or affirm some position or thesis.

- Using the correct format for your reports

  —Use the IMRD structure described above.

  —Make sure you give a detailed bibliography of your sources following whatever style your instructor requires. (When doing research, it is vital to write down all the bibliographic information you might need for your references. The best way to do this is to use an index card for each reference or approximate index cards on the computer.)

❖ CONCLUSIONS

The material discussed in this chapter is meant to guide you both in conceptualizing your research and in writing up your findings. There is a connection between thinking and writing: The quality of your writing reflects the quality of your thinking—and your knowledge of the rules of grammar is a key component of your writing.

The rules of grammar can be thought of as being similar in nature to the rules of the road. If you don't know what a stop sign means or a red light means or which side of the road to drive on, you'll cause all kinds of confusion and chaos when you're driving and probably won't live very long. You have to know the rules of the road (and the laws in the particular state you're driving in) to drive, and you have to know the rules of grammar to communicate with others clearly and effectively.

You must write correctly if your readers are to take your research seriously. It's a shame the way some students do excellent research and then write reports full of spelling mistakes, punctuation mistakes, and grammatical errors that make readers question their findings and their intelligence, as well. Some students think that just because their papers *look* good—that is, the quality of the printing is good and they've used some attractive typefaces—that their papers *are* good. That isn't the case. It isn't the quality of the uniforms of a football or baseball team that's important; it's the quality of the players wearing the uniforms.

The moral of this little disquisition is to be very careful about the correctness of your writing. It's a good idea to use your spell checker and your grammar checker if you are using a computer and have a word processor that has these features. *You must use the dictionary to look up the correct spelling for any word that you don't know, because the spell checker misses things.* Probably the best book (and also the shortest, at

92 pages) that will help you learn to write correctly is Strunk and White's (1999) *Elements of Style*. It is a classic work.

It also is a good idea to print out your research paper and make your corrections on the hard copy. That is what professional writers do. Then transfer your corrections from the hard copy to your diskette. (You cannot do a good job of revising a paper on your monitor; it simply doesn't work. You're more likely to catch errors when you look at hard copy, and you need to see what the printed pages look like so you can correct spacing and formatting problems.) If you repeat this process a few times, your reports will be much better. You must assume that you'll need to write several drafts to do a good job of writing up your findings.

❖ FURTHER READING

Ballinger, B. (1999). *The curious researcher: A guide to writing research papers* (2nd rev. ed.). Boston: Allyn & Bacon.

Barzun, J., & Graff, H. (1992). *The modern researcher* (5th ed.). Boston: Houghton Mifflin.

Becker, H. S. (1986). *Writing for social scientists: How to start and finish your thesis, book, or article.* Chicago: University of Chicago Press.

Berger, A. A. (1993). *Improving writing skills: Memos, letters, reports, and proposals.* Newbury Park, CA: Sage.

Berger, A. A. (2008). *The academic writer's toolkit: A user's manual.* Walnut Creek, CA: Left Coast Press.

Ellison, C. (2010). *McGraw-Hill's concise guide to writing research papers.* New York: McGraw-Hill.

Emerson, R. M., Fretz, R. L., & Shaw, L. L. (1995). *Writing ethnographic fieldnotes.* Chicago: University of Chicago Press.

Harvey, M. (2003). *The nuts and bolts of academic writing.* Indianapolis, IN: Hackett.

Lamott, A. (1995). *Bird by bird: Some instructions on writing and life.* New York: Anchor.

Lesley, J. D., Jr. (1998). *The essential guide to writing research papers.* White Plains, NY: Longman.

Queneau, R. (1981). *Exercises in style.* New York: New Directions.

Rivers, W. L., & Harrington, S. L. (1988). *Finding facts: Research writing across the curriculum.* Englewood Cliffs, NJ: Prentice Hall.

Strunk, W., Jr., & White, E. B. (1999). *Elements of style* (4th ed.). New York: Macmillan.

Turabian, K. (2010). *Student's guide for writing college papers* (4th ed.). Chicago: University of Chicago Press.

Williams, J. M. (1990). *Style: Toward clarity and grace.* Chicago: University of Chicago Press.

References

Adatto, K. (1993). *Picture perfect: The art and artifice of public image making*. New York: Basic Books.

Alasuutari, P. (1995). *Researching culture: Qualitative method and cultural studies*. Thousand Oaks, CA: Sage.

Allen, H. (1991). Everything you wanted to know about specs. *San Francisco Chronicle*. (Reprinted from the *Washington Post*)

Barthes, R. (1972). *Mythologies* (A. Lavers, Trans.). New York: Hill & Wang.

Barzun, J., & Graff, H. F. (1957). *The modern researcher*. New York: Harcourt, Brace & Company.

Berger, A. A. (1975). *The TV-guided American*. New York: Walker & Co.

Berger, A. A. (Ed.). (1989a). *Political culture and public opinion*. New Brunswick, NJ: Transaction Books.

Berger, A. A. (1989b). *Seeing is believing: An introduction to visual communication*. Mountain View, CA: Mayfield.

Berger, A. A. (1990). *Agitpop: Political culture and communication theory*. New Brunswick, NJ: Transaction Books.

Berger, A. A. (Ed.). (1991). *Media USA: Process and effect* (2nd ed.). White Plains, NY: Longman.

Berger, A. A. (1992). *Popular culture genres*. Newbury Park, CA: Sage.

Berger, A. A. (1994). *Cultural criticism: A primer of key concepts*. Thousand Oaks, CA: Sage.

Berger, A. A. (1995). *Essentials of mass communication theory*. Thousand Oaks, CA: Sage.

Berger, A. A. (1997). *Postmortem for a postmodernist*. Walnut Creek, CA: AltaMira.

Berger, A. A. (Ed.). (1998). *The postmodern presence*. Walnut Creek, CA: AltaMira.

Berger, A. A. (1999). *Signs in contemporary culture: An introduction to semiotics* (2nd ed.). Salem, WI: Sheffield.

Berger, A. A. (2007). *Ads, fads, & consumer culture* (3rd ed.). New York: Rowman & Littlefield.

Berger, J. (1972). *Ways of seeing*. London: British Broadcasting System and Penguin Books.

Berkhofer, R. F., Jr. (1969). *A behavioral approach to historical analysis*. New York: Free Press.

Bernard, H. R. (1994). *Research methods in anthropology: Qualitative and quantitative approaches* (2nd ed.). Walnut Creek, CA: AltaMira.

Best, S., & Kellner, D. (1991). *Postmodern theory: Critical interrogations.* New York: Guilford.

Bogdan, R. C., & Biklen, S. K. (1992). *Qualitative research in education: An introduction to theory and methods.* Boston: Allyn & Bacon.

Braudel, F. (1981). *The structures of everyday life: Civilization and capitalism, 15th–18th century* (Vol. 1). New York: Harper & Row.

Brenner, C. (1974). *An elementary textbook of psychoanalysis.* Garden City, NY: Doubleday.

Brewer, J., & Hunter, A. (1989). *Multimethod research: A synthesis of styles.* Newbury Park, CA: Sage.

Cashmore, E., & Rojek, C. (1999). *Dictionary of cultural theorists.* New York: Oxford University Press.

Certeau, M. (1984). *The practice of everyday life* (S. Rendall, Trans.). Berkeley: University of California Press.

Chase, M. (1982, June 16). Your suit is pressed, hair neat, but what do your molars say? *Wall Street Journal,* p. 1.

Cirksena, K. (1987). Politics and difference: Radical feminist epistemological premises for communication studies. *Journal of Communication Inquiry, 11*(1), 19–28.

Creswell, J. W. (1994). *Research design: Qualitative and quantitative approaches.* Thousand Oaks, CA: Sage.

Culler, J. (1976). *Structuralist poetics: Structuralism, linguistics, and the study of literature.* New York: Cornell University Press.

Culler, J. (1986). *Ferdinand de Saussure* (Rev. ed.). Ithaca, NY: Cornell University Press.

Dickey, M. (2006, April 27). Resources and tips for conducting online surveys. *The Chronicle of Philanthropy.* Retrieved February 10, 2010, from http://philanthropy.com/article/ResourseTips-for/52521

Dominick, J. R. (1993). *The dynamics of mass communication* (4th ed.). New York: McGraw-Hill.

Dundes, A. (1968). Introduction. In V. Propp, *The morphology of the folktale* (2nd ed., L. A. Wagner, Ed.; L. Scott, Trans.). Austin: University of Texas Press. (Original work published in 1928)

Eco, U. (1976). *A theory of semiotics.* Bloomington: Indiana University Press.

Ekman, P., & Sejnowski, T. J. (1992, August 1). *Facial expression understanding.* Report to the National Science Foundation, Arlington, VA. Retrieved July 14, 2005, from http://face-and-emotion.com/dataface/nsfrept/exec_summary.html

Eidelberg, L. (1968). *Encyclopedia of psychoanalysis.* New York: Free Press.

Freud, S. (1953). *A general introduction to psychoanalysis.* Garden City, NY: Doubleday.

Freud, S. (1963a). The antithetical sense of primal words. In *Character and culture: Vol. 9. The collected works* (P. Rieff, Ed.). New York: Collier. (Original work published 1910)

Freud, S. (1963b). *Character and culture: Vol. 9. The collected works* (P. Rieff, Ed.). New York: Collier. (Original work published 1910)

Freud, S. (1965a). *The interpretation of dreams.* New York: Avon. (Original work published in 1900)

Freud, S. (1965b). *New introductory lectures on psychoanalysis* (J. Strachey, Ed. & Trans.). New York: Norton.

Funk, J. B., & Buchman, D. D. (1996). Playing violent video and computer games and the adolescent self-concept. *Journal of Communication, 46*(2), 19–32.

Garfinkel, H. (1967). *Studies in ethnomethodology.* Englewood Cliffs, NJ: Prentice Hall.

Gerbner, G. (with Signorielli, N). (1988). *Violence and terror in the mass media: An annotated bibliography.* Lanham, MD: UNIPUB (distributor).

Gibaldi, J. (1995). *MLA handbook for writers of research papers* (4th ed.). New York: Modern Language Association of America.

Girard, R. (1991). *A theater of envy: William Shakespeare.* New York: Oxford University Press.

Grotjahn, M. (1957). *Beyond laughter.* New York: McGraw-Hill.

Hinsie, L. E., & Campbell, R. J. (1970). *Psychiatric dictionary* (4th ed.). New York: Oxford University Press.

Houston, B. (1996). *Computer assisted reporting.* New York: St. Martin's.

Ionesco, E. (1958). *The bald soprano.* In *Four Plays by Eugene Ionesco* (D. M. Allen, Trans.). New York: Grove.

Jameson, F. (1991). *Postmodernism; or, The cultural logic of late capitalism.* Durham, NC: Duke University Press.

Jung, C. G. (with von Franz, M.-L., Henderson, J. L., Jacobi, J., & Jaffe, A.). (1968). *Man and his symbols.* Garden City, NY: Doubleday.

Kantha, S. S. (1999). Sexual humor on Freud as expressed in limericks. *Humor, 12*(3), 288–299.

Kottak, C. (1982). *Researching American culture.* Ann Arbor: University of Michigan Press.

Lakoff, G., & Johnson, M. (1980). *Metaphors we live by.* Chicago: University of Chicago Press.

Lazere, D. (1977). Mass culture, political consciousness and English studies. *College English, 38,* 755–756.

Lifton, R. (1974). Who is more dry? Heroes of Japanese youth. In A. Berger (Ed.), *About man.* Dayton, OH: Pflaum.

Lotman, J. M. (1977). *The structure of the artistic text.* Ann Arbor: Michigan Slavic Contributions.

Lowenthal, L. (1944). Biographies in popular magazines. In P. F. Lazarsfeld & F. N. Stanton (Eds.), *Radio research 1942–1943.* New York: Essential Books.

Lyotard, J.-F. (1984). *The postmodern condition: A report on knowledge* (G. Bennington & B. Massumi, Trans.). Minneapolis: University of Minnesota Press.

Malinowski, B. (1961). *Argonauts of the Western Pacific.* New York: E. P. Dutton.

Mannheim, K. (1936). *Ideology and Utopia: An introduction to the sociology of knowledge* (L. Wirth & E. Shils, Trans.). New York: Harcourt Brace.

Marx, K. (1964). *Selected writings in sociology and social philosophy* (T. B. Bottomore & M. Rubel, Eds.; T. B. Bottomore, Trans.). New York: McGraw-Hill.

McKeon, R. (Ed.). (1941). *The basic works of Aristotle.* New York: Random House.

McKercher, R., & Fu, C. (2006). Living on the edge. *Annals of Tourism Research, 33*(2), 508–524.

McQuail, D., & Windahl, S. (1993). *Communication models for the study of mass communication* (2nd ed.). New York: Longman.

Medhurst, M. J., & Benson, T. W. (Eds.). (1984). *Rhetorical dimensions in media: A critical casebook.* Dubuque, IA: Kendall/Hunt.

Messaris, P. (1994). *Visual literacy: Image, mind and reality.* Boulder, CO: Westview.

Milgram, S. (1965). Liberating effects of group pressure. *Journal of Personality and Social Psychology, 1,* 127–134.

Mitchell, A. (1983). *The nine American lifestyles: Who we are & where we are going.* New York: Warner Books.

Mitchell, S., & Black, M. J. (1996). *Freud and beyond: A history of modern psychoanalytic thought.* New York: Basic Books.

Mueller, C. (1973). *The politics of communication: A study in the political sociology of language, socialization and legitimation.* New York: Oxford University Press.

Musil, R. (1965). *The man without qualities* (Vol. 1). New York: Capricorn.

Nietzsche, F. (1987). *The will to power* (B. Hollingdale & W. Kauffman, Trans.). New York: Random House.

Phifer, G. (1961). The historical approach. In C. W. Dow (Ed.), *An introduction to graduate study in speech and theatre.* East Lansing: Michigan State University Press.

Pines, M. (1982, October 13). How they know what you really mean. *San Francisco Chronicle.*

Propp, V. (1968). *The morphology of the folktale* (2nd ed., L. A. Wagner, Ed.; L. Scott, Trans.). Austin: University of Texas Press. (Original work published in 1928)

Radway, J. (1991). *Reading the romance: Women, patriarchy and popular literature.* Chapel Hill: University of North Carolina Press.

Rapaille, C. (2006). *The culture code: An ingenious way to understand why people around the world live and buy as they do.* New York: Broadway Books.

Riessman, C. K. (1993). *Narrative analysis.* Thousand Oaks, CA: Sage.

Root, R. L., Jr. (1987). *The rhetorics of popular culture: Advertising, advocacy, and entertainment.* New York: Greenwood.

Said, E. W. (1978). *Orientalism.* New York: Pantheon.

Saussure, F. (1966). *A course in general linguistics* (W. Baskin, Trans.). New York: McGraw-Hill.

Schellenberg, J. A. (1974). *An introduction to social psychology* (2nd ed.). New York: Random House.

Sebeok, T. A. (Ed.). (1977). *A perfusion of signs.* Bloomington: Indiana University Press.

Sherman, B. (1995). *Telecommunications management: Broadcasting/cable and the new technologies* (2nd ed.). New York: McGraw-Hill.

Solow, M. (1991). The case of the closet target. In A. A. Berger (Ed.), *Media USA: Process and effects* (2nd ed.). New York: Longman.

Stafford, W. (1978). *Writing the Australian crawl: View on the writer's vocation.* Ann Arbor: University of Michigan Press.

Steeves, H. L., & Smith, M. C. (1987). Class and gender in prime-time television entertainment: Observations from a socialist feminist perspective. *Journal of Communication Inquiry, 11*(1), 43–63.

Strunk, W., Jr., & White, E. B. (1999). *Elements of style* (4th ed.). New York: Macmillan.

Thompson, M., Ellis, R., & Wildavsky, A. (1990). *Cultural theory.* Boulder, CO: Westview.

Turner, R. (Ed.). (1974). *Ethnomethodology.* Baltimore, MD: Penguin.

Watson, J., & Hill, A. (1997). *A dictionary of communication and media studies* (4th ed.). New York: Arnold.

Wildavsky, A. (1982). *Conditions for a pluralist democracy, or cultural pluralism means more than one political culture in a country.* Unpublished manuscript, University of California–Berkeley, Department of Political Science.

Winick, C. (1995). *Desexualization in American life.* New Brunswick, NJ: Transaction.

Wiseman, J. P., & Aron, M. S. (1970). *Field projects for sociology students.* Cambridge, MA: Schenkman.

Wright, C. R. (1986). *Mass communication: A sociological perspective* (3rd ed.). New York: Random House.

Zaltman, G. (2003). *How customers think: Essential insights into the mind of the market.* Cambridge, MA: Harvard Business School Press.

Zeman, J. J. (1977). Peirce's theory of signs. In T. A. Sebeok (Ed.), *A perfusion of signs.* Bloomington: Indiana University Press.

Zito, G. V. (1975). *Methodology and meanings: Varieties of sociological inquiry.* New York: Praeger.

Glossary

Aberrant decoding This refers to the notion that audiences decode or interpret texts in ways that differ from the ways the creators of these texts expect them to be decoded. Aberrant decoding is the rule rather than the exception when it comes to the mass media, according to the semiotician Umberto Eco.

Aesthetics When applied to the media, aesthetics involves the way technical matters such as lighting, sound, music, kinds of shots and camera work, editing, and related matters in texts affect the way members of audiences react to texts.

Archetype According to Jung, archetypes are images found in dreams, myths, works of art, and religions all over the world. They are not transmitted by culture but are passed on, somehow, genetically, in a collective unconscious. We are not conscious of them directly, but they reveal themselves in our dreams and works of art. One of the most important archetypes is the hero.

Artist We will consider an artist to be not only someone who does paintings or sculptures or plays musical instruments but anyone involved in the creation or performance of a text.

Attitudes An *attitude*, as social psychologists use the term, refers to a relatively enduring state of mind in a person about some phenomenon or aspect of experience. Generally, attitudes are either positive or negative, have direction, and involve thoughts, feelings, and behaviors (tied to these attitudes).

Audience Audiences are generally defined as collections of individuals who watch a television program, listen to a radio program, or attend a film or some kind of artistic performance (symphony, rock band concert, etc.). The members of the audience may be together in one room or scattered or, in the case of television, each watching from his or her own set. In technical terms, audiences are addressees who receive mediated texts sent by some addresser.

Binary oppositions   According to the linguist Roman Jakobson, seeing things in terms of binary oppositions (hot/cold, on/off) is the fundamental way humans find meaning in the world. Oppositions are different from negations. Healthy/sick is an opposition; healthy/unhealthy is a negation.

Broadcast   We use the term to deal with texts that are made available over wide areas by using radio or television signals. Broadcasting differs from other forms of distributing texts such as cablecasting, which uses cables, and satellite transmission, which requires "dishes" to capture signals sent by the satellites.

Class   From a linguistic standpoint, a class is any group of things that have something in common. We use it to refer to social classes or, more literally, socioeconomic classes: groups of people who differ in terms of income and lifestyle. Marxist theorists argue that there is a ruling class that shapes the ideas of the proletariat, the working classes.

Codes   Codes are systems of symbols, letters, words, sounds, whatever . . . that generate meaning. Language, for example, is a code. It uses combinations of letters that we call words to mean certain things. The relation between the word and the thing the word stands for is arbitrary, based on convention. In some cases, the term *code* is used to describe hidden meanings and disguised communication.

Cognitive dissonance   The term *dissonance* refers to sounds that clash with one another. According to psychologists, people wish to avoid ideas that challenge the ones they hold, that create conflict and other disagreeable feelings. Cognitive dissonance refers to ideas that conflict with ones that people hold and generate psychological anxiety and displeasure.

Communication   There are many different ways of understanding and using this term. For our purposes, communication is a process that involves the transmission of messages from senders to receivers. We often make a distinction between communication using language, verbal communication, and communication using facial expressions, body language, and other means, or nonverbal communication.

Communications   The plural of the term refers to what is communicated in contrast to the process of communication, described above.

Concept   We will understand concept to be a general idea or notion that explains or helps us understand some phenomenon or phenomena. I make a distinction in this book between theories, concepts, and the application of concepts.

Connotations   This term deals with the ideas or cultural meanings associated with a term, an object, or some phenomenon. *Connotation* comes from the Latin term *connotare*, "to mark along with." It is different from *denotation*, which refers to the literal meaning of a term.

Content analysis   This is a methodology for obtaining statistical data from a collection of texts that are similar in some respect. Content analysis is a nonintrusive way of conducting research.

Control group   In experiments, the control group is left alone and doesn't experience any kind of intervention, in contrast to the experimental group, to whom something is done. Then the two groups are compared to see whether there are significant differences found in the experimental group, which can then be attributed to the intervention.

Cultural imperialism (also media imperialism)   This theory describes the flow of media products (such as songs, films, and television programs) and popular culture from the United States and a few other capitalist countries in Western Europe to the Third World. Along with these texts and popular culture, it is alleged that values and beliefs (and bourgeois capitalist ideology) are also being transmitted, leading to the domination of these people.

Cultural studies   This is a multidisciplinary approach (using concepts from literary theory, semiotic theory, sociology, psychoanalytic theory, political theory, and other social sciences and humanities) to analyze and interpret phenomena such as the media, popular culture, literature, social movements, and related matters.

Culture   There are hundreds of different definitions of this term. Generally speaking, from the anthropological perspective, it involves the transmission from generation to generation of specific ideas, arts, customary beliefs, ways of living, behavior patterns, institutions, and values. When applied to the arts, it is generally used to specify "elite" kinds of art works, such as operas, poetry, classical music, and serious novels.

Culture codes   According to Clotaire Rapaille, young children from the time they are born until they are age 7 become "imprinted" with certain codes that are distinctive to where they grow up, and these codes shape their tastes, behavior, and attitudes.

Data (plural of datum)   Data are conventionally understood to be forms of information, frequently of a numerical nature, that can be organized and tabulated and used as the basis for decision making.

Defense mechanisms   These are methods used by the ego to defend itself against pressures from the id or impulsive elements in the psyche and superego elements such as conscience and guilt. Some of the more common defense mechanisms are repression (barring unconscious instinctual wishes, memories, etc. from consciousness), regression (returning to earlier stages in one's development), ambivalence (a simultaneous feeling of love and hate for some person), and rationalization (offering excuses to justify one's actions).

Demographics   Demographics refers to similarities found in selected groups of people in terms of matters such as race, religion, gender, social class, ethnicity, occupation, place of residence, and age.

Denotation   When we give the literal or explicit meaning of a word or a description of an object, we give its denotation. Denotation is the opposite of connotation (see above), which deals with the cultural meanings of a term or object.

Desexualization   The argument by Charles Winick and others that differences between males and females are lessening, with men getting weaker and women getting stronger and that American society is becoming desexualized—that is, the sexes are losing their distinctive characteristics and a unisex culture is evolving.

Ego   In Freud's theory of the psyche, the ego functions as the executant of the id and as a mediator between the id and the superego. The ego is involved with the perception of reality and the adaptation to reality.

Emotive functions   According to Roman Jakobson, messages have a number of functions. One of them is the emotive function, which involves expressing feelings by the sender of a message. (Other functions are referential and poetic.)

Ethnomethodology   A branch of sociology that studies the everyday activities of people, seeing these activities as phenomena worth investigating in their own right. The focus is on how people make sense of the world and on commonsense attitudes, as revealed in conversation and behavior.

Evidence   As defined in this book, evidence is material that a reasonable person would find worth considering that supports some contention or theory. Evidence can be qualitative or quantitative.

Facial expression   According to Paul Ekman, a psychologist who is an authority on the subject, there are eight universal facial expressions showing emotions: anger, determination, disgust, fear, neutral (no expression), pouting, sadness, and surprise. He developed a Facial Action Coding System that deals with the 43 muscles in the human face that are used to show emotions.

False consciousness   In Marxist thought, false consciousness refers to mistaken ideas that people have about their class, status, and economic possibilities. These ideas help maintain the status quo and are of great use to the ruling class, which wants to avoid changes in the social structure. Marx argued that the ideas of the ruling class are always the ruling ideas in society.

Feminist criticism   Feminist criticism focuses on the roles given to women and the way they are portrayed in general in texts of all kinds. Feminist critics argue that women are typically used as sexual objects and are portrayed stereotypically in texts, and this has negative effects on both men and women.

Focal points   These refer to the five general topics or subject areas we can concentrate on in dealing with mass communication: (a) the work of art or text, (b) the artist, (c) the audience, (d) America or the society, and (e) the media.

Focus groups   Focus groups involve relatively small numbers of people, usually around 8 or 10 people, who are selected to participate in group discussions on topics of interest to marketers. They have been criticized for not getting at people's deepest thoughts and feelings and for providing ideas that have little of value to the companies paying for the focus groups.

Functional   In sociological thought, the term *functional* refers to the contribution an institution makes to the maintenance of society. Something functional helps maintain the system in which it is found.

Gender   This term refers to the sexual category of an individual, masculine or feminine, and to behavioral traits connected with each category.

Genre   *Genre* is a French term that means "kind" or "class." As we use the term, it refers to the kind of formulaic texts found in the mass media: soap operas, news shows, sport programs, horror shows, detective programs, and so on. I have dealt with this topic at length in my book, *Popular Culture Genres* (A. A. Berger, 1992).

Grid-Group theory   Based on the work of social anthropologist Mary Douglas, this theory argues that in modern societies, there are four mutually antagonistic lifestyles that shape people's choices in consumption and other areas of social and political life. Group involves the strength of the bounds in the units in which people find themselves (strong or weak), and grid involves the number of rules that they must obey (many or few).

Hypothesis   A hypothesis is something assumed to be true for the purposes of discussion or argument or further investigation. It is, in a sense, a guess or supposition used to explain some phenomenon.

Icon   In Peirce's trichotomy, an icon is a sign that conveys meaning by resemblance. Photographs are iconic, and so are the various stylized drawings used in airports to help people find toilets or luggage.

Id   The id in Freud's theory of the psyche (technically known as his structural hypothesis) is that element of the psyche that is the representative of a person's drives. Freud (1965b) called it, in *New Introductory Lectures on Psychoanalysis,* "a chaos, a cauldron of seething excitement." It also is the source of energy, but lacking direction, it needs the ego to harness it and control it. In popular thought, it is connected with impulse, lust, and "I want it all now" kind of behavior.

Ideology   An ideology refers to a logically coherent, integrated explanation of social, economic, and political matters that helps establish the goals and direct the actions of some group or political entity. People act (and vote or don't vote) on the basis of some ideology they hold, even though they may not have articulated it or thought about it.

Image   Defining images is extremely difficult. In my book, *Seeing Is Believing: An Introduction to Visual Communication,* I define an image as "a collection of signs and symbols that we find when we look at a photograph, a film still, a shot of a television screen, a print advertisement, or just about anything" (A. A. Berger, 1989b, p. 38). The term is also used for mental as well as physical representations of things. Images often have powerful emotional effects on people as well as having historical significance. Two recent books that deal with images in some detail are Kiku Adatto's (1993) *Picture Perfect: The Art and Artifice of Public Image Making* and Paul Messaris's (1994) *Visual Literacy: Image, Mind and Reality.*

Index   For Peirce, an index is a kind of semiotic sign that conveys meaning based on a cause-and-effect relationship. Smoke is indexical in that it signifies fire.

Internet   The Internet is a system of interlinked computer networks that enables people to send e-mail (electronic mail) and access all kinds of sites on the World Wide Web.

Interpretation   We distinguish between interpretation and analysis. Interpretation involves applying concepts and methods from one or more disciplines to a literary text or to some phenomenon of interest. Analysis involves studying something—a literary text or something else—by separating it into its components.

Intertextuality   In literary theory, the term *intertextuality* is generally used to deal with borrowings by one text of other texts. This borrowing can involve content and style. In some cases, intertextual borrowings are not consciously made, whereas in other cases, such as parody, the borrowing is done on purpose.

Jokes   Jokes are conventionally defined as short narratives, meant to amuse and create mirthful laughter, that have a punch line.

Lifestyles   This term, which means, literally, style of life, refers to the way people live from the decisions they make about matters such as how to decorate their apartments or homes (and where they are located) to the kind of cars they drive, the clothes they wear, the kinds of foods they eat and the restaurants they attend, where they go for vacations, and what kind of pets they have.

Likert scale   Likert scales enable respondents to indicate degrees or strength of attitude by using (most commonly) a numerical 5- or 7-point scale.

Marxism   This system of thought developed by Karl Marx (and elaborated on by numerous others) deals with the relationship that exists between the economic system in a country (the base) and the institutions that develop out of this economic system (the superstructure). Marxist media critics focus on the role of the media in capitalist societies and the way the media help prevent class conflict and defuse alienation by generating consumerist cultures.

Mass   For our purposes, *mass* as in *mass communication* refers to a large number of people who are the audience for some communication. There is considerable disagreement about how to understand the term *mass*. Some theorists say it comprises individuals who are heterogeneous, do not know one another, are alienated, and do not have a leader. Others attack these notions, saying they are not based on fact or evidence but on theories that are not correct.

Mass communication   This term refers to the subject of this book—the transfer of messages, information, and texts from a sender of some kind to a large number of people, a mass audience. This transfer is done through the technologies of the mass media, such as newspapers, magazines, television programs, films, records, computers, and CD-ROMs. Often, the sender is a person in some large media organization, the messages are public, and the audience tends to be large and varied.

Medium (plural: media)   A medium is a means of delivering messages, information, and texts to audiences. There are different ways of classifying the media. Some of the most common are print (newspapers, magazines, books, billboards), electronic (radio, television, computers, CD-ROMs), and photographic (photographs, films, videos).

Metaphor   A metaphor is a figure of speech that conveys meaning by analogy. It is important to realize that metaphors are not confined to poetry and literary works but, according to some linguists, are the fundamental way in which we make sense of things and find meaning in the world. A simile is a weak form of metaphor that uses either *like* or *as* in making an analogy.

Metonymy   According to linguists, metonomy is a figure of speech that conveys information by association and is, along with metaphor, one of the most important ways people convey information to one another. We tend not to be aware of our use of metonymy, but whenever we use association to get an idea about something (Rolls Royce = wealthy), we are thinking metonymically. A form of metonymy that involves seeing a whole in terms of a part or vice versa is called *synecdoche*. Using "The White House" to stand for the presidency is an example of synecdoche.

Mimetic desire   A theory of a French literary theorist René Girard that argues that people often imitate the "desire" of celebrities, sports heroes, and others when they purchase things, not their behavior.

Model   Models, in the social sciences, are abstract representations that show how some phenomenon functions. Theories are typically expressed in language, but models tend to be represented graphically or by statistics or mathematics. Denis McQuail and Sven Windahl (1993) define *model* in *Communication Models for the Study of Mass Communication* as "a consciously simplified description in graphic form of a piece of reality. A model seeks to show the main elements of any structure or process and the relationships between these elements" (p. 2).

Modernism   This term is used in criticism to deal with the arts in the period from approximately the turn of the century until around the 1960s. The modernists rejected narrative structure for simultaneity and montage and explored the paradoxical nature of reality. Some of the more important modernists were T. S. Eliot, Franz Kafka, James Joyce, Pablo Picasso, Henri Matisse, and Eugene Ionesco.

Paradigmatic analysis   The paradigmatic analysis of texts involves finding the pattern of binary oppositions that are (allegedly, some would argue) found in these texts. These oppositions enable people to find meaning in texts.

Participant observation   Participant observation is a qualitative form of research in which a researcher becomes a member (to varying degrees) in some group or entity being studied. Being a participant enables a researcher to gain a better sense of the views and objectives of the group being studied.

Personal journal   A record of one's ideas, thoughts, and speculations that can be used to play with ideas and think up new ideas that can be used in scholarly research. My suggestions are that these journals be kept in bound notebooks, with the pages numbered and an index on the last page to facilitate access to ideas and thoughts that may be of interest and use when involved in scholarly writing.

Phallic symbol   An object that resembles either by shape or function the penis is described as a phallic symbol. Symbolism is a defense mechanism of the ego that permits hidden or repressed sexual or aggressive thoughts to be expressed in a disguised form. For a discussion of this topic, see Freud's (1900/1965a) book *An Interpretation of Dreams*.

Phallocentric theory   This term is used to suggest that societies are dominated by males and that the ultimate source of this domination, that which shapes our institutions and cultures, is the male phallus. In this theory, a link is made between male sexuality and male power. A more detailed discussion of this concept is found in my book, *Cultural Criticism: A Primer of Key Concepts* (A. A. Berger, 1994).

Pilot study   The term is used to refer to a small-scale test study made to determine whether the questions in a survey or questionnaire are easily understood. More generally, a pilot study refers to any small study that helps researchers refine their techniques and gain a sense of whether a full-scale study might be effective.

Poetic functions   In Jakobson's theory, poetic functions are those that use literary devices such as metaphor and metonymy. Poetic functions differ, Jakobson suggests, from emotive functions and referential functions.

Political cultures   According to Aaron Wildavsky, all democratic societies have four political cultures and need these cultures to balance off one another. These political cultures are (a) individualists, (b) hierarchical elitists, (c) egalitarians, and (d) fatalists. A political culture is made up of people who are similar in terms of their political values and beliefs and, for Wildavsky, similar in relation to group boundaries and rules and prescriptions they observe. For an example of how Wildavsky's theories can be applied to mass media and popular culture, see my book *Agitpop: Political Culture and Communication Theory* (A. A. Berger, 1990).

Political theory   Political theory is the branch of philosophy (or of political science) that deals with the theories of philosophers about the nature of government and the role of the state.

Popular   *Popular* is one of the most difficult terms used in discourse about the arts and the media. Literally speaking, the term means appealing to a large number of people. It comes from the Latin term *popularis*, "of the people."

Popular culture   *Popular culture* is a term that identifies certain kinds of texts that appeal to a large number of people—that is, texts that are popular. But mass communication theorists often identify (or should we say confuse) popular with *mass* and suggest that if something is popular, it must be of poor quality, appealing to some mythical "lowest common denominator." Popular culture is generally held to be the opposite of *elite* culture—that is, arts that require certain levels of sophistication and refinement to be appreciated, such as ballet, opera, poetry, classical music, and so on. Many critics now question this popular culture/elite culture polarity.

Postmodernism   We are, some theorists suggest, all living in a post-modern era and have been doing this since the 1960s, more or less. Literally speaking, the term means after modernism, the period from approximately 1900 to the 1960s. Postmodernism is charac-terized by, as a leading theorist of the subject, Jean-Francois Lyotard (1984), put it, "incredulity toward metanarratives" (p. xxiv). By this, he means that the old philosophical belief systems that had helped people order their lives and societies are no longer accepted or given credulity. This leads to a period in which, more or less, anything goes. See my books *Postmortem for a Postmodernist* (a mystery novel that explains postmodernism; A. A. Berger, 1997) and *The Postmodern Presence* (a reader; A. A. Berger, 1998) for more on this subject.

Power   Power is, politically speaking, the ability to implement one's wishes as far as policy in some entity is concerned. When we use the term to discuss texts, we use it to describe their ability to have an emotional impact on people—readers, viewers, or listeners.

Primary research   Primary research is research personally done by someone investigating some subject of interest. Primary research differs, then, from secondary research, which is research done using and citing the work (often the primary research) of others.

Psychoanalytic theory   Psychoanalytic theory is based on the notion that the human psyche has what Freud called the "unconscious," which, ordinarily speaking, is inaccessible to us (unlike conscious-ness and the preconscious) and continually shapes and affects our mental functioning and behavior. We can symbolize this by imagin-ing an iceberg: The tip of the iceberg, showing above the water, represents consciousness. The part of the iceberg we can see, just below the surface of the water, represents the preconscious. And the rest of iceberg (most of it, which cannot be seen, but we know it is there) represents the unconscious. We cannot access this area of our psyches because of repression. Freud also emphasized matters such as sexuality and the role of the Oedipus complex in everyone's lives.

Public   Instead of the term *popular culture*, we sometimes use the terms *the public arts* or *public communication* to avoid the negative connotations of the terms *mass* and *popular*. A public is a group of people, a community. We can contrast public acts, those meant to be known to the community, with private acts, which are not meant to be known to others.

Qualitative research   Qualitative research techniques are those (such as semiotic analysis, psychoanalytic criticism, ideological criticism, rhetorical interpretation, interviewing, and participant observation) designed primarily to yield nonquantitative or nonnumerical data. As such, they differ from quantitative research methods, although in some kinds of research, both approaches can be used.

Quantitative research   Quantitative research techniques are those (such as content analysis, surveys and questionnaires, and experiments) designed to yield numerical data.

Random sample   This term refers to a sample generated by using a table of random numbers and designed to select representative samples for surveys and questionnaires.

Ratings   In media research, ratings refer to the percentage of households or of people in an area who have tuned their televisions or radios to a specific station, program, or network. Ratings differ from shares, which refer to the number of people or households tuned to a station, program, or network correlated with sets in use.

Rationalization   In Freudian thought, a rationalization is a defense mechanism of the ego that creates an excuse to justify some action (or inaction when an action is expected). Ernest Jones, who introduced the term, used it to describe logical and rational reasons that people give to justify behavior that is really caused by unconscious and irrational determinants.

Reactivity   We use this term to describe the impact or effect of researchers on those who are being studied. When people are being studied, they often behave differently from the way that they do under ordinary circumstances.

Referential functions   In Jakobson's theory, the referential function of speech deals with the way it helps speakers relate to their surroundings. He contrasts this with emotive and poetic functions of speech.

Research   In this book, I define research as the use of various qualitative or quantitative methods to obtain desired information about some group of people or subject of interest. Sometimes this information is in the form of numerical data, but not always.

Rhetoric   In essence, rhetoric is the study of effective expression and of style in language. Rhetoric is also used to deal with the means by which people are persuaded. In recent years, rhetoric has also been used to study the mass media and popular culture.

Role   Sociologists describe a role as a way of behavior that we learn in a given society and that is appropriate to a particular situation. A person generally plays many roles with different people during a given day, such as parent (family) and worker (job).

Samples   In this book, I define representative samples as small groups of people held to have the same attributes as larger populations. In general terms, a sample is a part that is representative of some larger whole.

Secondary research   This term is used for research done by others that is cited by researchers to make some point or provide information. Secondary research differs, then, from primary research, which is original research done by an individual or group of people.

Semiotics   The term *semiotics* means, literally, the science of signs. *Semion* is the Greek term for sign. A sign is anything that can be used to stand for anything else. According to C. S. Peirce, one of the founders of the science, a sign "is something which stands to somebody for something in some respect or capacity." My book *Signs in Contemporary Culture: An Introduction to Semiotics* (A. A. Berger, 1999) discusses many of the more important semiotic concepts and shows how they can be applied to popular culture.

Shadow   In Jungian thought, the shadow represents the dark side of the psyche, which we attempt to keep hidden. It contains repressed and unfavorable aspects of our personalities as well as normal instincts and creative impulses. Thus, in all people, there is a continual battle between shadow aspects of our personalities and our egos, which also contain some negative features.

Share   Share is used to designate the number of people or households tuned to a specific program, station, or network correlated with sets in use. It differs from ratings, which are tied to households tuned to a specific program, station, or network in a certain area.

Sign   In semiotics, a sign is defined as anything that can be used to stand for something else. Semiotics is the science of signs and studies how they are used to generate meaning. As Umberto Eco has pointed out, if signs can be used to tell the truth, they can also be used to lie.

Simile   Similes are weak forms of metaphor that use *like* or *as*. The statement "My love is like a rose" is a simile; the statement "my love is a rose" is a metaphor.

Social media   We will understand the social media to be those Internet companies and corporations, such as Facebook, Twitter, and YouTube, that enable individuals to communicate, at no cost, textual material, images, and videos to potentially large numbers of people.

Socialization   This term refers to the processes by which societies teach individuals how to behave: what rules to obey, roles to assume, and values to hold. Traditionally, socialization was done by the family, by educators, by religious figures, and by peers. The mass media seem to have usurped this function to a considerable degree nowadays, with consequences that are not always positive.

Sociology   Sociology is a social science that studies groups, institutions, and collectivities—that is, the social behavior of human beings. As such, it differs from psychology, which focuses on the mind, the psyche, and individual behavior.

Stereotypes   Stereotypes are commonly held, simplistic, and inaccurate group portraits of categories of people. These stereotypes can be positive, negative, or mixed, but generally, they are negative in nature. Stereotyping always involves making gross overgeneralizations (all Mexicans, Chinese, Jews, African Americans, Native Americans, WASPs, Americans, lawyers, doctors, and professors, to cite just a few groups, are held to have certain characteristics, usually something negative).

Subculture   Subcultures are cultural subgroups whose religion, ethnicity, sexual orientation, beliefs, values, behaviors, and lifestyles vary in certain ways from those of the dominant culture. In any complex society, it is normal to have a considerable number of subcultures. Some subcultures are deviant and others criminal.

Superego   In Freud's typology, the superego is the agency in our psyches related to conscience and morality. The superego is involved with processes such as approval and disapproval of wishes on the basis or whether they are moral or not, critical self-observation, and a sense of guilt over wrongdoing. The functions of the superego are largely unconscious and are opposed to id elements in our psyches. Mediating between the two, and trying to balance them, is the ego.

Surveys   Surveys generally take the form of lists of questions (technically known as "instruments") addressed to representative samples of some population to obtain valid numerical data about the larger population as a whole.

Symbol   In Peirce's trichotomy, a symbol is anything that has a conventional meaning—that is, whose meaning must be taught to others and is not natural. Saussure disagrees with this notion and sees the symbol as only partially conventional.

Synecdoche   Synecdoche is a weak form of metonymy in which, generally speaking, a part is used to stand for the whole and vice versa. Thus, we use the term *Pentagon* to stand for the armed forces and military establishment in the United States.

Syntagmatic analysis   A syntagmatic analysis of a text deals with its linear structure. The term *syntagm* means "chain," and thus, a syntagmatic analysis looks at the sequence of actions in a text. It differs from a paradigmatic analysis, which seeks out the binary oppositions that inform the text.

Text   For our purposes, a text is, broadly speaking, any work of art in any medium. The term *text* is used by critics as a convenience so they don't have to name a given work all the time or use various synonyms. There are problems involved in deciding what the text is when we deal with serial texts, such as soap operas or comics.

Theory   *Theories,* as I use the term, are expressed in language and systematically and logically attempt to explain and predict phenomena being studied. They differ from concepts, which define phenomena being studied, and from models, which are abstract, usually graphic in nature, and explicit about what is being studied.

Typology   A typology is a classification scheme or system of categories that someone uses to make sense of some phenomena. My list of 45 techniques of humor is a typology.

Values   Values are abstract and general beliefs or judgments about what is right and wrong, what is good and bad, that have implications for individual behavior and for social, cultural, and political entities. There are a number of problems with values from a philosophical point of view. First, how does one determine which values are correct or good and which aren't? That is, how do we justify values? Are values objective or subjective? Second, what happens when there is a conflict between groups, each of which holds central value that conflicts with that of a different group?

Values and Lifestyles (VALS)   This refers to a typology of groups in America based on a survey of American values and lifestyles developed by the Stanford Research Institute. The VALS typology was used by advertising agencies seeking to understand what motivated consumers.

Violence   This term is extremely difficult to define. Conventionally, it is used to describe the use of physical force by a person or by persons to hurt or harm someone or prevent someone from hurting or harming a person or a group of persons. Many media researchers are interested in the relation that may exist between watching television and violent behavior in people, and there have been numerous studies made on this subject.

Index